IMAGES
of Rail

PLANO AND THE INTERURBAN RAILWAY

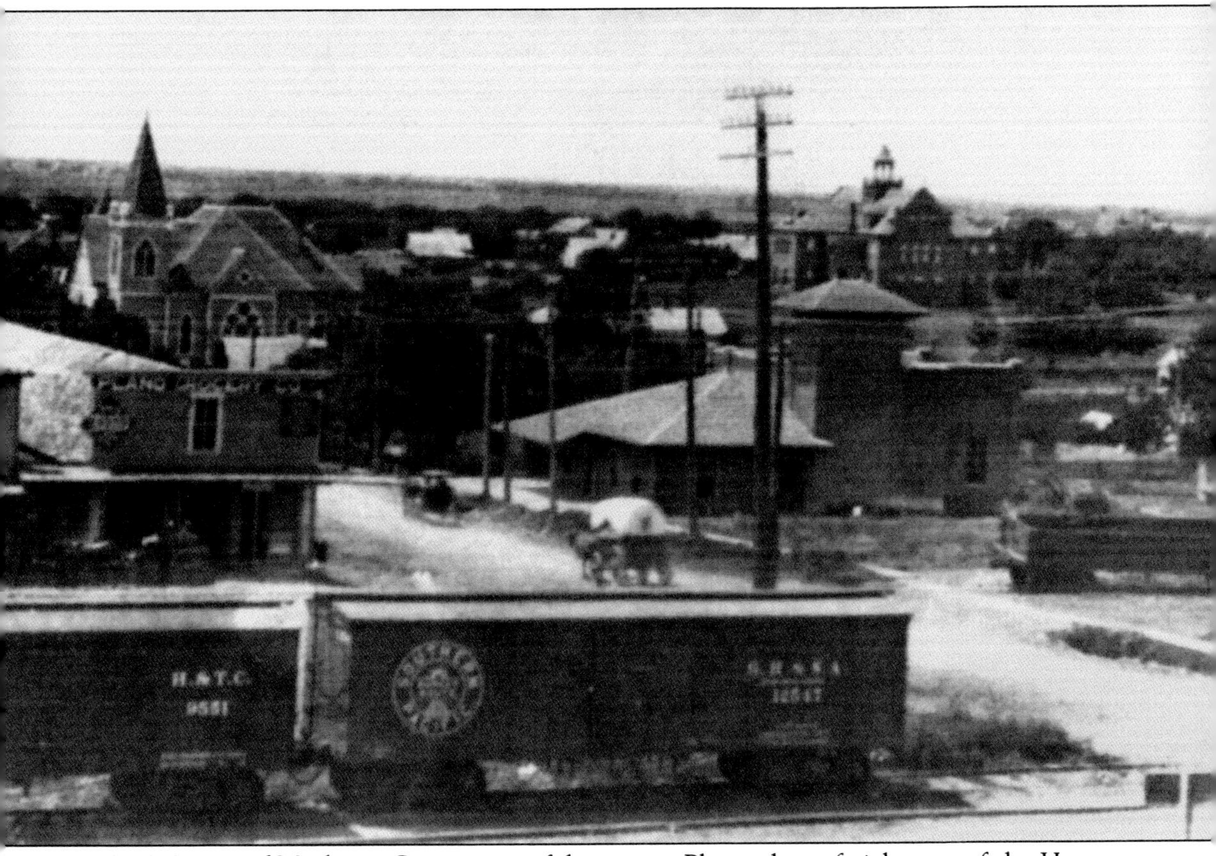

A 1910 view of Mechanic Street, west of downtown Plano, shows freight cars of the Houston and Texas Central and Southern Pacific Railroads. The recently constructed Plano Interurban depot and substation are in the center right frame. (Courtesy of the Wells Collection, Plano Public Library.)

On the Cover: A promotional campaign to persuade passengers to leave their automobiles at home and ride the Texas Electric Railway included advertisements showing affluent and fashionably dressed passengers riding in ease and comfort aboard luxuriously appointed railcars. (Courtesy of the Interurban Railway Museum/Johnnie J. Myers Collection.)

IMAGES
of Rail

PLANO AND THE INTERURBAN RAILWAY

The Plano Conservancy
for Historic Preservation, Inc.

ARCADIA
PUBLISHING

ISBN 978-0-7385-7136-2

Published by Arcadia Publishing
Charleston, South Carolina

Printed in the United States of America

Library of Congress Control Number: 2008941567

For all general information contact Arcadia Publishing at:
Telephone 843-853-2070
Fax 843-853-0044
E-mail sales@arcadiapublishing.com
For customer service and orders:
Toll-Free 1-888-313-2665

Visit us on the Internet at www.arcadiapublishing.com

Our family is honored to have this book dedicated in memory of our great-great-grandfather, Frank J. Sprague, a pioneer and genius who shined a light into the 20th century that lighted the way for many to follow.

—Robert C. Sprague IV
Suzanne K. Sprague-Trammell
Sara E. Sprague

"Transportation is the key of civilization—in fact it is civilization—for without it our existing social structure would collapse."

—Frank J. Sprague
July 25, 1932

Contents

ACKNOWLEDGMENTS

We wish to thank the Plano Conservancy for Historic Preservation, Inc., Russell C. Kissick, codirector, and Margaret M. Sprague, codirector; Robert Haynes, Interurban Railway Museum, curator, and Debbie Calvin, technical assistant, for their dedication to researching, writing, and laying out this book. All photographs in this book, unless otherwise noted, are from the Interurban Railway Museum/Johnnie J. Myers Collection.

We wish to acknowledge the generosity of the City of Plano, Department of Parks and Recreation for use of images from the Johnnie J. Myers Collection and the Plano Public Library System for use of images from the Wells Collection. We also wish to express our gratitude to the following individuals and organizations for their inspiration and support and generous donation of their time. Without their assistance, this project could not have been completed. These include the Plano Conservancy for Historic Preservation Board of Directors: Duane Peter, Alexander "Pete" Schoemann, Harry Kepner, Jim Ryan, Russell C. Kissick, Margaret M. Sprague, Sid S. Wall Jr., and Fred Frawley; Bonnie J. Peter; City of Plano, Department of Parks and Recreation; John J. Myers; Library of Congress; Plano Public Library; *Dallas Morning News* Archives; Dallas Public Library; Dallas Public Library History Division; *Handbook of Texas History*; Robert C. Sprague IV, University of Pennsylvania; Suzanne K. Sprague Trammell; Kevin Kendro (Irving Archives, Irving Public Library); Cindy Boyd; Tina Bashor; Bryan McKinney (Dallas Public Library, Texas/Dallas History and Archives Room); Brian Collins (Dallas Public Library, Texas/Dallas History and Archives Room); Cheryl Smith (Plano Public Library); Tom Turner (Plano Public Library); Frank J. Conahan (archivist, Massachusetts Institute of Technology Museum); Baylor University Library (Gildersleeve Collection); Gayle Moran; Tom Petr; Kristie Kelly; Dana Conklin; Ron Smith; Rev. Dr. James J. Showers Jr.; Phillip Myers; Bryan Lean (North Texas History Century); John Humiston; Richard Humiston; Jeff Lingo; Lynda Morley; Alice Bogdan; and David Lerry.

To those whose names should be included in this list but are not, please forgive us for this oversight. You know who you are, and we thank you, too.

INTRODUCTION

In the late 19th century, development of interurban and street rail travel had been spreading rapidly along the East Coast of the United States, in Boston, New York, Philadelphia, and throughout the Midwest in cities such as Chicago, Cleveland, and Cincinnati. In heavily industrialized Midwestern cities, large populations lived in cities where the industrial revolution had created huge manufacturing complexes to produce the goods and products for a rapidly expanding population. Workers needed transportation to and from work.

Charles L. Henry, an Indiana lawyer and electric railway promoter, is generally credited with popularizing the word "interurban." It is believed that Henry coined the term by making an analogy to the intramural railway at the 1893 World's Columbian Exposition (also known as the Chicago World Fair), although some evidence exists that it had been used before.

By 1880, the basic technical knowledge for electric traction had been developed and pioneering names such as Nicola Tesla, George Westinghouse, Thomas Edison, and Frank J. Sprague became synonymous with the discoveries. Frank Sprague's inventions and techniques such as attaching the electric motor onto the truck and axle of a railcar to generate stronger and more direct torque, the development of series parallel switches, and the trolley pole to carry current to the motors were critical technological improvements. Sprague drew much attention with his innovative work and created an important system for the New York Elevated Railway in 1886. In 1888, he worked to equip an electric rail line in St. Joseph, Missouri, as well as developed a system for the Union Passenger Railway of Richmond, Virginia.

The demonstrated efficiency of the Sprague system encouraged other cities to have similar systems built. Effective and low-cost electric public transportation helped solve the problems of moving about urban populations and bringing cities and distant rural areas together. Sprague's successful Electric Railway and Motor Company was eventually absorbed by Edison's General Electric Company, but Sprague's contributions to electric rail transportation and modern urbanization continue to be legendary.

In North Texas, the first interurban system was chartered August 27, 1900, a single-track system to run between the cities of Denison and Sherman. Streetcar lines and interurban systems were developed by private investors who sold stock in the proposed venture to raise the capital necessary to pay for the project. Promoters and developers looked everywhere across the country to find growing urban areas that could benefit from an interurban railway system and generate a return on the investment. Fred Fitch, an Iowa entrepreneur, thought an interurban line that ran the 10-mile distance between Denison and Sherman would be feasible and bring a profit. Working with other promoters, some of whom were local to North Texas, the necessary capital was raised to begin the project, and the first interurban car began operation on May 1, 1901.

The Denison and Sherman Interurban line became successful by linking two thriving cities and expanding business transportation during the week, but its success also was due in part to weekend leisure patronage by residents traveling to and from Woodlake and Coursing Parks.

The parks had originally been built not only as weekend and holiday recreational destinations for railway employees and their families, but also as an attraction for residents in the surrounding area. Heavily promoted to the public as wholesome relaxation, the parks had swimming pools, camping, picnic areas, and one of the best theaters in the North Texas area. Built at the end of city streetcar and interurban car lines, they were called "trolley parks." In most cities, trolley parks served urban populations seeking recreation outside the city. Neither Woodlake nor Coursing Parks added the then popular electric or mechanical amusement rides. Amusement rides provided a strong source of revenue for other trolley parks.

J. F. Strickland

Horace Greely's call, "Go West young man and grow up with the country," must have rung true in the ear of an 18-year-old Alabama farm boy, John F. Strickland.

As did so many others who sought a new life away from Civil War–devastated Southern states, Strickland joined a wagon train in 1878 headed for Texas. Texas had not suffered from major invasion by Union forces during the war and offered many opportunities for anyone willing to work hard and live by thrift.

Working as a farmhand and saving every penny, Strickland soon bought a team of oxen to move cotton to the local gins in Waxahachie, where he had settled. He soon acquired a cotton gin, but it caught fire and burned. Starting all over, Strickland worked at a series of jobs and soon gained a reputation for being a shrewd businessman in new electric technologies and above reproach in his ethics.

By 1880, electrification of cities was growing rapidly in Texas. Strickland soon found himself managing an electricity generating plant and a mule-drawn streetcar system and was chosen as a director of the local bank.

One business success led to another. Strickland and his close circle of business associates moved from Waxahachie to Dallas in 1904. With an eye on developing electric traction transportation, in that same year, he founded and organized the Dallas Securities Company, which bought up several small electricity generating companies in North Texas.

By 1909, through stock transfers, bond issues, and consolidation, Strickland founded Texas Power and Light Company. Strickland acquired power companies at the same time that he was working to merge all of North Texas's interurban systems. The companies he controlled then acquired a dominant interest in the Denison and Sherman Railway. Two years later, Strickland's other company, Texas Traction, bought outright the Denison and Sherman Railway. The race to combine electricity generation and electric rail systems was growing fiercely competitive.

Utilizing stock subscriptions and cash, Strickland quickly moved to acquire the interurban built by Stone and Webster, a company founded by two young, recently graduated, enterprising electrical engineers from Massachusetts Institute of Technology. Stone and Webster's Northern Texas Traction Company was reaping handsome profits from building the line connecting Dallas to Waxahachie and Fort Worth in 1913. Strickland masterfully interceded to take ownership and consolidated Texas Traction Company, Southern Traction Company, and Dallas Traction Company to create the largest interurban system in the South, the Texas Electric Railway, on January 1, 1917.

The Golden Age

The golden age of the interurban railway in Plano and North Texas was a short but exuberant and financially successful period. It began with creation of the Texas Electric Railway on January 1, 1917, continued into the Roaring Twenties, and chilled with a whimper at the Great Depression in 1929. The company entered receivership in 1931, emerged in 1935, enjoyed brief prosperity during World War II, and finally ended all passenger service at midnight on December 31, 1948.

During this Golden Age, Texas Electric Railway Company commanded railcars over 226 miles of track through towns and cities and across the spacious North Texas prairie. Built to high standards, with track running mostly over private rights-of-way land, the rich and powerful, the hardworking, the pleasure seeking, the average, and the not-so-well-off rode in comfort and convenience at speeds of up to 60 miles per hour.

Soon after organization, Texas Electric Railway took possession of a gleaming new eight-story, $1.5-million terminal in downtown Dallas. Functioning as the headquarters and nerve center for the complex rail operation, the terminal building boasted a seven-track yard that could accommodate an astounding 24 interurban railcars at one time. The system and the headquarters were the pride of the South and rivaled the most impressive terminal building in the country, the 1904 Indianapolis Traction Terminal, which had a nine-track yard. The steel and brick structure was situated almost directly across the street from the Texas Power and Light Company Building where J. F. Strickland was also president.

Financially, the Texas Electric Railway during the Golden Age was one of the most successful interurban systems in the South and may have actually justified the $10-million investment. Although created in an era when many interurban systems in other parts of the country were in decline, and some even had been abandoned, Texas Electric became an outstanding example. In terms of profitability, the operating ratio stayed about 60 percent (operating expenses/revenues) throughout the 1920s and the rate of return on investment at over four percent. For interurban systems and railroads, an operating ratio of 80 percent or lower was considered desirable.

The Rise of Plano

Plano, a small settlement 20 miles north of Dallas, was a U.S. postal stop in the 1850s served by a stagecoach line. The stagecoach was replaced by the steam train in the 1870s. Eventually mail also arrived by way of Interurban Railway Post Office cars beginning in 1913 under a postal contract after the U.S. government introduced Rural Free Delivery mail.

First settled in the 1840s and incorporated in 1873, early Plano was a sparsely populated agricultural community that grew to have plumbing, stove, garment, and electric wire manufacturing industries. Originally a part of the Peters Land Grant Colony established to help settle Texas, Plano grew slowly at first. Plano's agricultural products were cotton, livestock, wheat, corn, oats, and the abundant and ubiquitously rich prairie grass for livestock. In 1872, further growth occurred when the Houston and Texas Central Railroad arrived and connected the community to Dallas. When the St. Louis, Arkansas, and Texas Railway Company laid track that intersected the Houston and Texas Central, Plano became an important center for the highly productive blackland prairie farmers.

The rich blackland prairie soil yielded abundant crops for the early Plano settlers, and soon the town had created a small but prosperous and precocious merchant class. News of the city's prosperity spread, and the Plano National Bank was founded in 1887 by investors who also held stock in other ventures in Dallas and North Texas. George Bowman, who was one of the first directors of the bank, would become a colleague of John Strickland and later sit on the boards of both the Southern Traction Company and Texas Electric Railway. The businessmen of Plano were a visionary group and sought out early opportunities to advance the fortunes of the city.

This close group of businessmen formed a fraternal, social, and business group known as the '44 Club. The main prerequisite for membership was to have been born in 1844. Many of the members had served on the side of the Confederacy during the War Between the States, as it was commonly referred to. Through their guidance, Plano grew to be an important community in North Texas.

Because it was so well situated, and due in no small part to the influential '44 Club, Strickland chose Plano as a substation and depot stop on the new Southern Traction Company interurban line that ran from Sherman to Dallas. The Plano depot was dedicated and opened with music, banners, and much fanfare for the first interurban car loaded with stockholders, investors, and company officers on the grand inspection ride, June 30, 1908. Almost the entire Plano community showed up on Mechanic Street (now Fifteenth Street) to celebrate the momentous occasion.

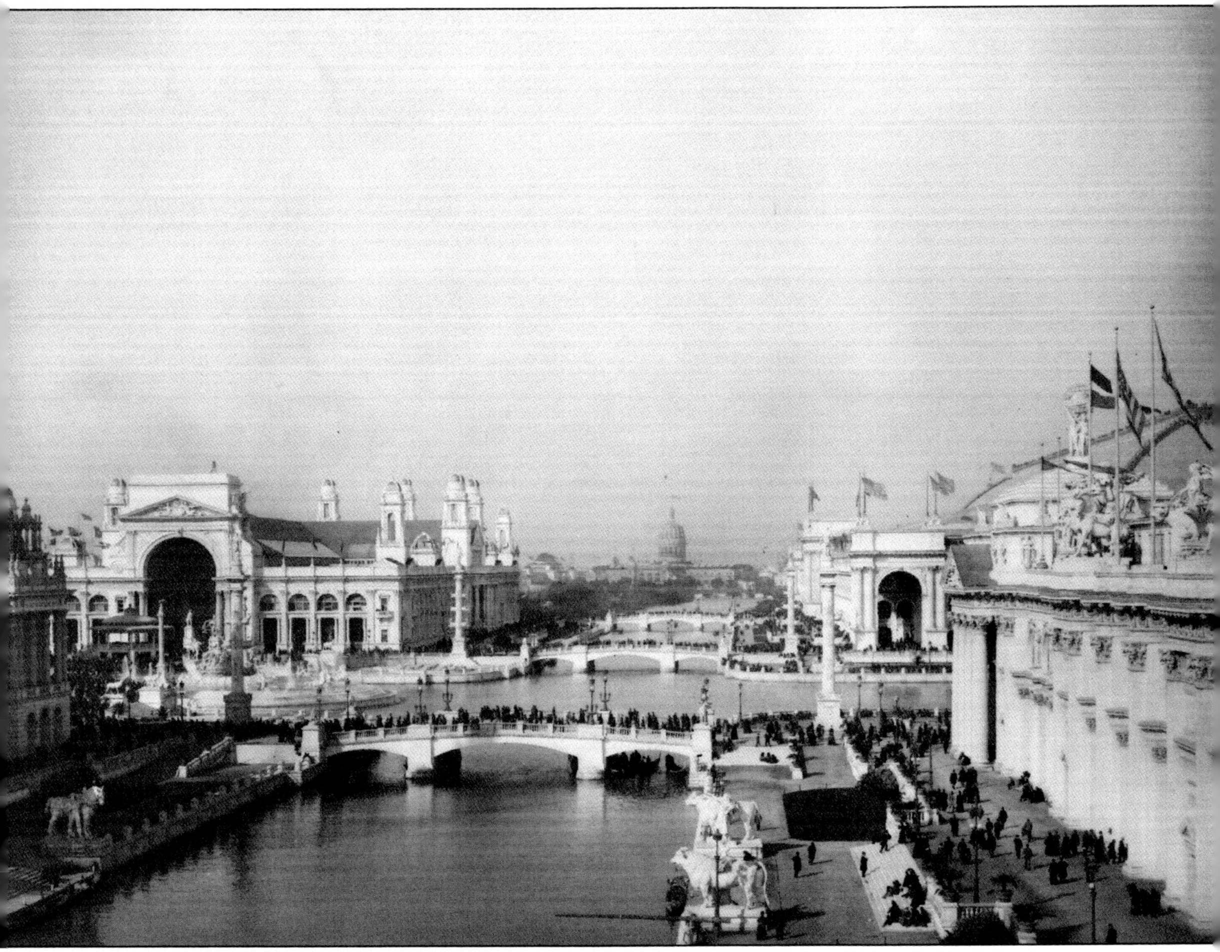

The 1893 World's Columbian Exposition introduced the miracle of Nicola Tesla's alternating current method of electric illumination. Tesla's high-frequency, high-voltage lighting was chosen to illuminate the entire exposition as demonstration of its superiority over Thomas Edison's direct current method. Tesla's method has become the world standard. (Courtesy of the Library of Congress.)

One

A Vision for Modernization Takes Root

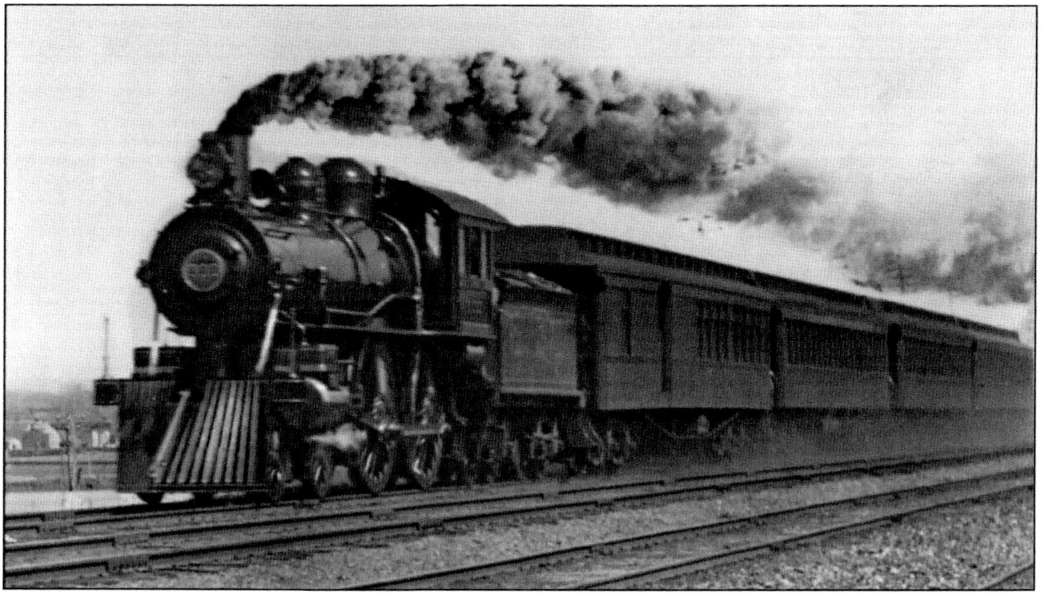

Texas and Pacific Railroad "Flier" arrives at Dallas in 1905 in a cloud of smoke, steam, and ash. Steam-powered locomotives were noisy, and they polluted the air. They were also slow to stop and were difficult to navigate through the center of cities, where transportation was needed to convey urban populations. (Courtesy of the Library of Congress.)

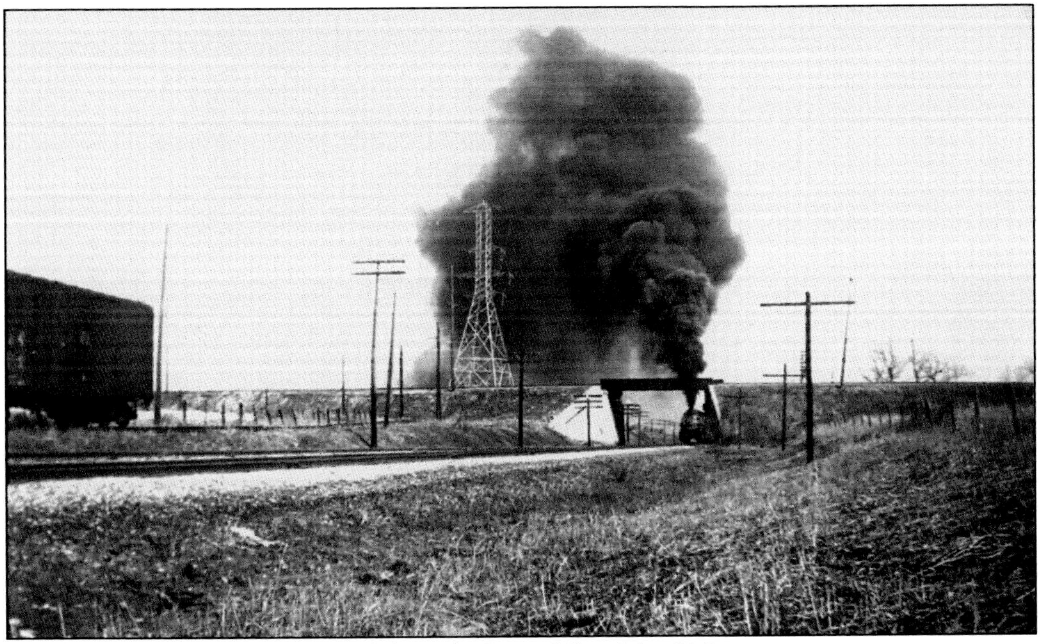

Steam trains continued to be used through the middle of the 20th century.

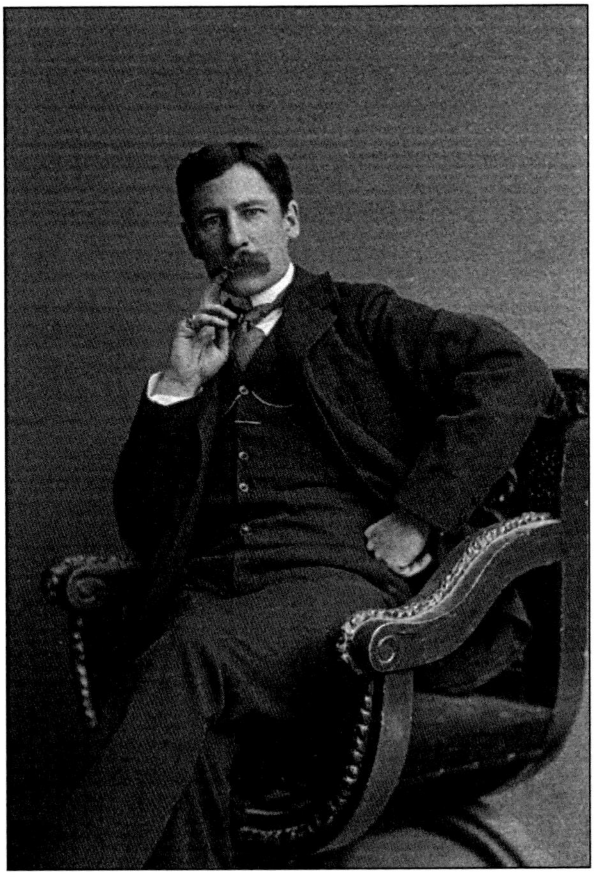

Frank Julian Sprague was born in Milford, Connecticut, on July 25, 1857, and attended the U.S. Naval Academy, where he learned about electricity and mechanical engineering. He resigned from the navy in 1885 and joined Thomas A. Edison for a time. Eventually Sprague left Edison and founded the Sprague Electric Railway Motor Company. He soon invented a spring-loaded trolley pole that had a wheel attached to the end. The wheel traveled along the electric wire and carried current to the motor on the railway car. He then solved the problem of delivering torque to railway cars. In 1888, he installed the first successful major electric street railway system in Richmond, Virginia. Sprague also developed the constant speed motor and the multiple unit, regenerative, and remote control systems. He invented the first electrically trained gun, as well as unique automatic signaling brake and train control systems, and generally laid the groundwork for the interurban railway system as it is known today. (Courtesy of a private collection.)

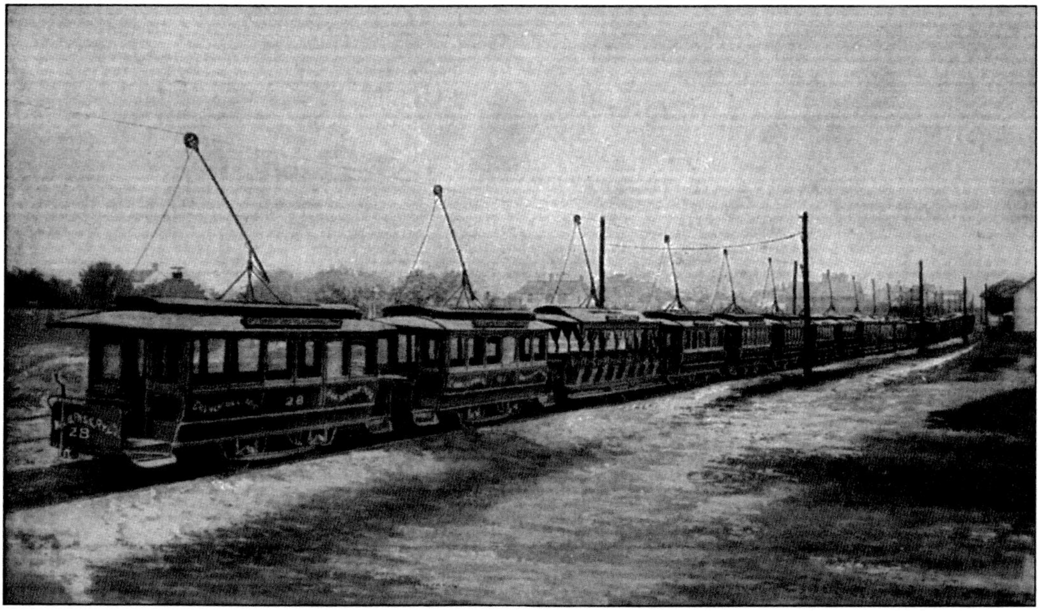

In 1888, Sprague installed the Richmond Union Passenger Railway in Richmond, Virginia. He achieved the breakthrough by demonstrating the ability to start up and move 22 trolley cars all at once. The system was so successful that within a year over 100 urban rail systems were using his inventions and techniques. By 1901, some 15,000 miles of electric rails had been laid in America's cities. The electric car was so clearly superior to the mule car that by 1902, a full 97 percent of urban street railways were electrically equipped. The mule car almost instantly had become an echo from a bygone era. (Courtesy of the Hagley Museum and Library.)

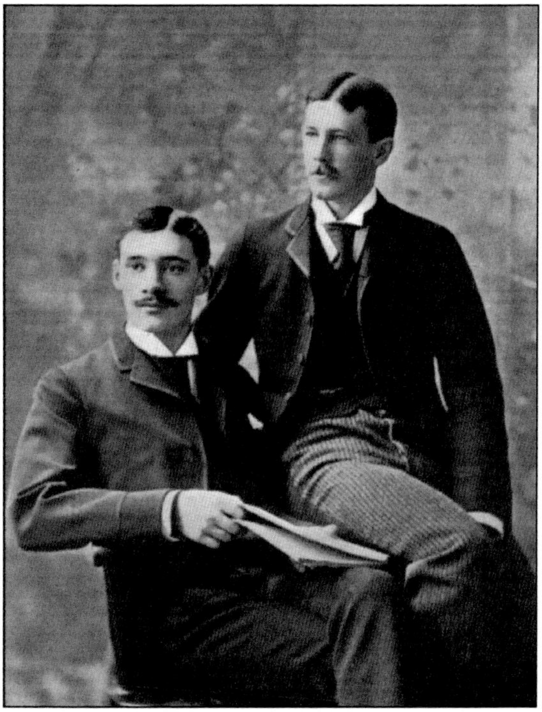

Upon graduation from MIT (Massachusetts Institute of Technology), earning degrees in the brand-new field of electrical engineering, these two very bright young men recognized a need for an engineering consulting firm to evaluate the potential for financial success of construction projects and to manage construction of numerous proposed interurban rail systems and electric power generating plants throughout the country. In an age of unrestrained capitalism, when financiers frequently lost their investments in the scramble to reap huge profits in new electric technologies, Charles A. Stone (left) and Edwin Webster (right) became the first and most successful of a new breed of company to specialize in project analysis by scientific means, much in the same manner that Nicola Tesla showed Thomas Edison how to perform laboratory experimentation mathematically rather than by trial and error. (Courtesy of the Massachusetts Institute of Technology Museum.)

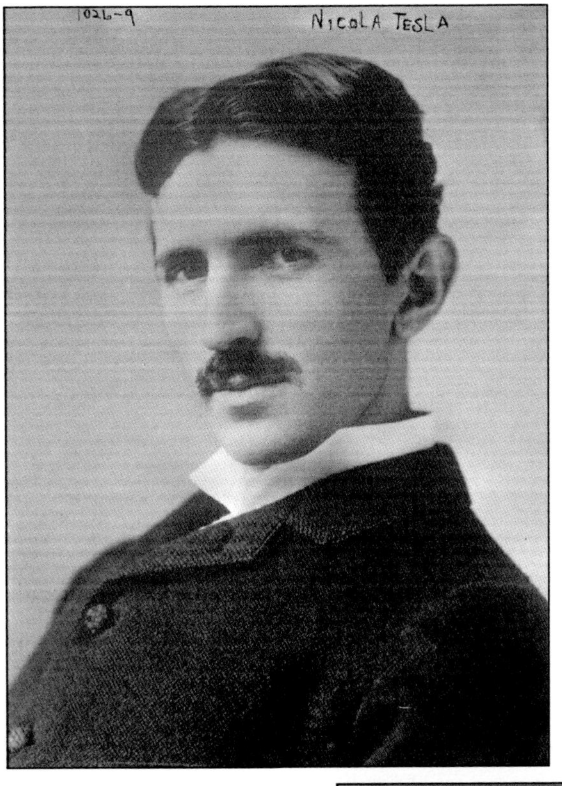

Nicola Tesla (1856–1943) was perhaps the greatest electrical genius of all time. Tesla's landmark 1888 paper, "A New System of Alternating Current Motors and Transformers," revolutionized the world of electricity. By applying the principle of the rotating magnetic field in physics, Tesla was led to discover how to construct alternating current induction motors and develop the polyphase system for generation, transmission, and distribution of electrical power. Tesla pioneered the "Tesla coil," used modernly in radio, television, and electronics. His discoveries include fluorescent light, laser beams, wireless communications, robotics, and many other conveniences that are considered commonplace in the 21st-century world. (Courtesy of the Library of Congress.)

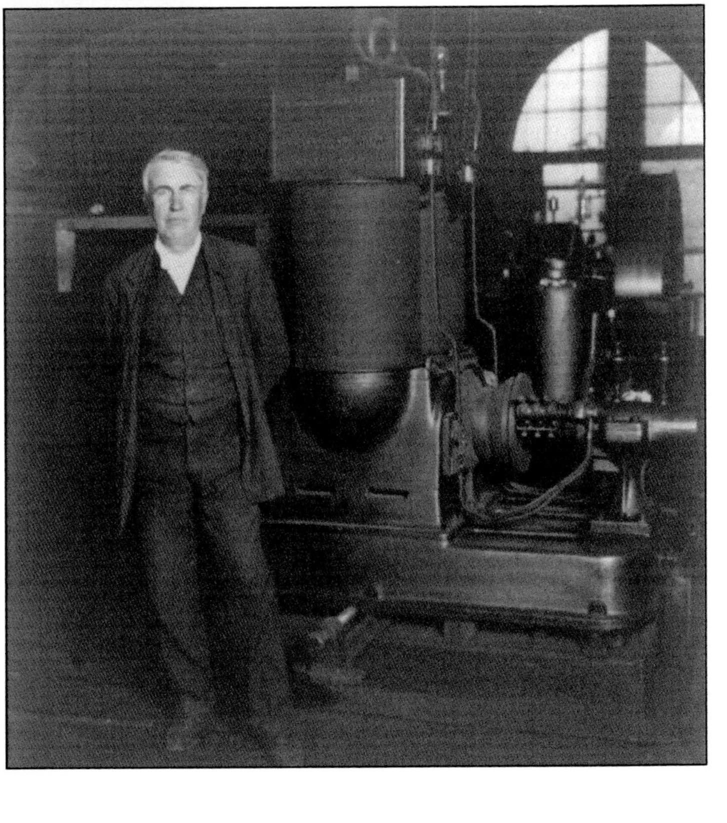

In 1906, Thomas A. Edison stands beside his dynano for making electricity. (Courtesy of the Library of Congress.)

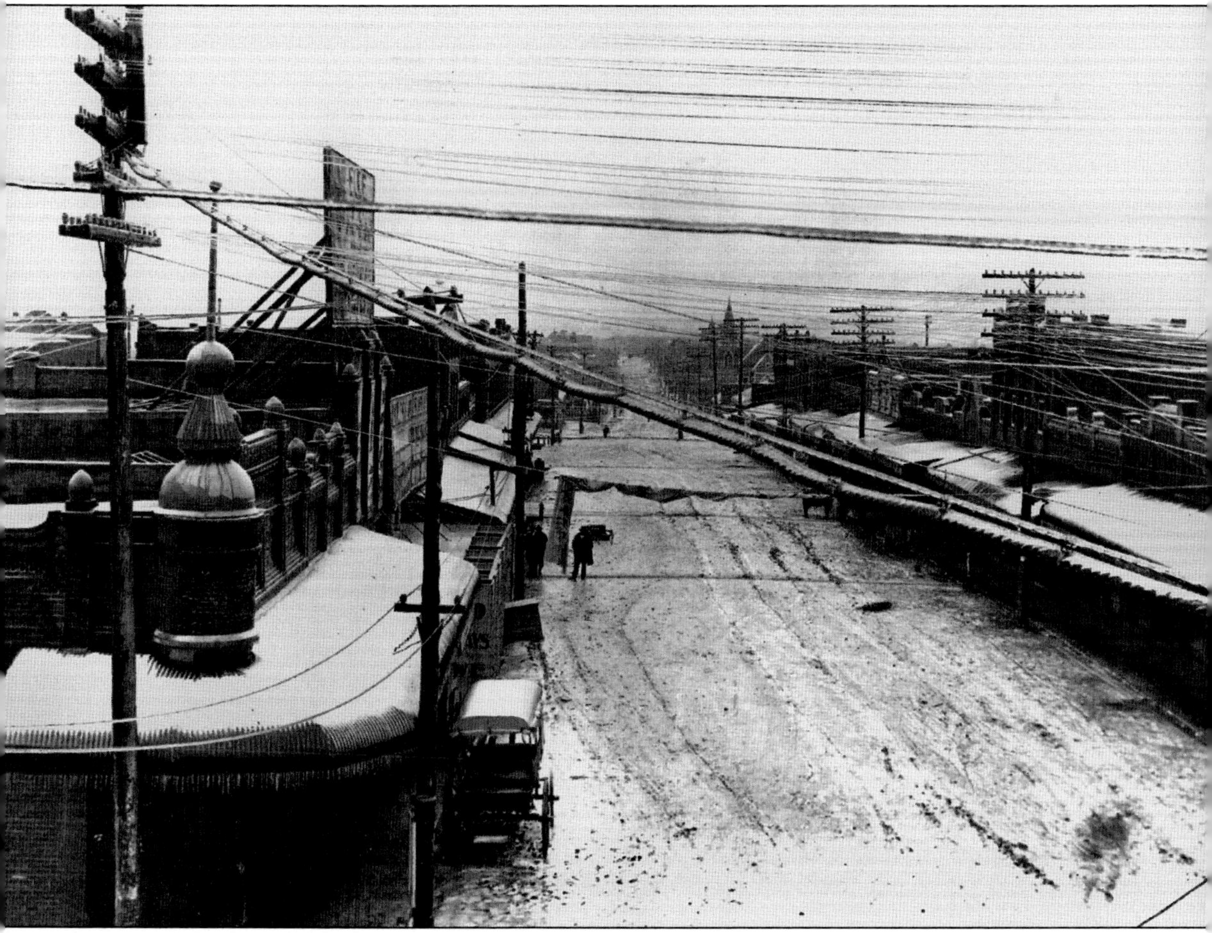

In a *c.* 1908 unusual winter scene in Plano, Texas, looking west, Mechanic Street (now Fifteenth Street) is covered with snow. Horses and wagons are carefully making their way through the center of town on this main thoroughfare. Note the electric overhead wires that indicate the downtown area has been electrified. By this time, the Texas Traction Company would have laid rails and strung wires for the interurban line to stop at Plano. (Courtesy of the Wells Collection, Plano Public Library.)

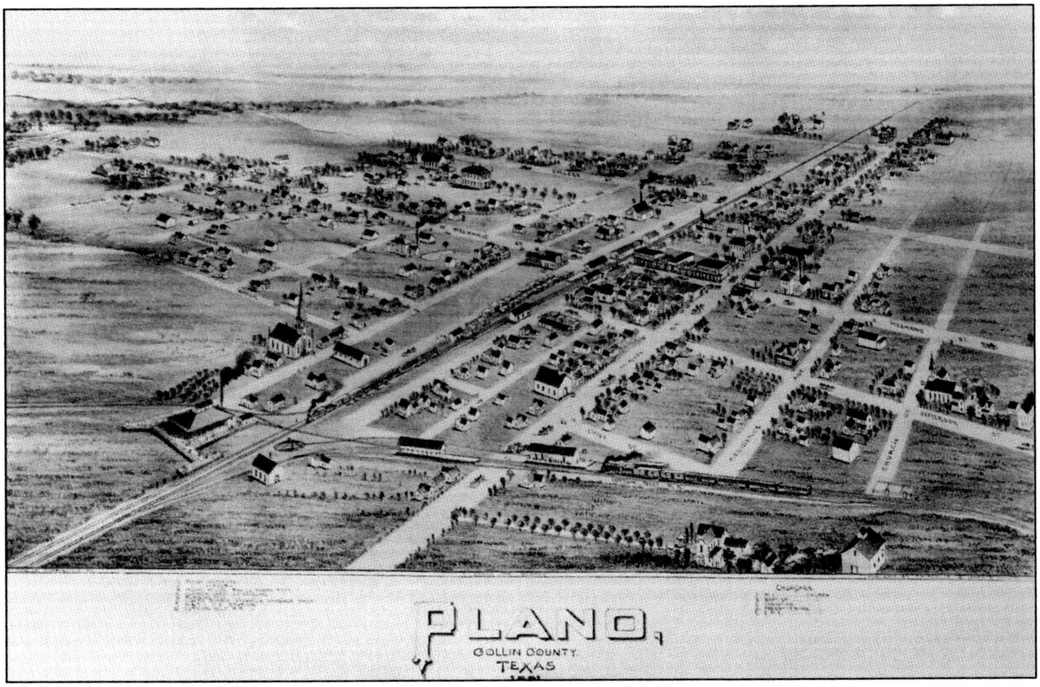

This early, c. 1891 Plano bird's-eye-view lithograph is by A. E. Downs of Boston. (Courtesy of the Plano Public Library.)

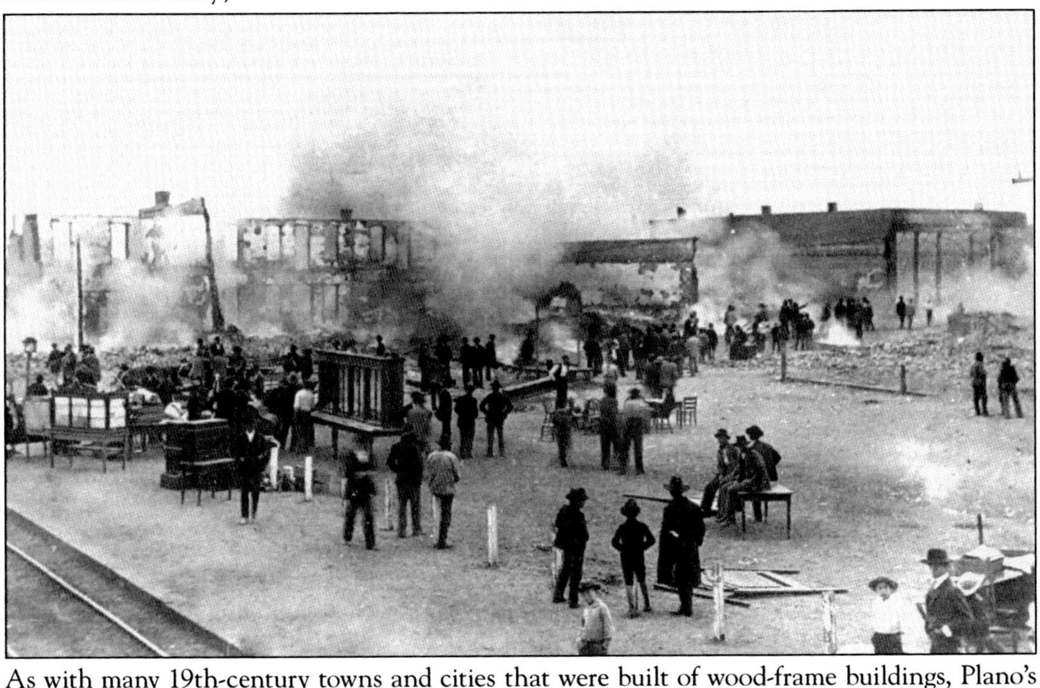

As with many 19th-century towns and cities that were built of wood-frame buildings, Plano's eventually fell victim to fire. Plano residents and businessmen salvaged what they could, but for the most part, the buildings and the contents in this 1895 fire were a total loss. Plano suffered several major fires in its early history, occurring in 1881, 1893, 1895, 1897, and 1911. (Courtesy of the Wells Collection, Plano Public Library.)

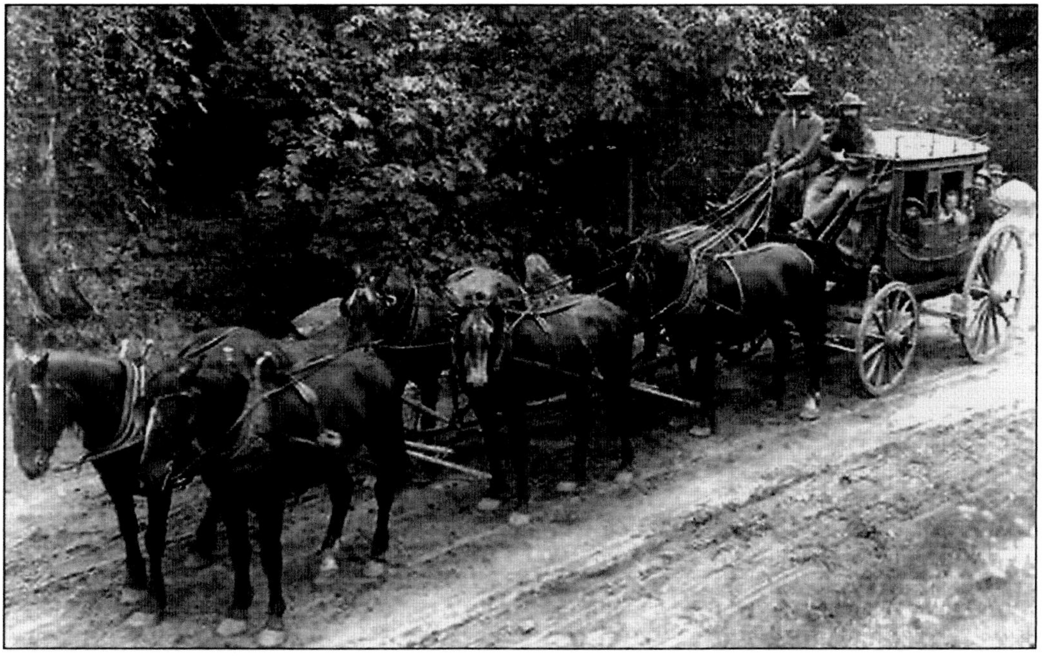

Before completion of the vast railroad network throughout Texas, mail was handled by stagecoaches as shown above. Plano was barely a settlement in the 1850s but did receive mail from a local stop by rider on horseback. The old stage road was from Bonham, in Fannin County, Texas, and continued south, crossing Wilson Creek south of McKinney. The route followed a southerly direction through the prairie and across Rowlett Creek near Highway 75. (Courtesy of *Collin County in Pioneer Times* by R. B. Whisenant, Library of Congress.)

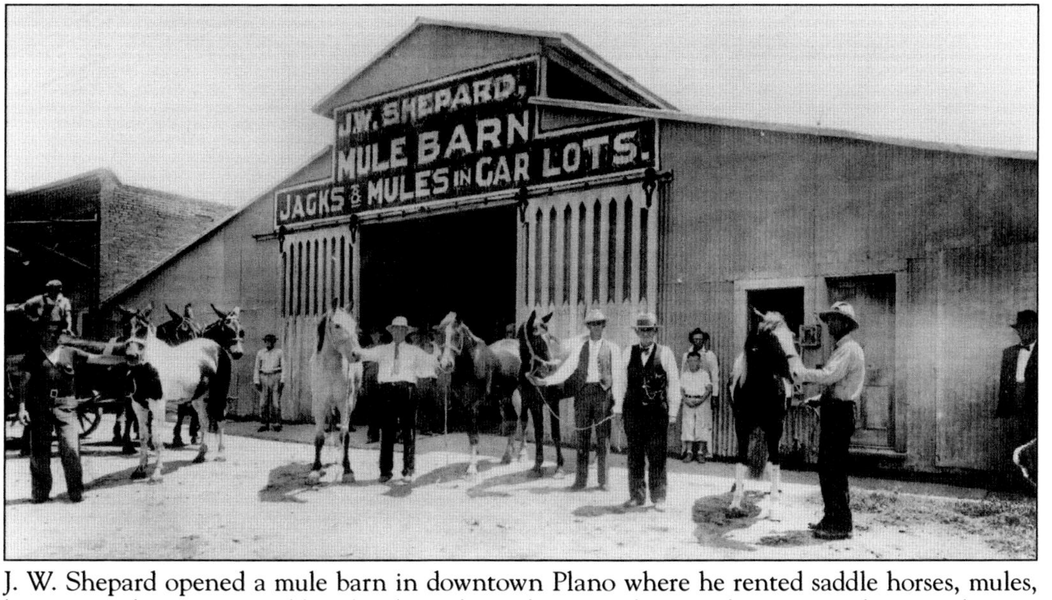

J. W. Shepard opened a mule barn in downtown Plano where he rented saddle horses, mules, buggies, and teams. He sold mules throughout the United States, bringing acclaim to Plano as an important trade center for raising and training prime mules. Mules were superior to horses as work animals and were also better suited to the Texas heat than horses. (Courtesy of the Wells Collection, Plano Public Library.)

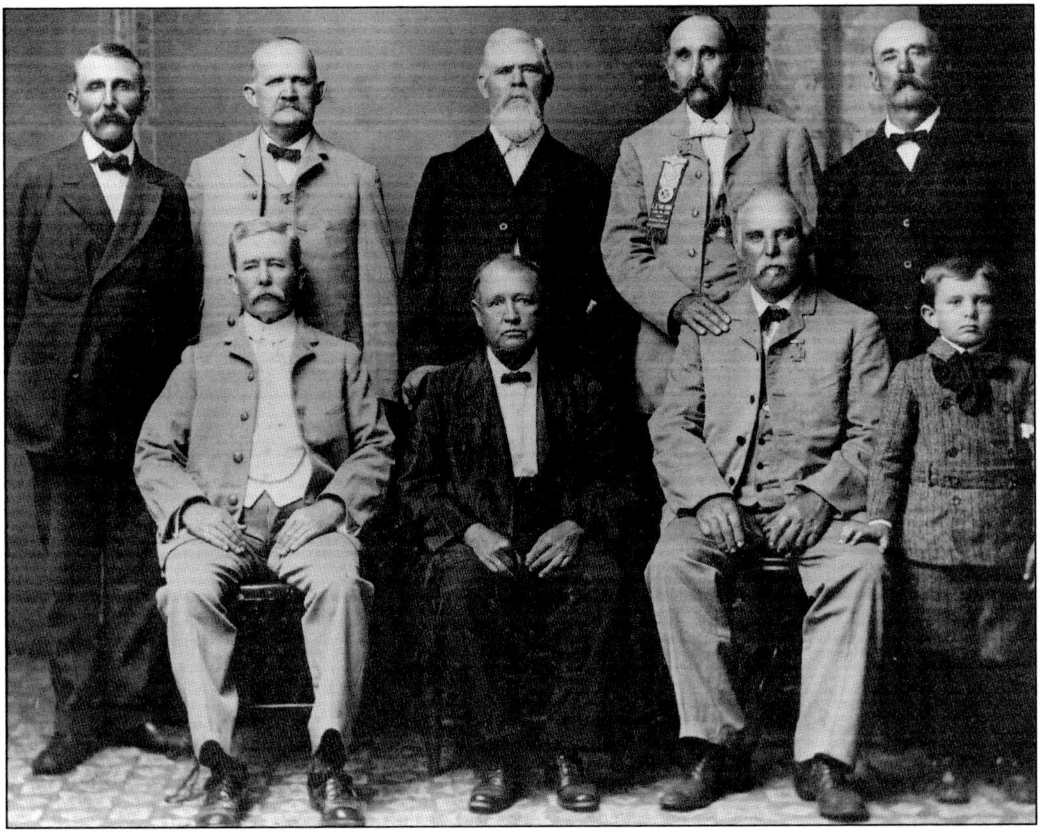

George W. Bowman (back row, third from the left) was a member of the '44 Club and one of the important civic leaders in Plano. He played an important role in helping to bring the Texas Traction rail station to Plano. (Courtesy of the Wells Collection, Plano Public Library.)

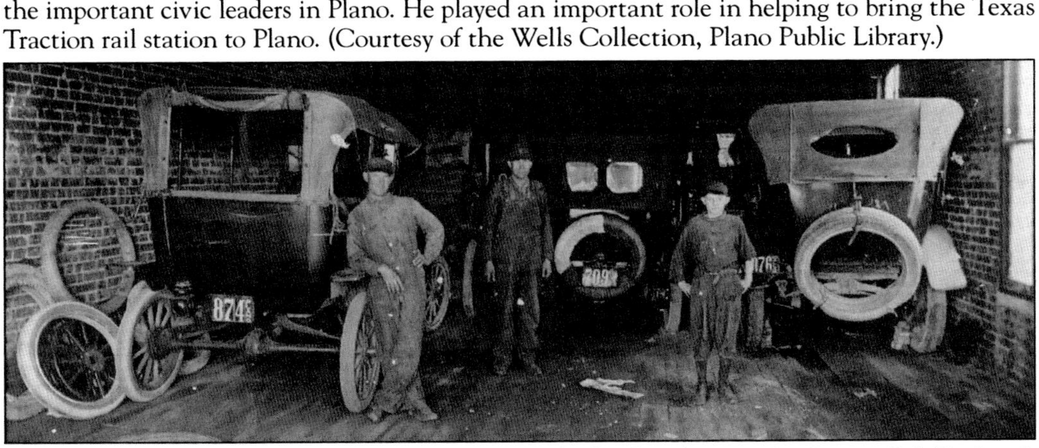

The first automobile to arrive in Plano came on a flatbed railroad car on the Cotton Belt Railroad. It drew a large crowd, for many people had heard of automobiles but had not seen one. As automobiles became more common, in January 1912, the *Plano Star Courier* wrote, "The honk of the automobile in Collin County is as common as the bray of the mule. The farmer who owns a 'car' and they have learned to call it that in old Collin—has no excuse for not holding his cotton if the price is not right." It was not suspected at the time that with each new automobile brought onto the streets of Plano, a step closer was taken to the future demise of the recently completed interurban railway. (Courtesy of the Wells Collection, Plano Public Library.)

At Christmastime 1917, troop trains filled with furloughed soldiers for the holidays arrived at Union Station in Dallas, and the khaki-clad warriors crowded onto Texas Electric Railway trains to get to their North Texas hometowns. The interurban was a useful part of the victory effort. Texas Electric management gave permission to anyone who wanted to do so to plant a war garden along the route of the interurban right-of-way. A special office at the interurban building in Dallas was set up to handle plots of land designated for war gardens. (Courtesy of the Plano Public Library.)

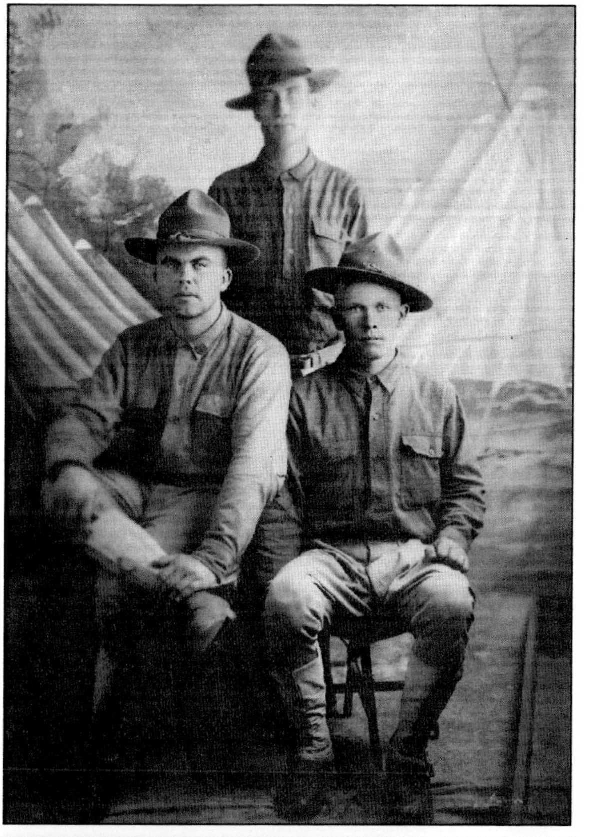

Employees pictured in this mercantile shop in Plano, Texas, were prosperous businessmen. (Courtesy of the Wells Collection, Plano Public Library.)

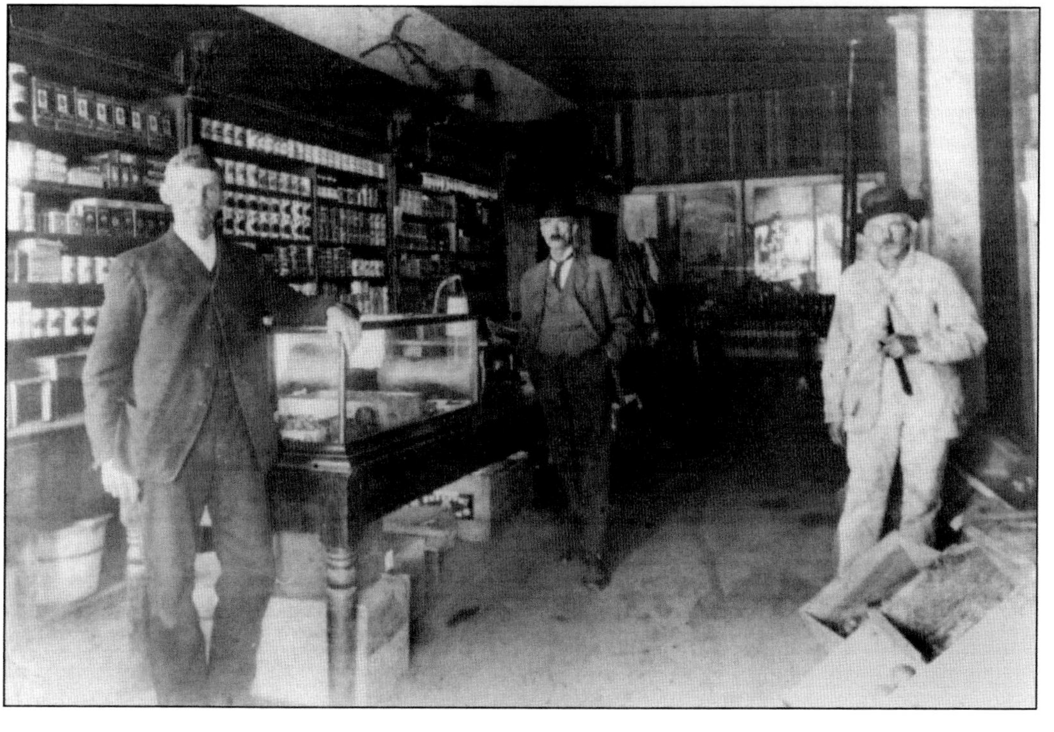

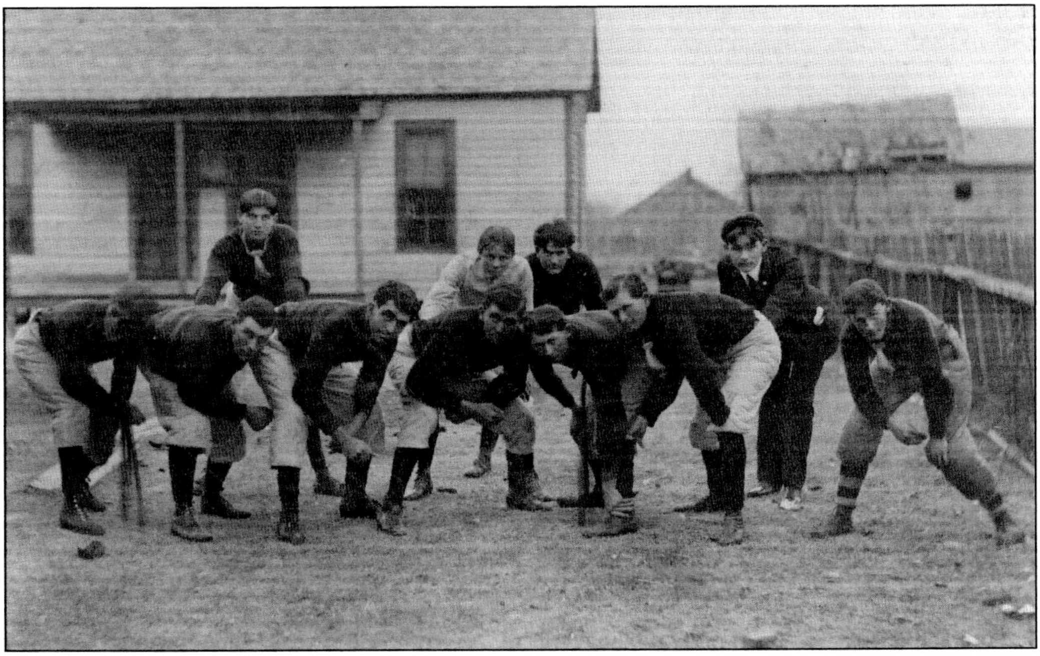

Plano was always a tightly knit community where "everybody knew everybody else," and young people from the farm-based community spent time together whenever they had an opportunity. (Courtesy of the Wells Collection, Plano Public Library.)

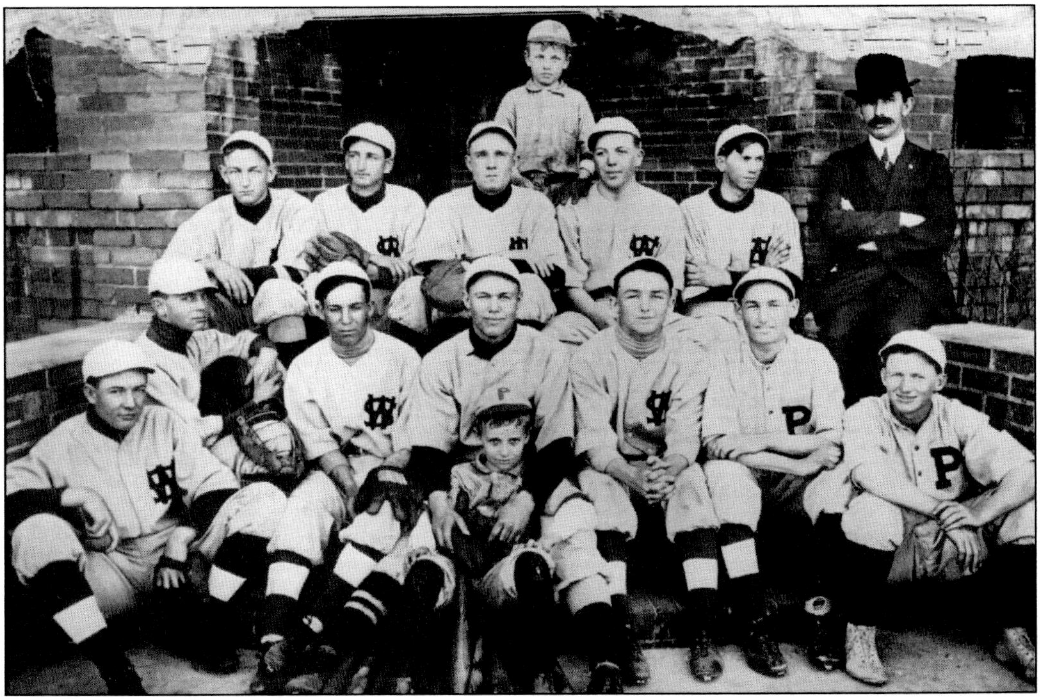

As baseball grew in popularity nationally, so did it grow in Plano. Two Plano baseball teams are represented in this 1915 photograph. (Courtesy of the Wells Collection, Plano Public Library.)

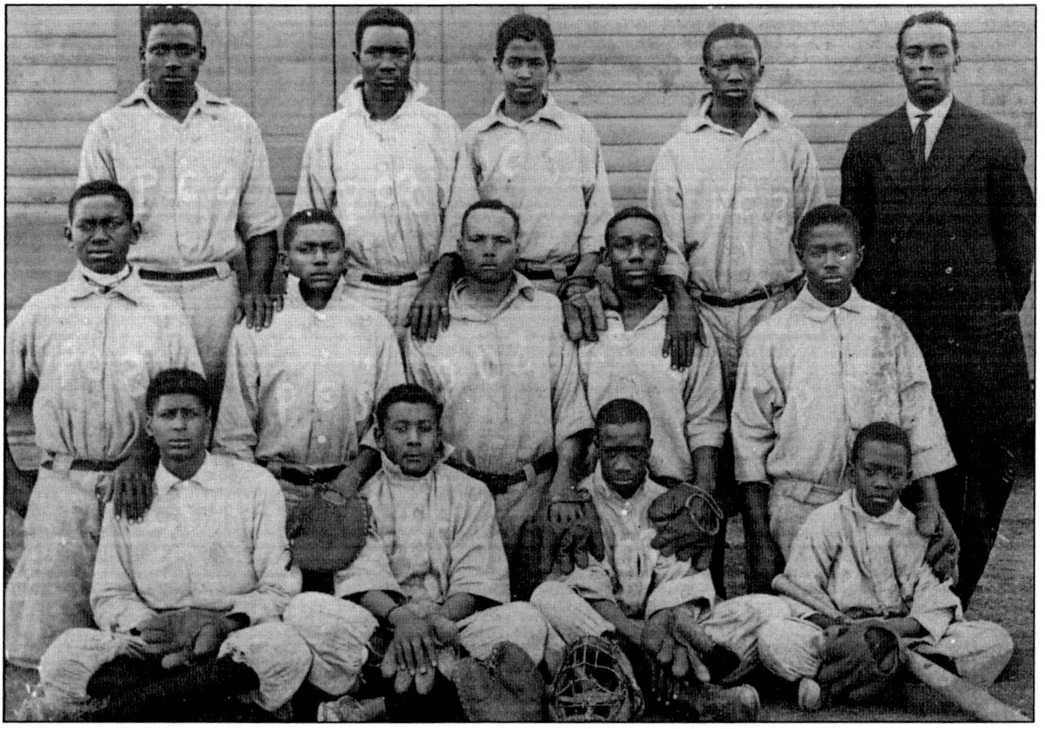

Plano African American baseball teams organized informally for special events, such as the annual Juneteenth celebration to commemorate Gen. Gordon Granger's proclamation declaring all slaves in Texas free. (Courtesy of the Wells Collection, Plano Public Library.)

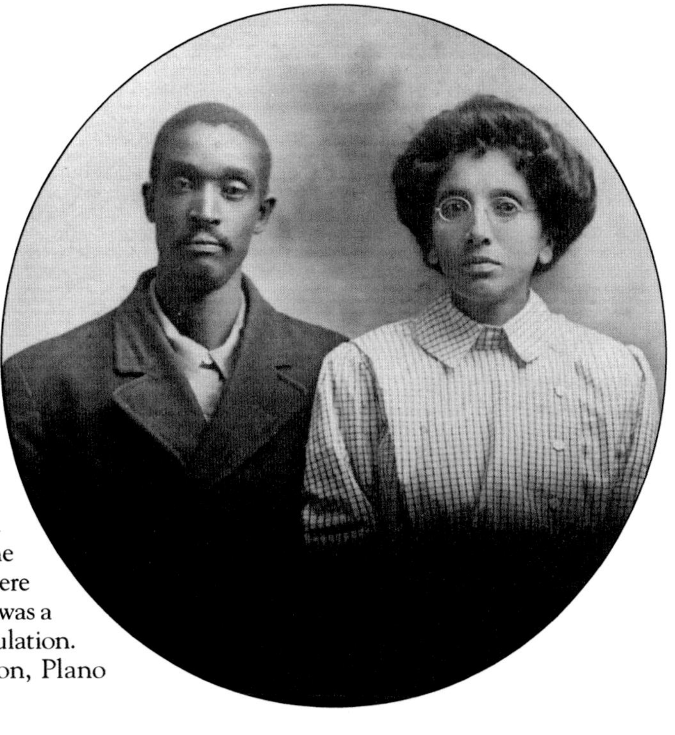

Pioneer Plano families trace their roots back to the 19th century; some Plano African American families trace their roots from the era of Reconstruction. Although there were no plantations in Plano, there was a small farm and domestic slave population. (Courtesy of the Wells Collection, Plano Public Library.)

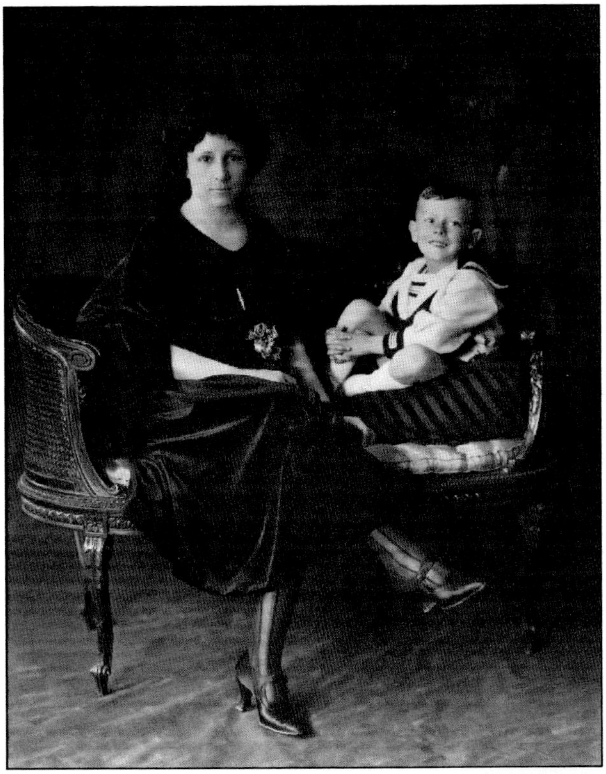

Interurban travel connected Plano residents with the modern and progressive urban centers of Dallas and Fort Worth. Pioneer-descended Plano residents such as Bess Shelton and her son Robert typify the golden age. (Courtesy of the Wells Collection, Plano Public Library.)

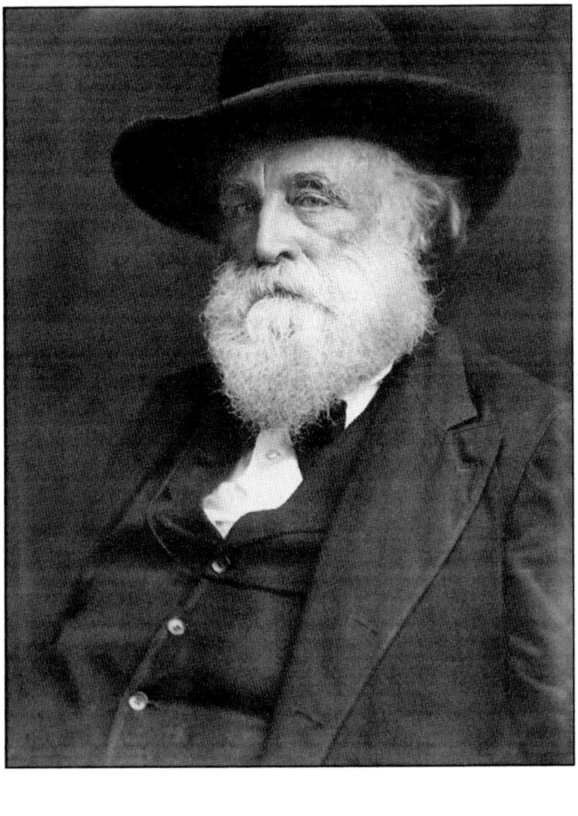

C. S. (Clinton Shepard) Haggard, an early pioneer in Texas and one of the largest landowners in Collin County, came to Texas shortly after Texas joined the union. Coming from Kentucky in 1856 with his father, they settled on a large section of land that was probably part of the Land Grant Act of 1854. Early Texas pioneers came from nearby Southern states such as Tennessee and Kentucky and often had known or were related to each other before resettling in Texas. Haggard was famous for raising mules and horses, and by 1866, Collin County became the leading mule market west of the Mississippi. (Courtesy of the Wells Collection, Plano Public Library.)

Maude Goode Shepard was the wife of Clint Shepard of Shepard Ranch. She held a leadership role in Plano's Women's Clubs, which sought social uplift for the community. (Courtesy of the Wells Collection, Plano Public Library.)

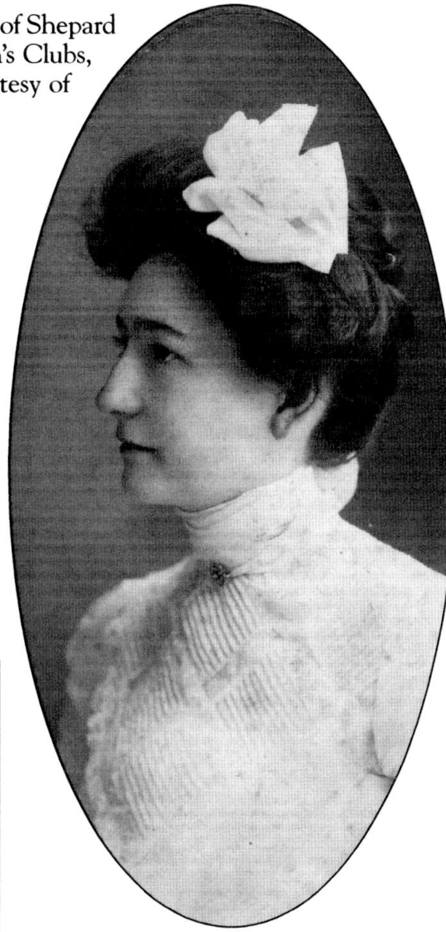

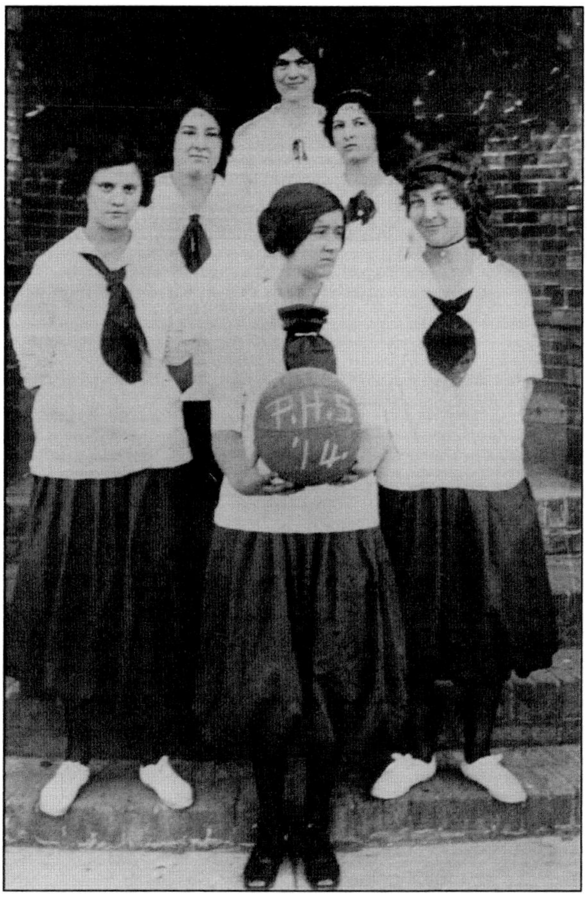

Sports enthusiasm in the schools and community was an important factor in welding the Plano community together. Part of the Plano High School 1914 girls' basketball team and their coach pose on the school steps to have their photograph taken for the annual yearbook. (Courtesy of the Wells Collection, Plano Public Library.)

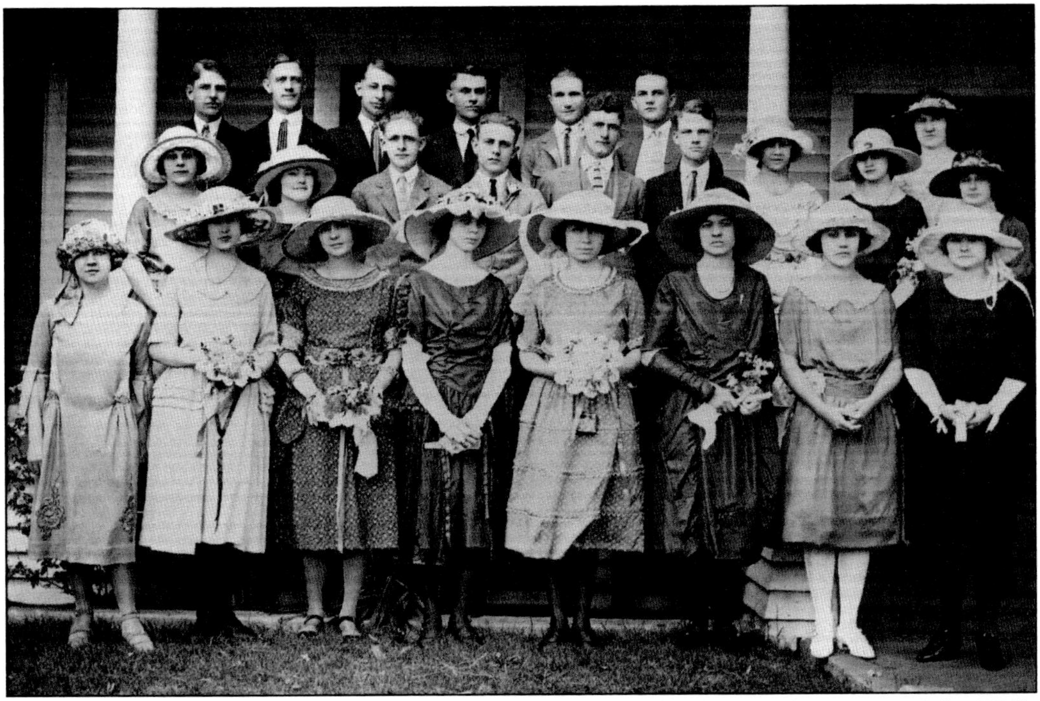

Pictured here is the Plano High School graduating class of about 1925. (Courtesy of the Wells Collection, Plano Public Library.)

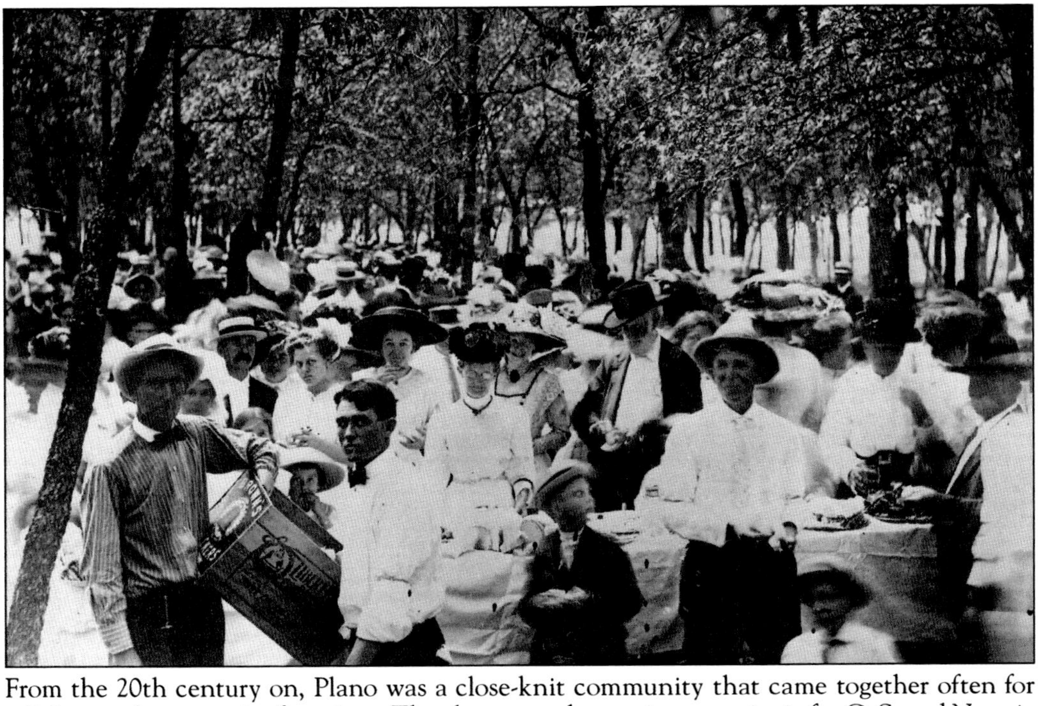

From the 20th century on, Plano was a close-knit community that came together often for religious and community functions. The above was the anniversary picnic for C. S. and Nannie Kate Haggard in 1909. The celebration was held in the grove next to their home. (Courtesy of the Wells Collection, Plano Public Library.)

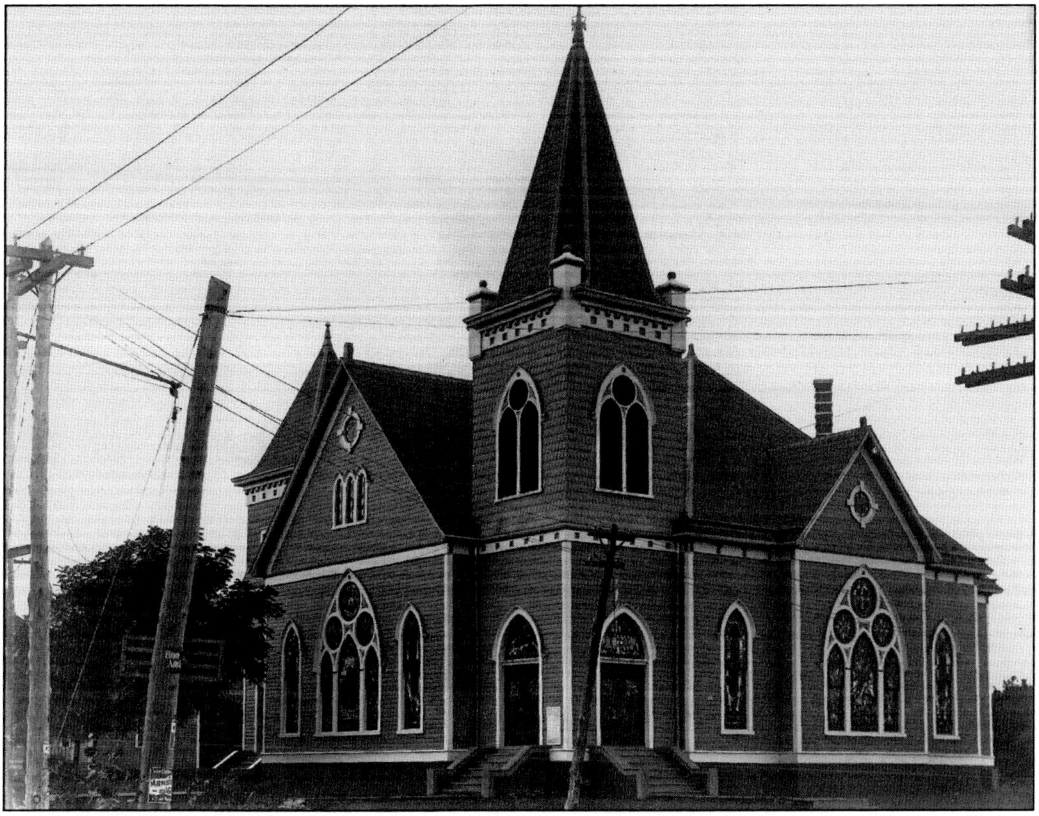

Religion played an important role in the life of the citizens of Plano. Built in the 19th century, the Christian Church of Plano is a fine example of a wood-frame church with a tower and well-designed stained-glass windows. By 1900, Plano could support many church congregations, including an African American congregation, Shiloh Baptist Church, which still exists today.

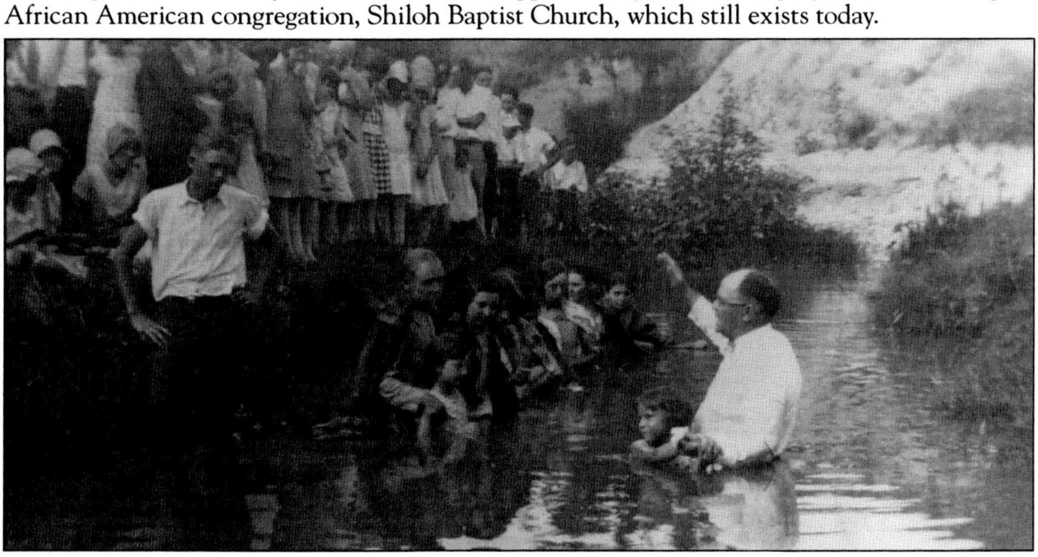

Religious revivals were often held in Plano and drew large attendances. During a revival, most saloons in town would close during the services and often the saloon owners would come to get the spirit. (Courtesy of the Plano Public Library.)

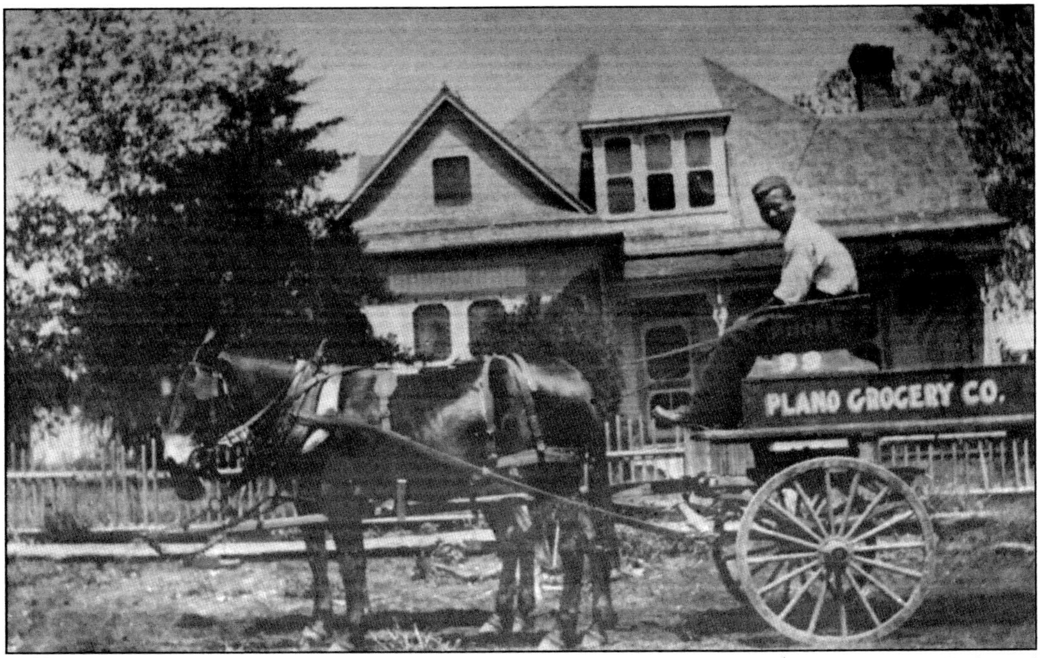

As Plano grew into a larger town, citizens needed expanded services such as grocery, fuel, and ice delivery to their homes. Founded by Manley Carlisle and his father, Henry B. Carlisle, after 1896, Plano Grocery became one of the main businesses in town and prospered with the city. (Courtesy of the Wells Collection, Plano Public Library.)

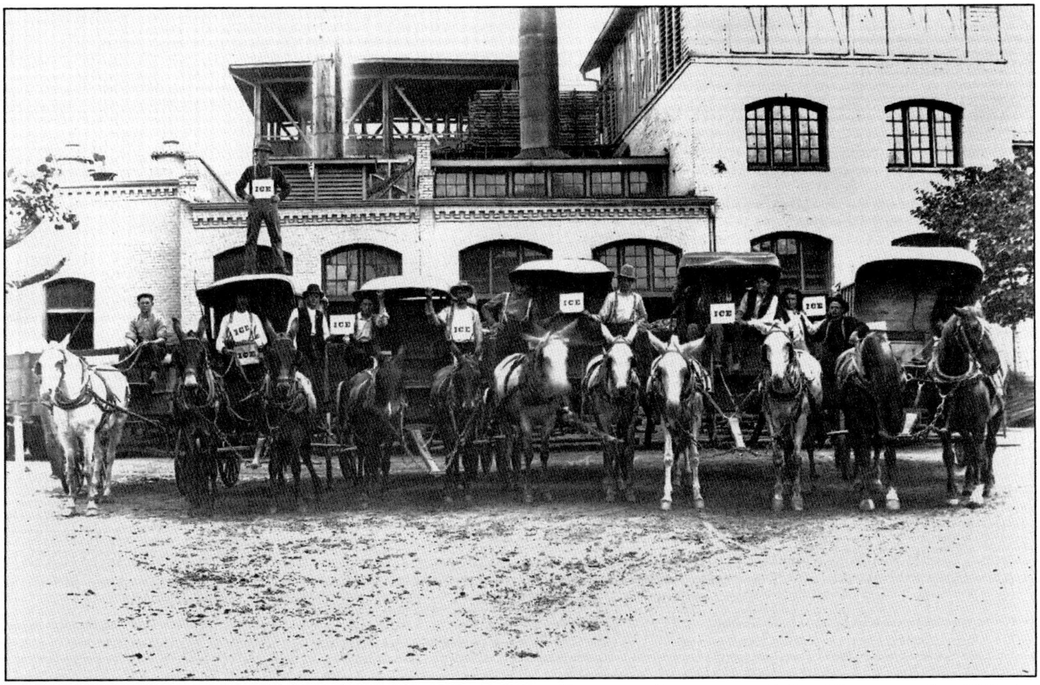

For the warm summers on the Texas prairie, ice was always welcome, and the Sherman Ice Works was ready to deliver. In this 1905 photograph, young delivery men are lined up for the day's work of delivering blocks of ice to their customers in town.

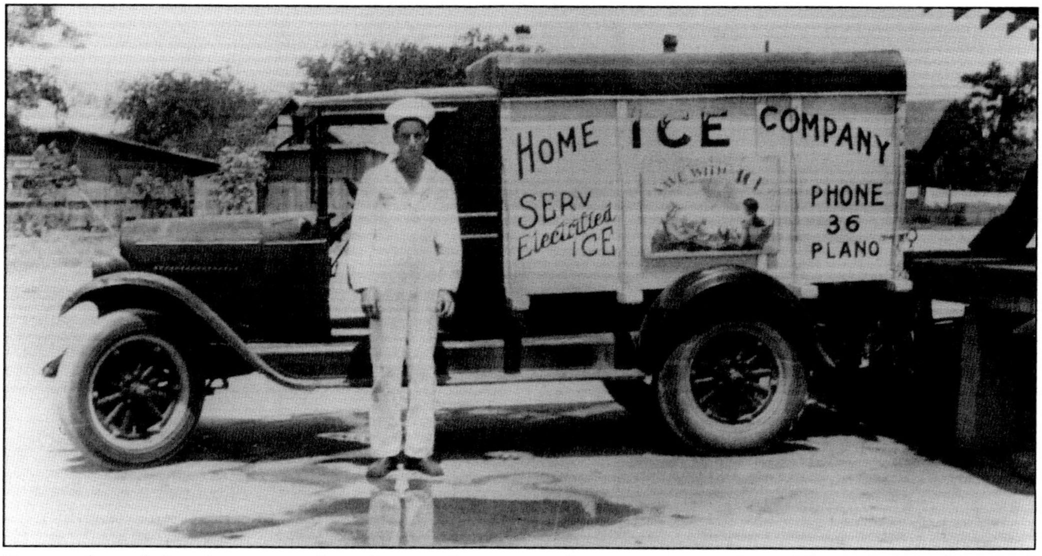

Research and development of mechanical ice manufacture grew early in Texas during the Civil War, when ice harvesting from the North was interrupted. The first ice plant in Plano was built in the 1880s and probably used ammonia compression technology, developed by Charles Zilker in San Antonio. Ice delivery wagons and later trucks were common sights on the streets of Plano and other cities in North Texas from the late 19th through the mid-20th century. In 1891, iceboxes (called refrigerators now) in Plano sold from as little as \$9.75 up to and beyond \$30 each. (Courtesy of the Wells Collection, Plano Public Library.)

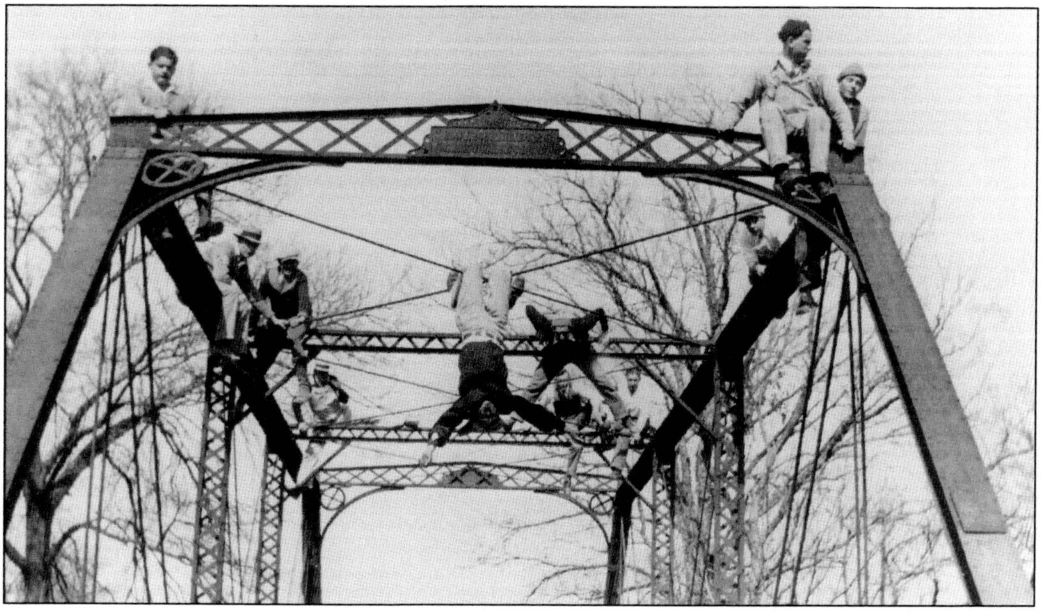

Here are 11 members of the Plano group called the "Twenty Tough Tamales." The young men all attended Plano High School and came together for fun and to perform good deeds for the community on the sly. After graduating from high school, they stayed in touch. Especially loyal was Lefty Creekmore, who moved to Oak Cliff in 1927. He returned on weekends for many years on the Texas Electric Railway to visit his friends in Plano. (Courtesy of the Wells Collection, Plano Public Library.)

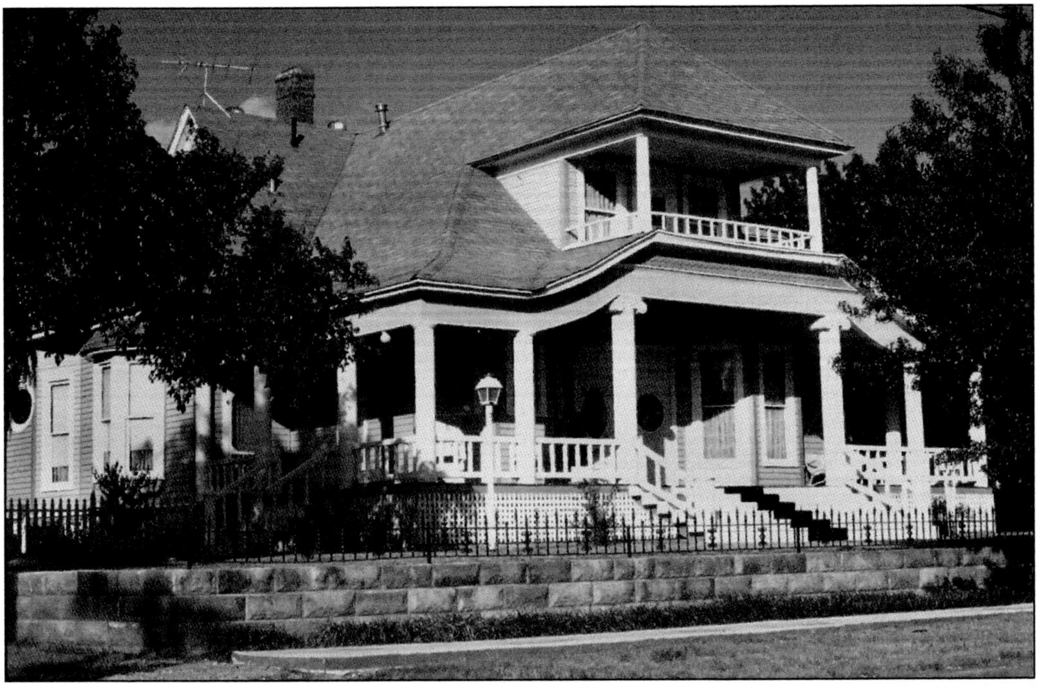

Although none of the titans of the Texas interurban railway ever achieved the lofty financial and social status of the great financiers of the East, such as J. P. Morgan, John Astor, and Cornelius Vanderbilt, they were wealthy at their own level and in their communities. At an age in Texas when wealth was manifested by land ownership, the interurban developers built splendid homes for themselves as evidence of their success. Restored to its 19th-century stateliness, the Waxahachie home of James Andrew Beall, born in 1866, is still an imposing sight. Beall taught school and practiced law in Ellis County from 1890 until elected to the Texas Legislature and later to the U.S. Congress (1903–1915). After the death of his friend and business associate James F. Strickland, Beall became president of Texas Electric Railway from 1921 until his death in 1929.

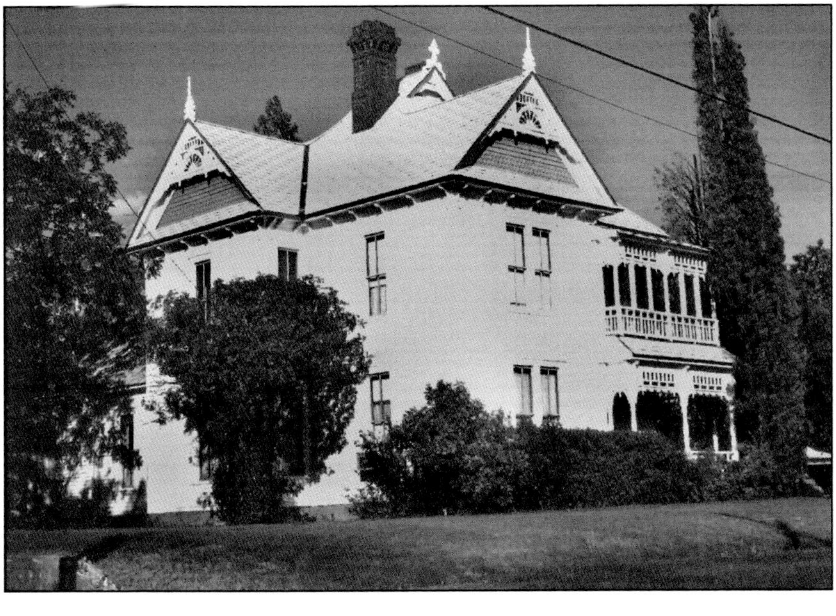

Also living in Waxahachie was James Griffin, nephew of James Beall, who succeeded Beall as the last president of Texas Electric Railway. He had a home that was more modest than his colleagues but nonetheless very striking in its architectural style and detail.

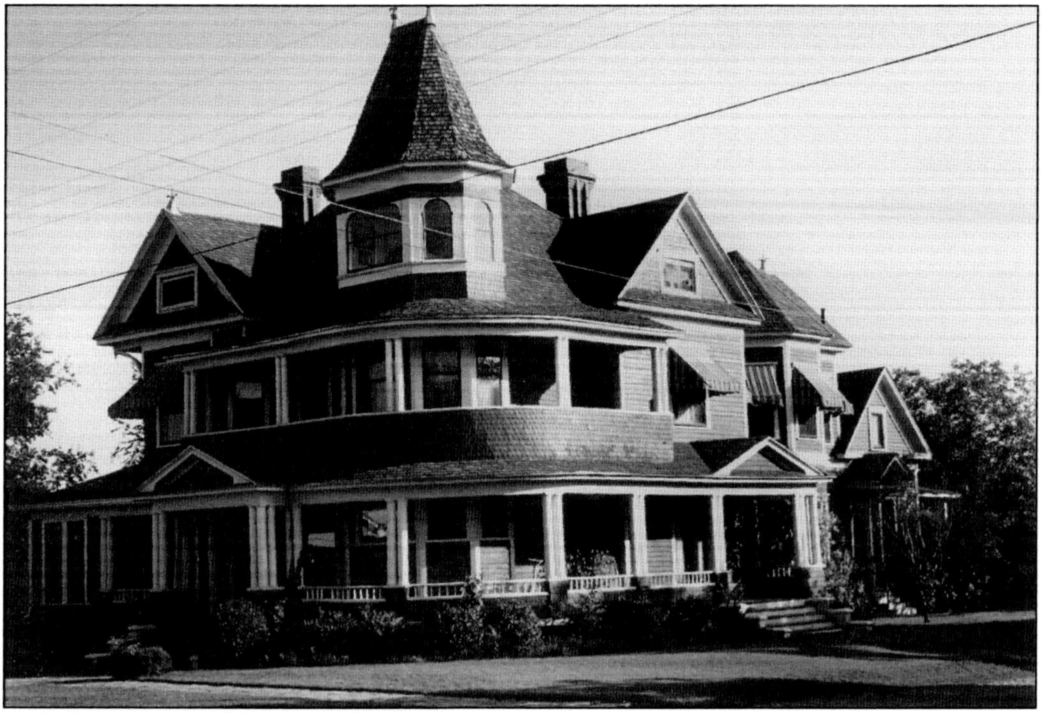

Perhaps the most magnificent of the houses of the interurban magnates was that of John F. Strickland. He lived here in Waxahachie until he moved to Dallas in 1904.

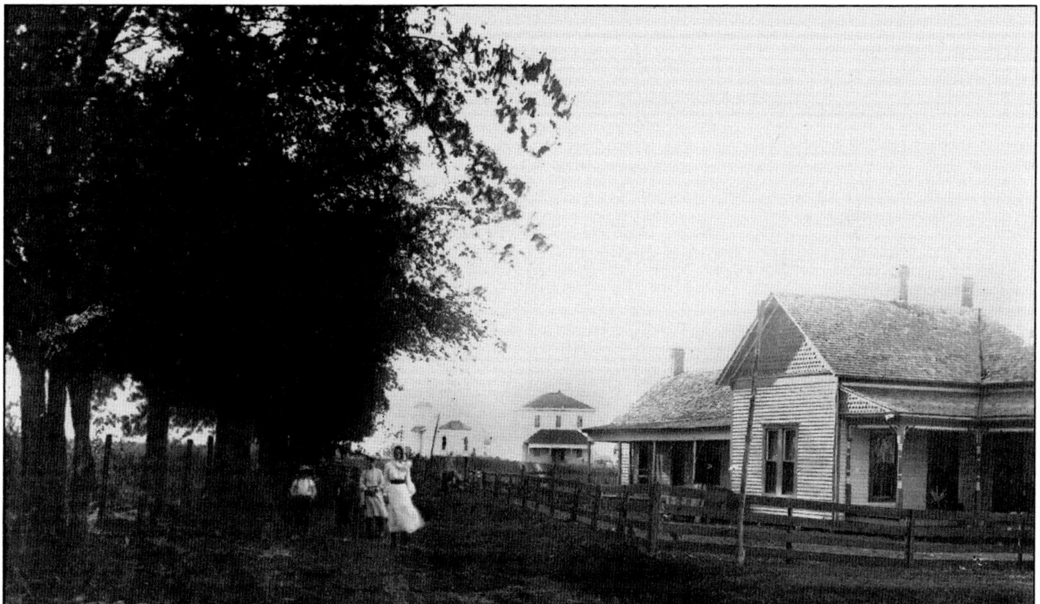

Renner was one of the many agricultural communities that ended its isolation by being close to the new Texas Traction interurban railway system. Founded in 1888 as a stop on the Cotton Belt Line, it never grew beyond 300 people until the mid-20th century and was annexed by Dallas in 1983. Due to the interurban, Sunday afternoons could be spent at Woodlake, the Texas State Fair, Waco, or Dallas.

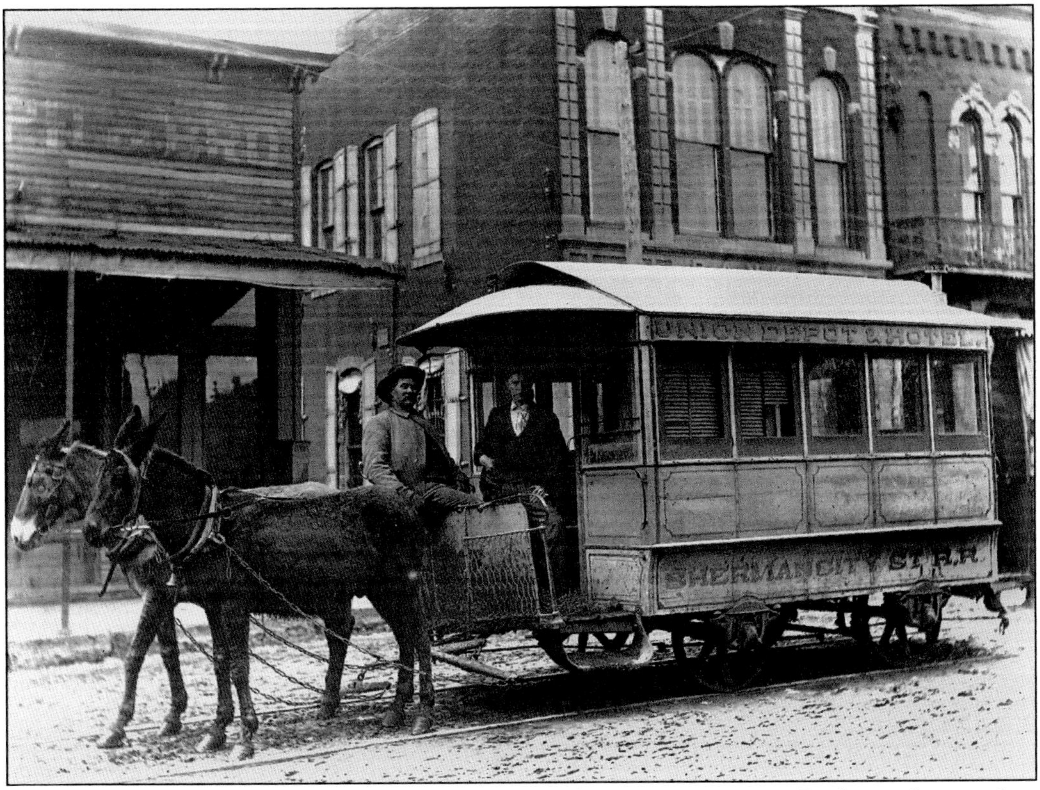

The first electric rail line in Texas was called the Sherman City Street Railway, chartered in 1877. The car was pulled by mules traveling through the business district. The driver would stop anyplace on the line and wait for passengers. The driver of the mule car is M. P. "Dad" Hill. The last mule car ran in 1900.

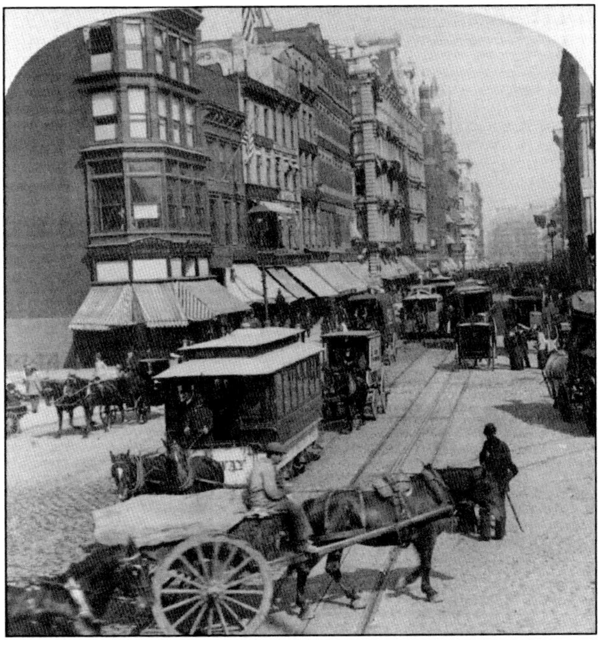

In the early 19th century, the horse omnibus began to appear in city streets, and as rails were laid, the horse- or mule-powered street railway in cities gained widespread popularity. By the 1880s, this type of railway even penetrated small towns. These early transport systems would soon give way to electric traction systems. (Courtesy of the Library of Congress.)

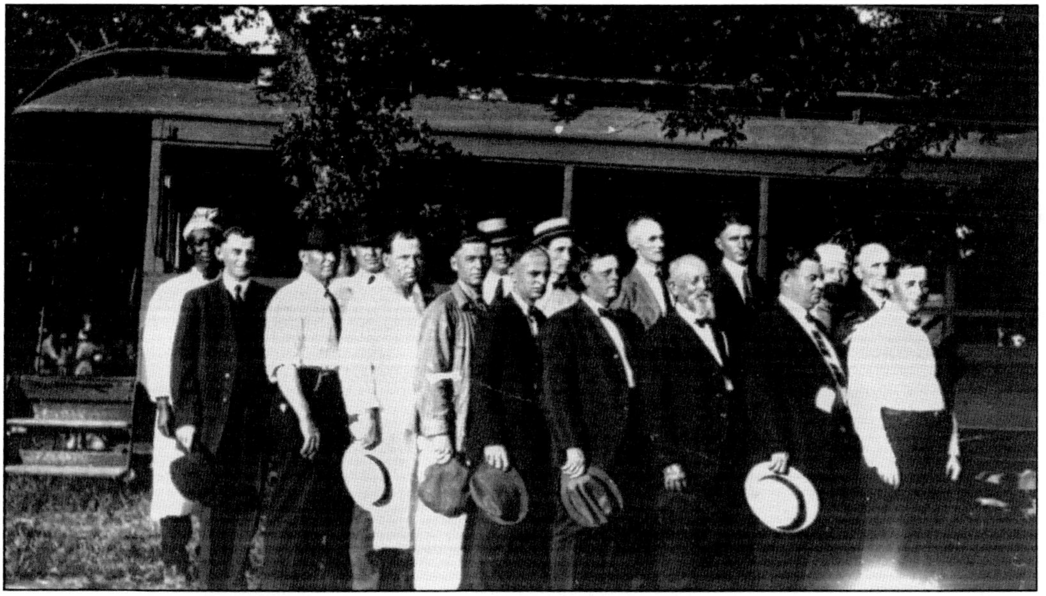

Probably at Woodlake Trolley Park, the company-owned recreation park for employees, Texas Traction men in management are posed for a photograph taken about 1912. From left to right are (first row) Dick Hawkins, cook; ? Roy; Beck Lofton; Bob Hunter; unidentified; Happy Summers; ? Hayden and his son; C. Smith, claim agent; and M. J. Loftus, superintendent; (second row) five unidentified, Stanley Reynolds, and ? Silvus.

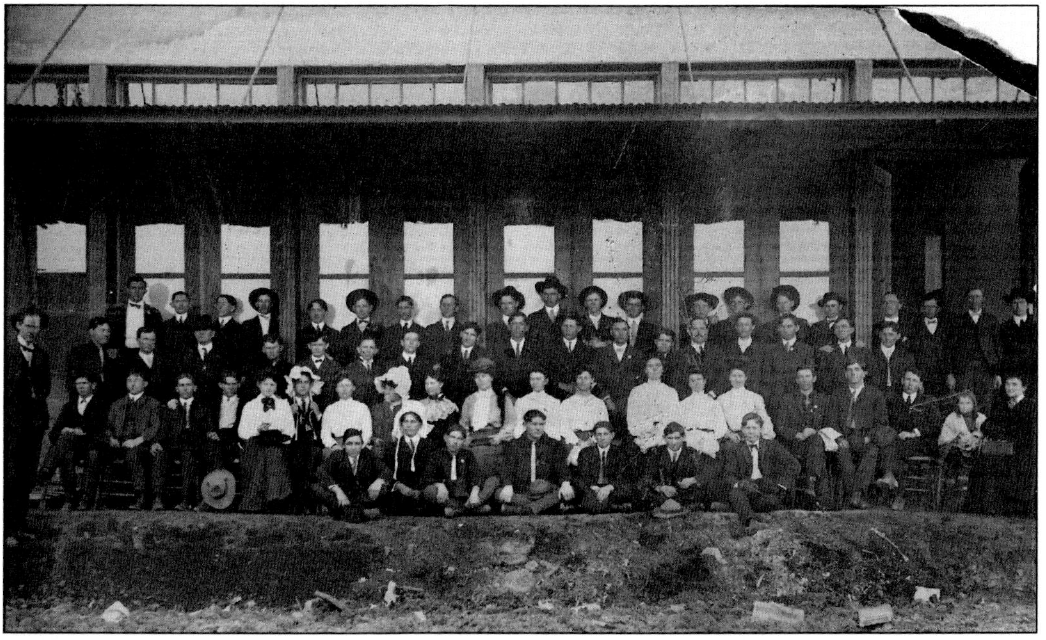

These are probably Texas Traction employees at the Woodlake Casino around 1910.

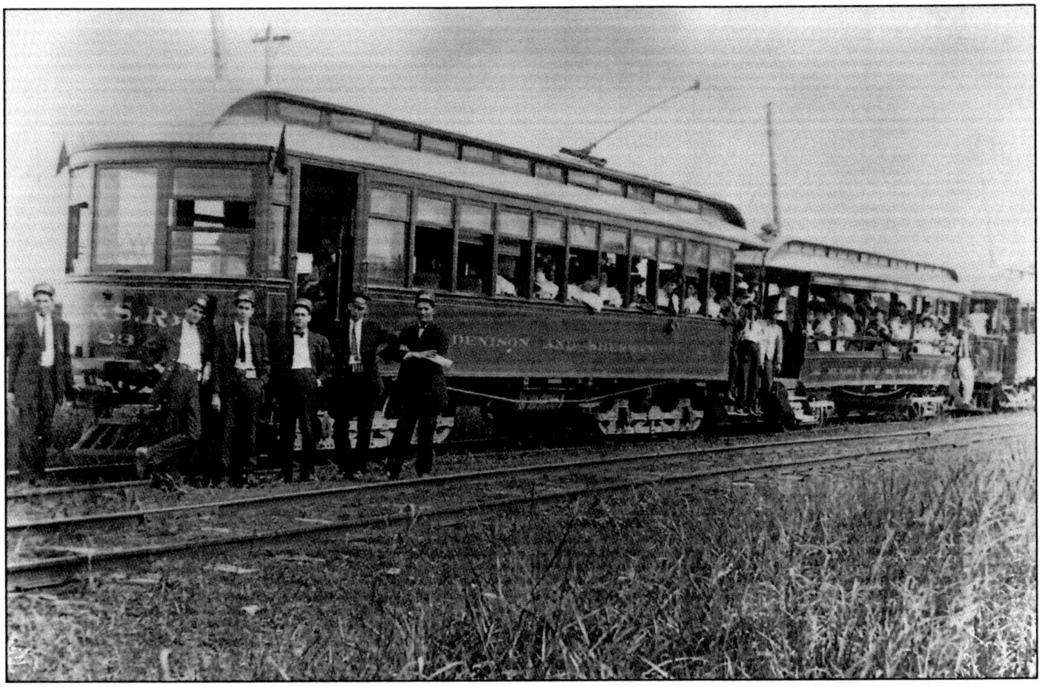

Passengers are shown at Woodlake Park in 1902. It was common for groups to charter two, three, or even four cars for a daylong excursion at the park.

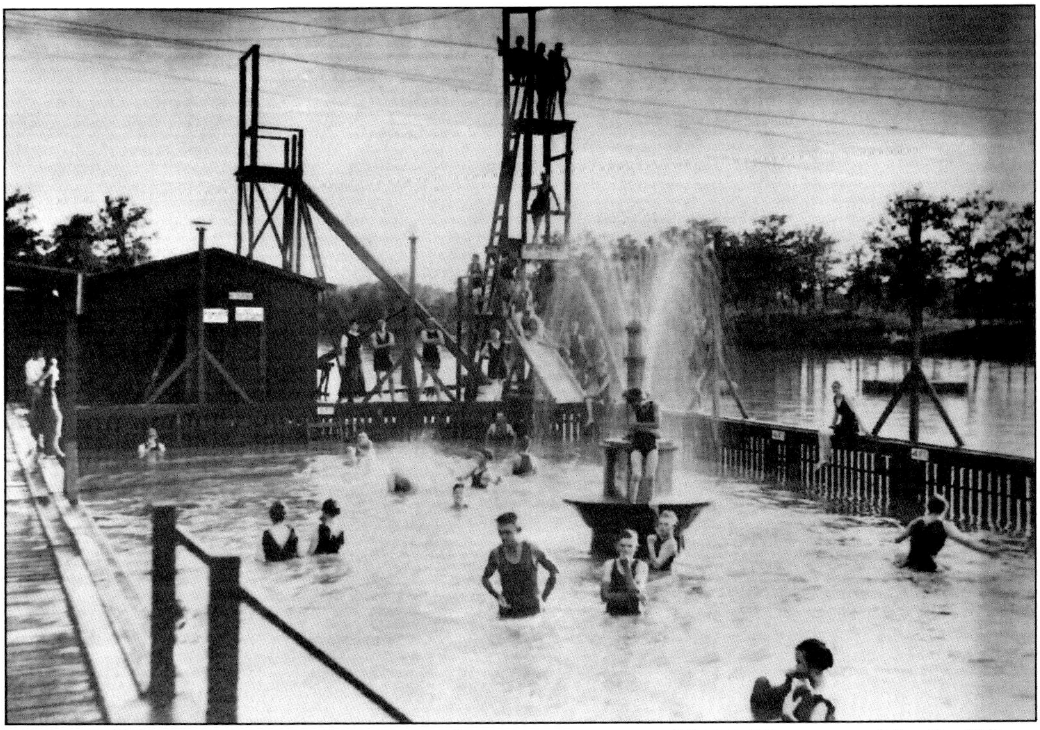

The Woodlake swimming pool was a popular attraction around 1905. (Courtesy of the Red River Historical Museum.)

J. F. Strickland, president of the Texas Traction Company, came to Plano on the evening of October 14, 1905, to meet with city officials from Plano and Allen to execute the contracts for the interurban electric railway from Sherman to Dallas. Plano and Allen furnished 10.5 miles of right-of-way, 60 feet in width and, where there were cuts and fills to be made, 100 feet if necessary.

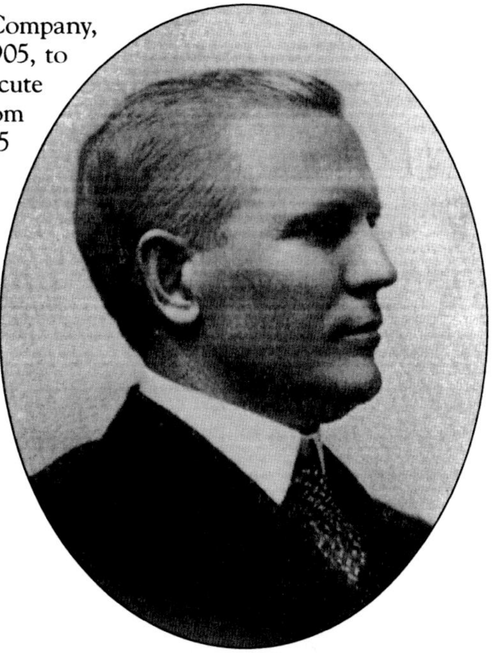

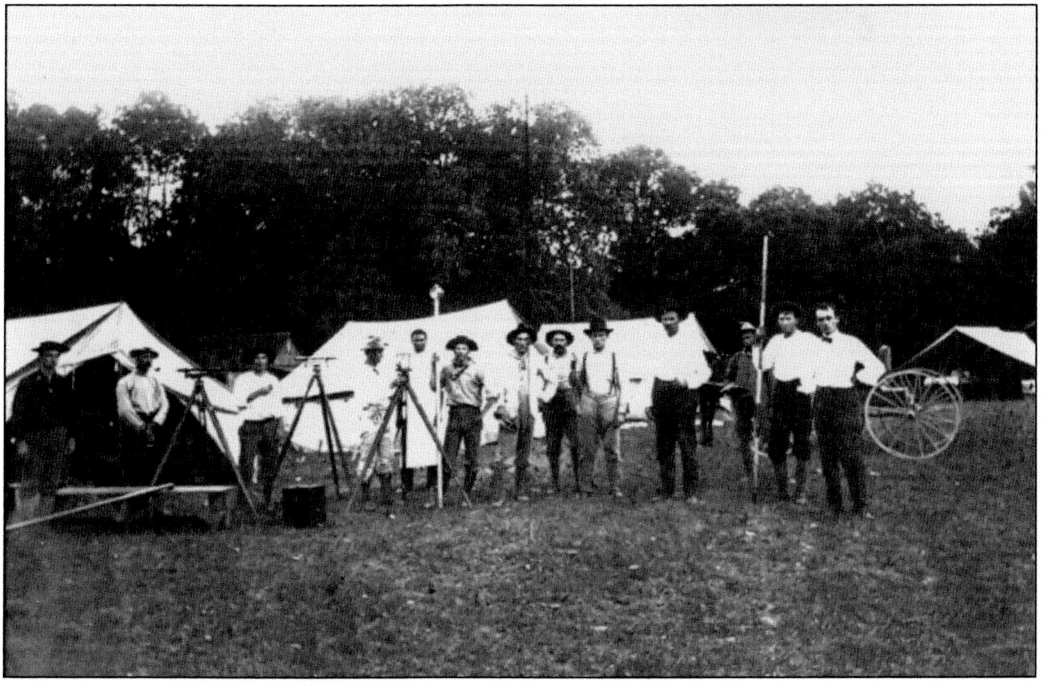

Before an interurban line linking Sherman to Dallas could be built, John Strickland commissioned a comprehensive survey that showed the justification for building such a line. The survey team laid out the line in exact form with boundaries and rights-of-way. The practice of using engineering consulting firms such as Stone and Webster and Fred A. Jones Consulting Engineers had grown out of the need to determine what the economic prospects for a proposed interurban project would be. Many early interurban systems in other parts of the country had been hastily built and had lost money for investors.

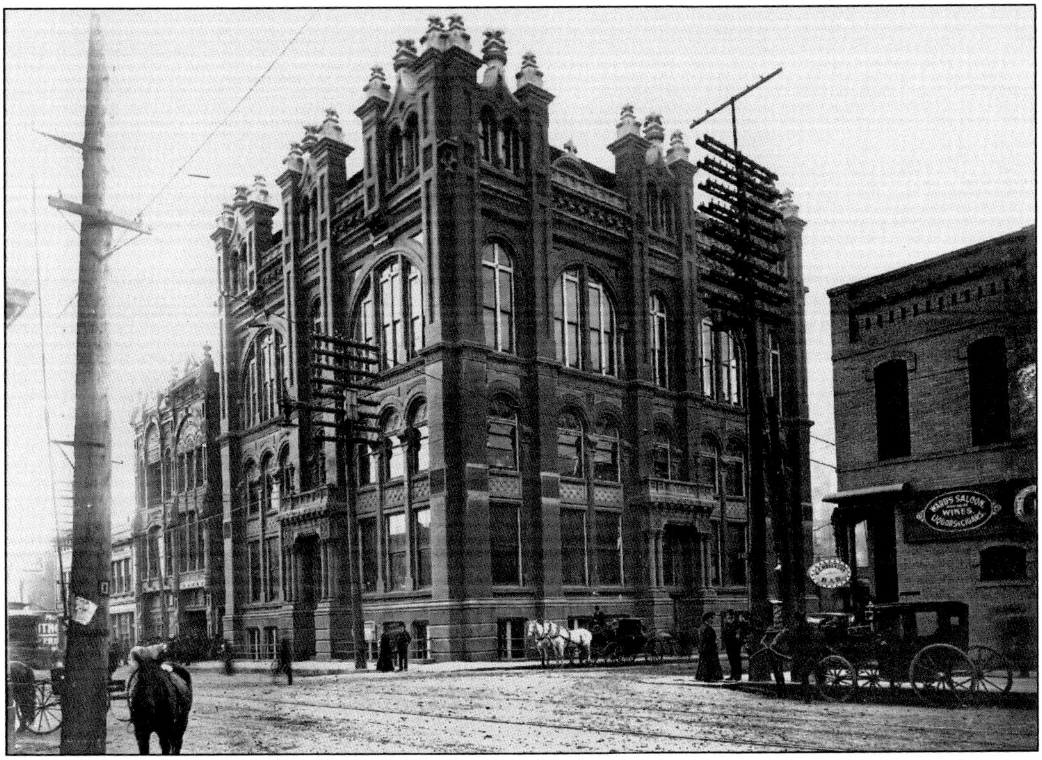

Built in 1888, Dallas City Hall, at the time of the interurban survey in 1905, stands adjacent to its architectural companion, the Dallas Police Station. The Dallas Consolidated Railway tracks run in front of city hall, and two carriages wait outside Ward's Saloon Wines Liquors and Cigars for their VIP owners.

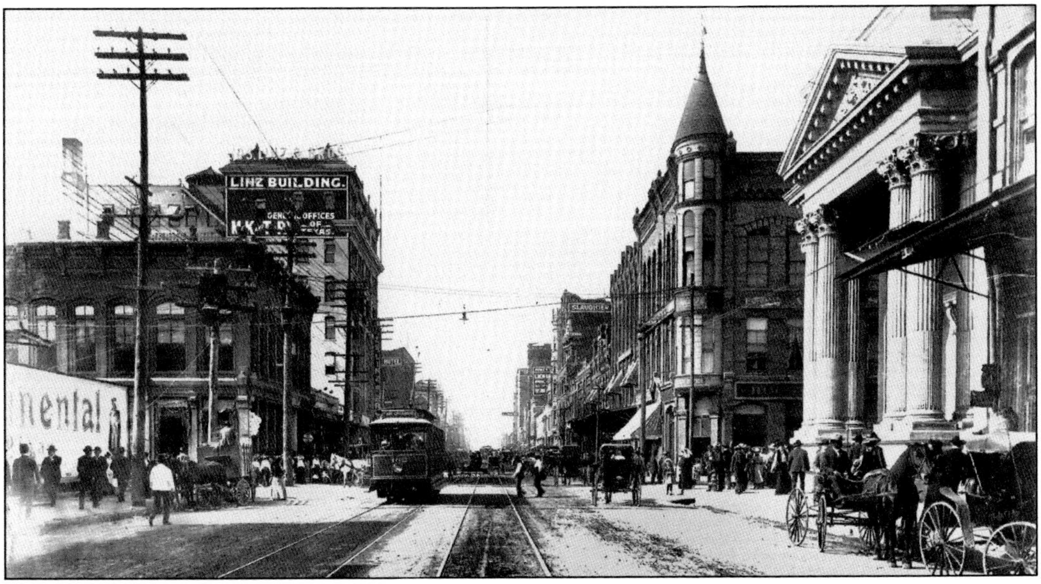

This photograph of Main Street looks west from the new Dallas Post Office building. Carriage and wagon traffic congestion is already becoming apparent in the business district, and the need for an interurban system linking North Texas business and farm communities with Dallas is obvious.

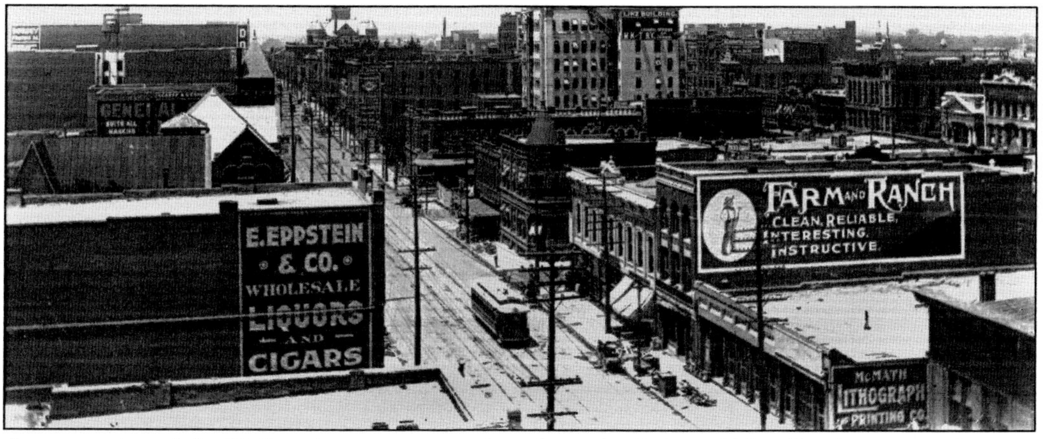

A survey view of the Dallas city center was taken from the Oriental Hotel looking west, showing the development of electricity and the electric rail system.

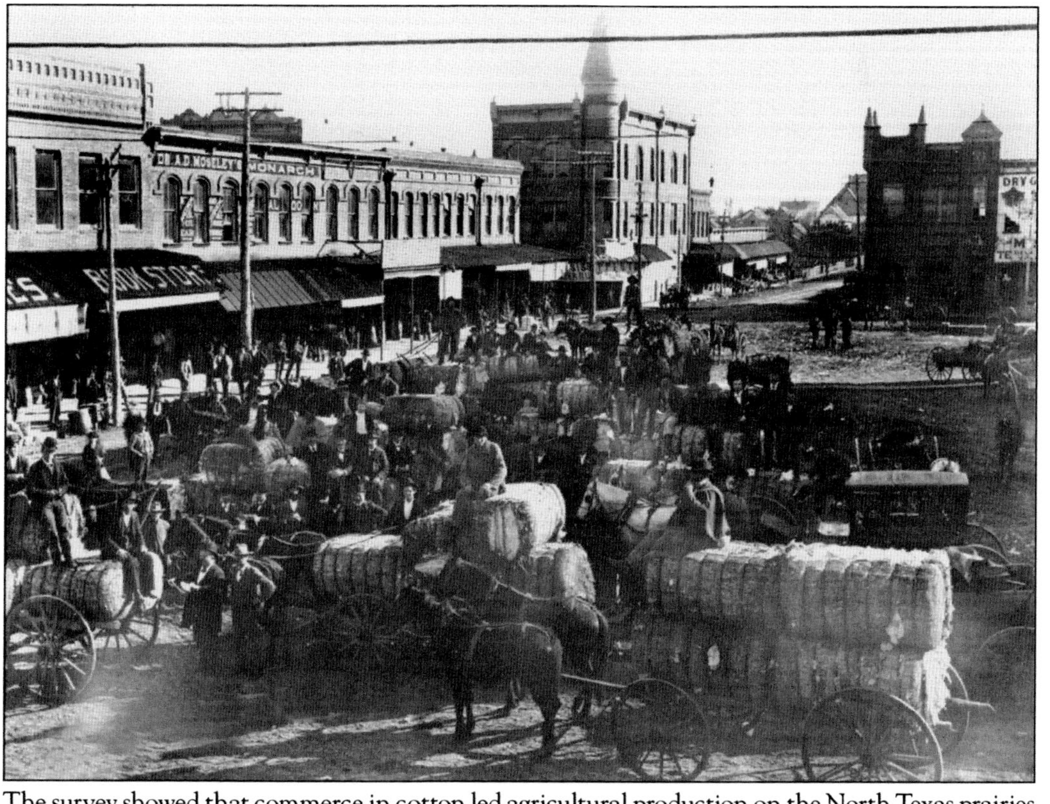

The survey showed that commerce in cotton led agricultural production on the North Texas prairies in the early years of the 20th century. Cotton producers and workers, such as those pictured here in the McKinney Square, often needed to travel to Plano, Denison, Sherman, Dallas, and Waco to conduct their business. A horse and wagon was not fast enough, and railroad trains were not frequent enough. The arrival of the interurban solved their problem.

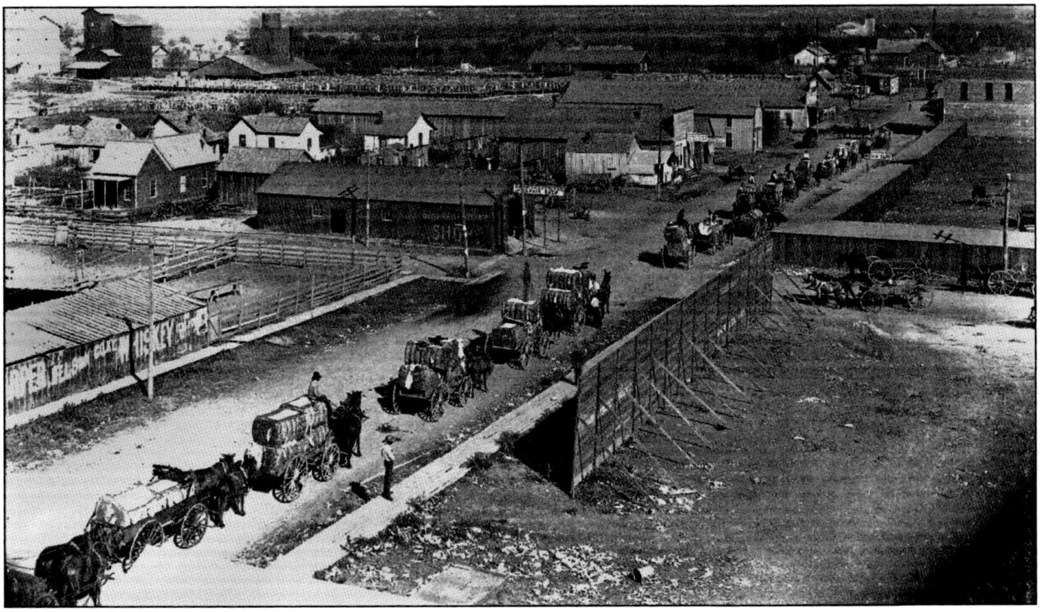

Wagons laden with bales of cotton line up for the compress and elevator. The agricultural abundance of the region brought riches to many in Texas and drove the development of more efficient transportation, such as electric interurban systems. In one day, businessmen could easily travel to major commercial centers such as the Dallas Cotton Exchange and then go on to the Waco Cotton markets or even to the Fort Worth Stock Exchange and return in the evening.

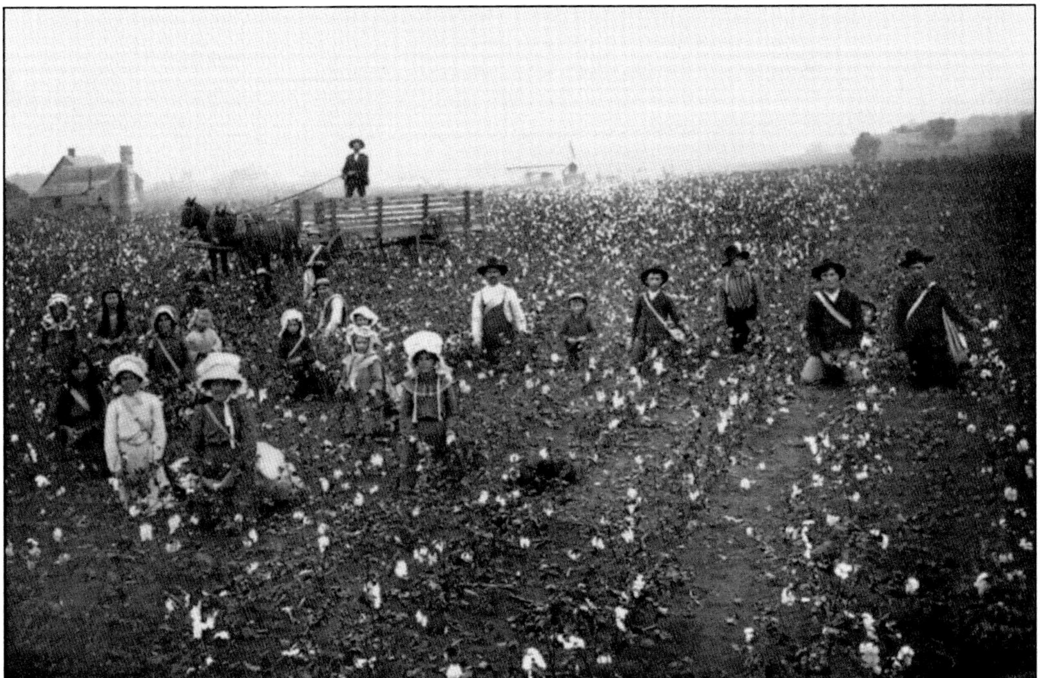

Early Plano was a simple agricultural community before the arrival of the railroad and the interurban. Whole families participated in the cotton harvest, including small children and elders. Migrant farm workers went from farm to farm.

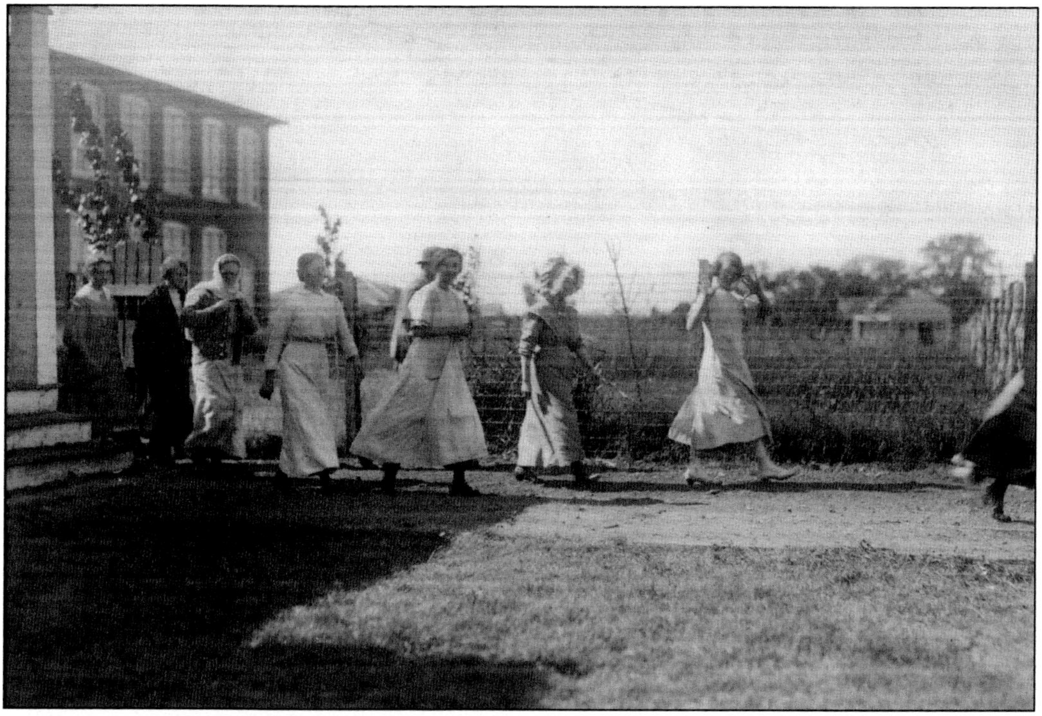

North Texas cotton mills drew workers from farms and homesteads to process cotton and create wealth for many in the region. (Courtesy of the Library of Congress.)

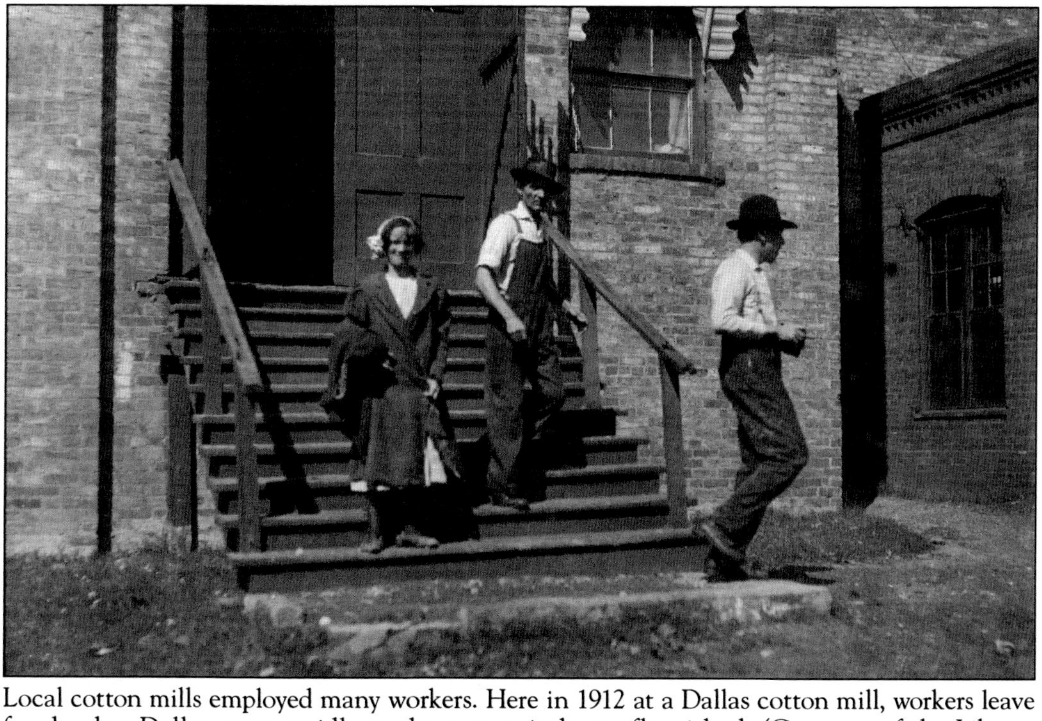

Local cotton mills employed many workers. Here in 1912 at a Dallas cotton mill, workers leave for the day. Dallas grew rapidly as the cotton industry flourished. (Courtesy of the Library of Congress.)

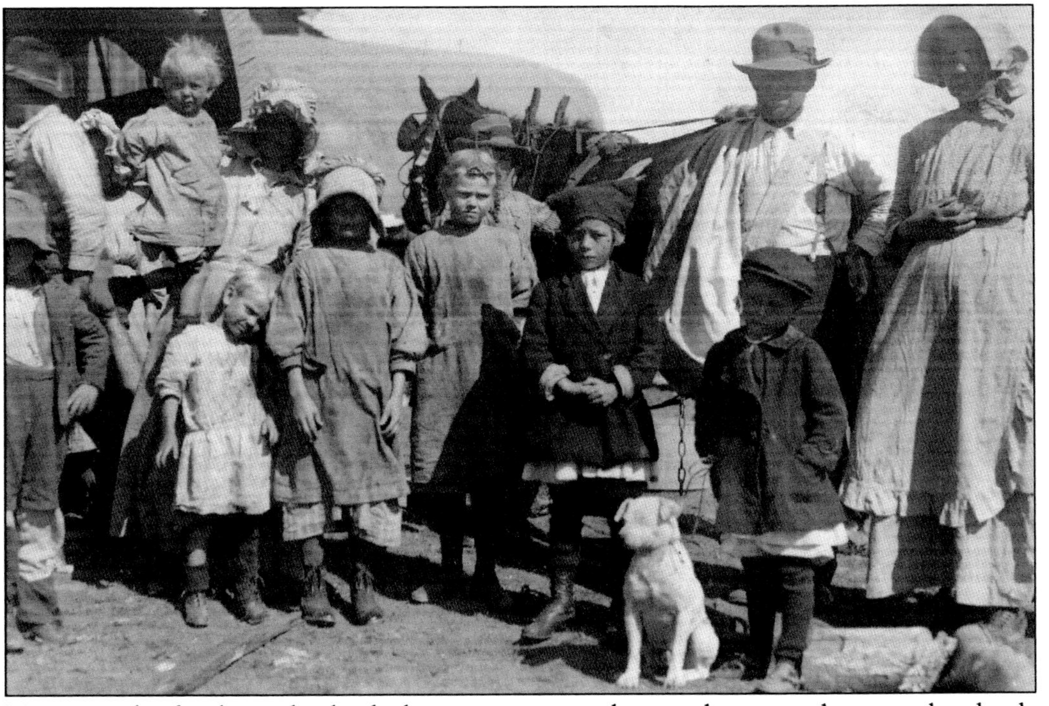

Migrant worker families and individuals were necessary to harvest the cotton that grew abundantly on the blackland prairie. This 1912 photograph shows a family group migrating by wagon from one farm to another. (Courtesy of the Library of Congress.)

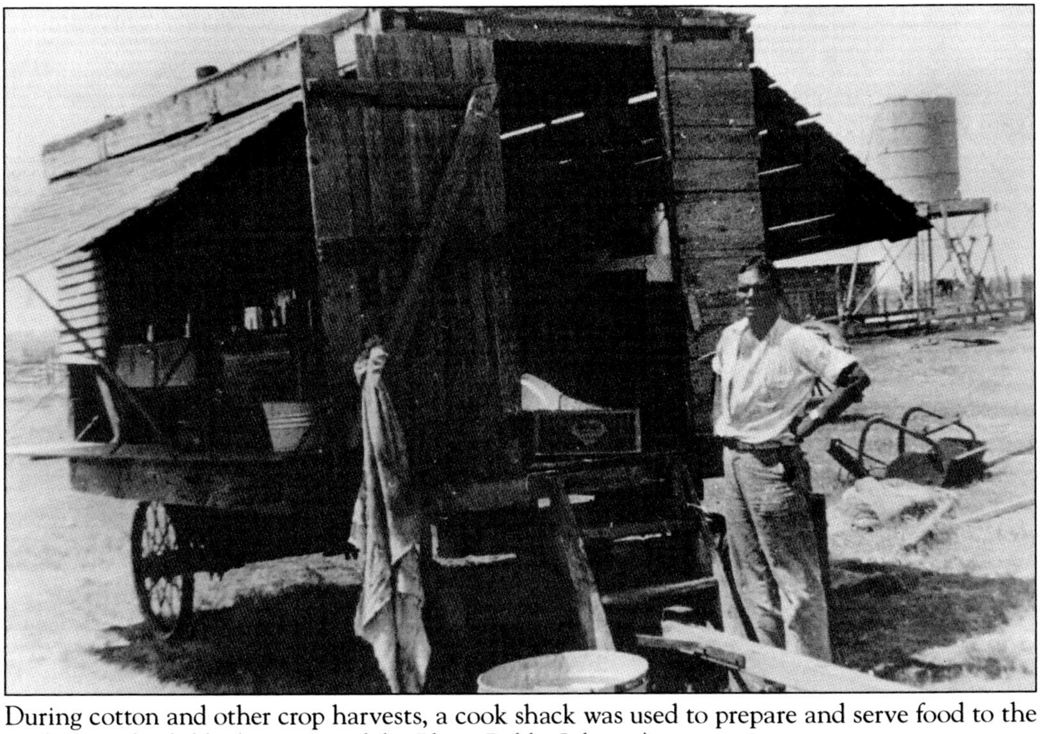

During cotton and other crop harvests, a cook shack was used to prepare and serve food to the workers in the fields. (Courtesy of the Plano Public Library.)

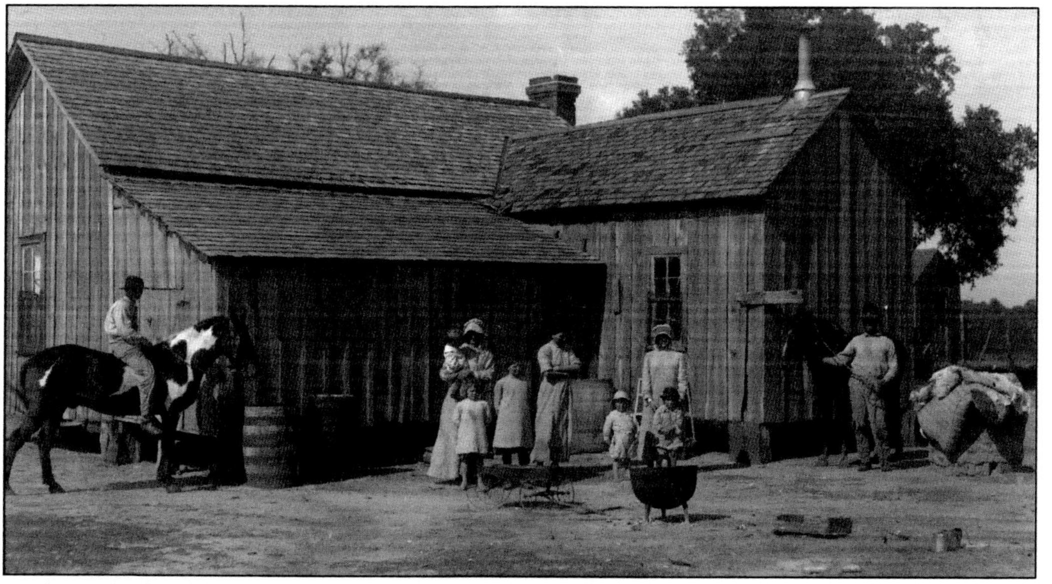

Without the hard work and perseverance of the plain and simple folk who worked the farms and picked the cotton, the wealth of North Texas and Plano could not have emerged. This picture dates to around 1912. (Courtesy of the Library of Congress.)

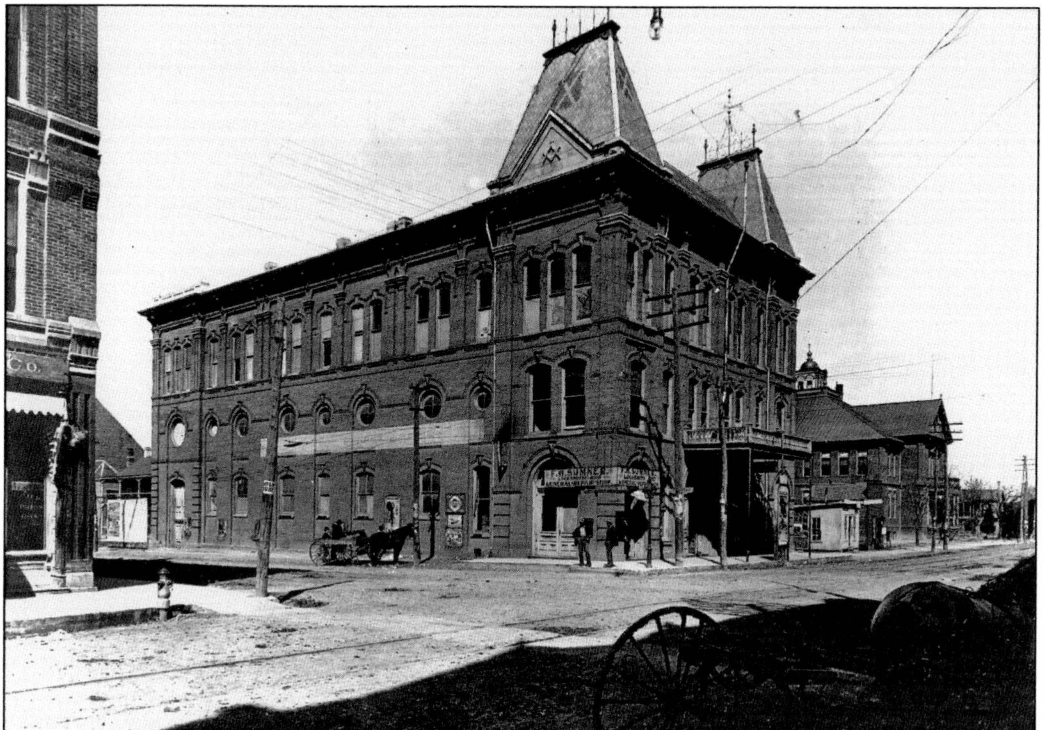

An objective of the Fred Jones Survey was to show the level of cultural and economic development of the region. An opera house was a strong indicator of a town's cultural progress. In past times, an opera house was a building used for public performances. Plano had had several opera houses at various times since 1881, all of which burned at one time or another.

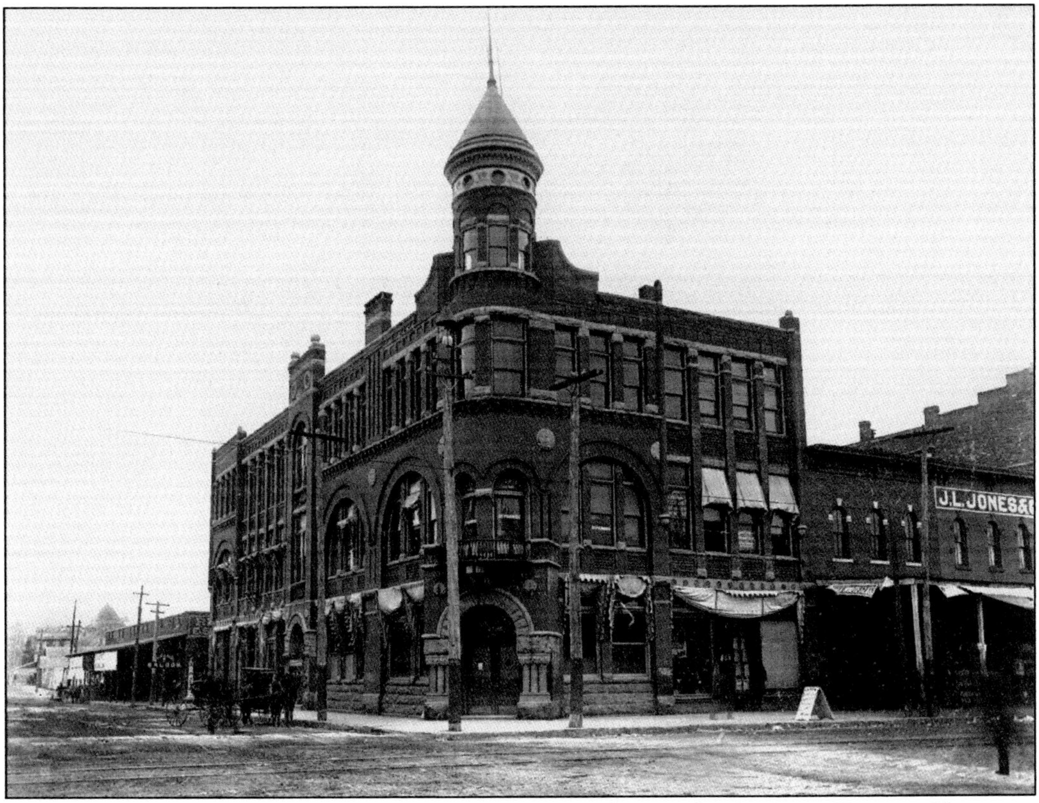

In the John Strickland survey to determine financial justification for the Texas Traction Sherman-to-Dallas Interurban, officials sought to show that the community had growth and financial potential. The existence of brick and stone bank buildings such as the National Bank of Denison helped to tell the story.

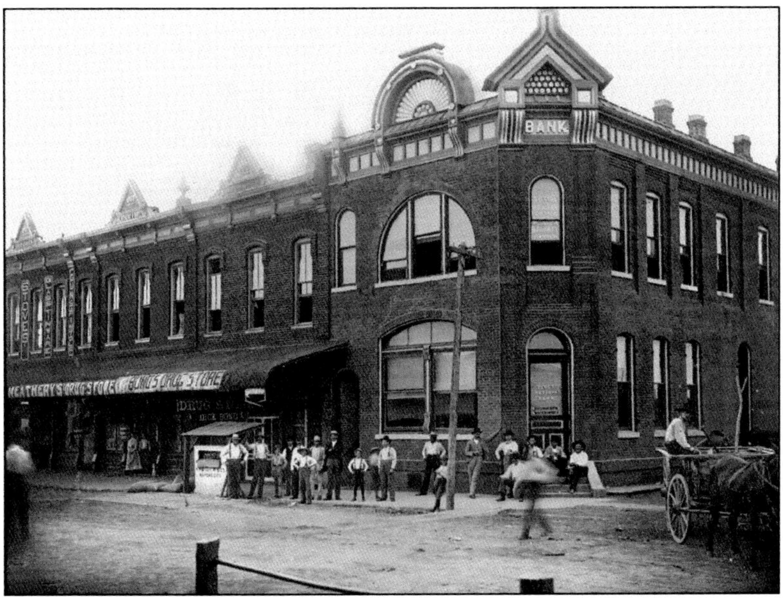

In the small town of Van Alstyne, a formidable bank building indicated substantial progress.

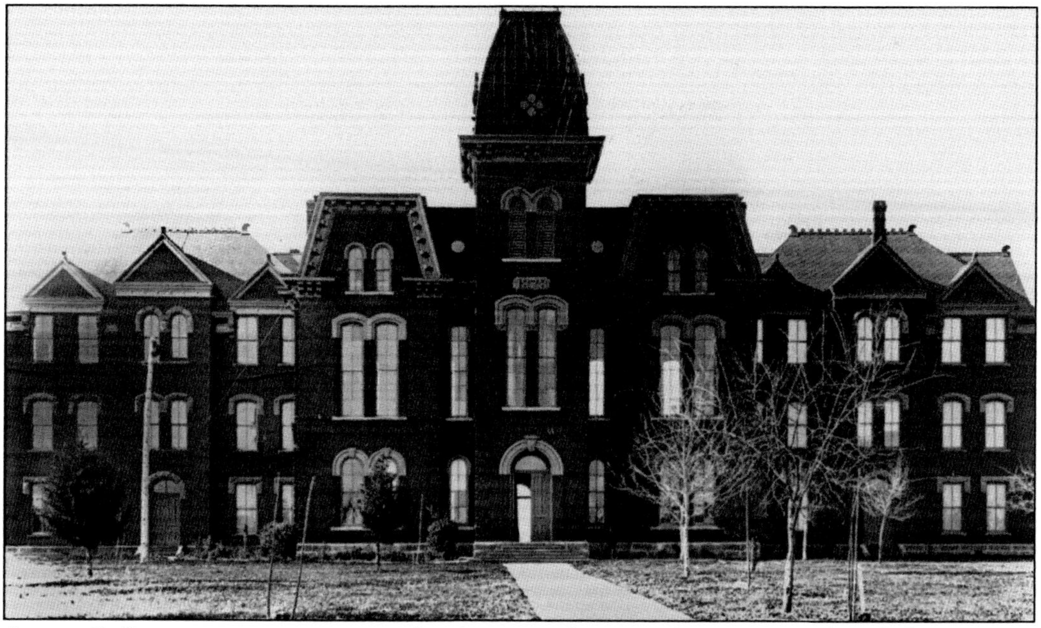

Austin College was a prestigious and important educational institution, founded in 1849 in Huntsville. The college was modeled after Princeton University. Two presidents of the Republic of Texas, Sam Houston and Anson Jones, served on the original board of trustees. In 1876, the institution moved to Sherman and was the first college in Texas to grant a graduate degree. Including Austin College in the survey showed the educational strength of the region.

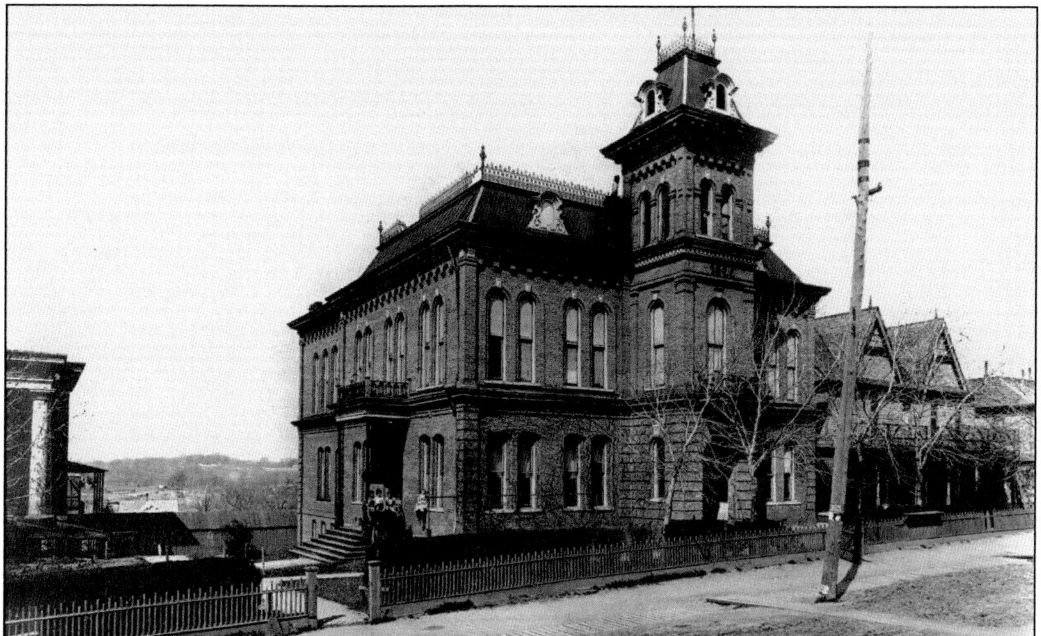

The survey further showed the educational strength of the North Texas region by including the North Texas Female College and Conservatory of Music in Sherman. Formalized in 1874, the institution boasted ownership of 120 pianos and a library of 1,000 volumes with an enrollment of 500 by 1914.

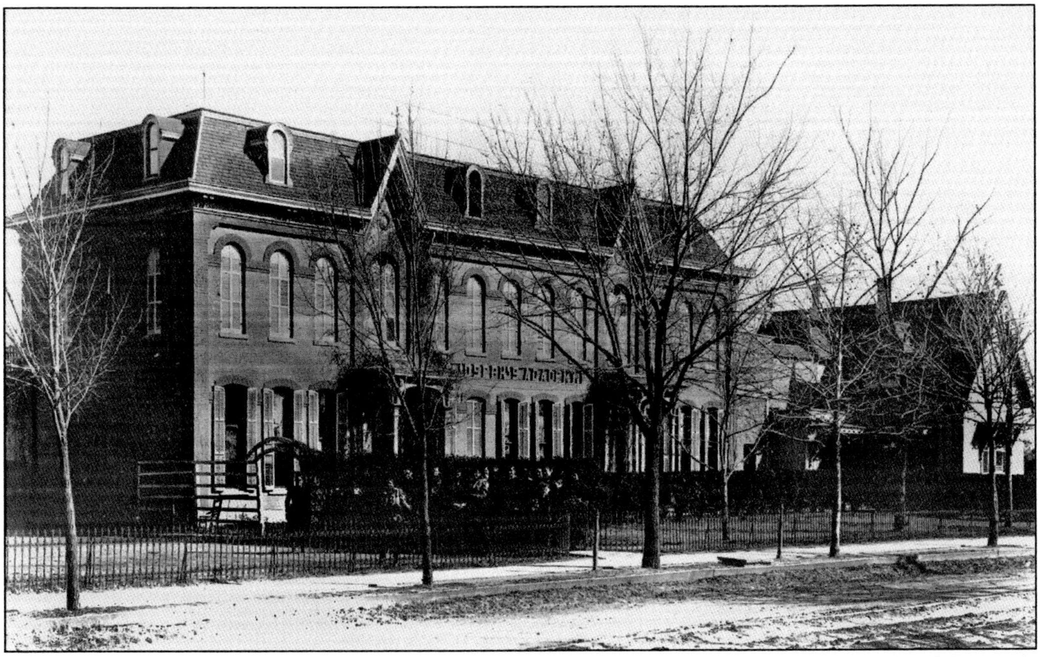

Religious schools often were the basis of educational institutions. The Catholic School for Girls in Sherman was considered one of the finest.

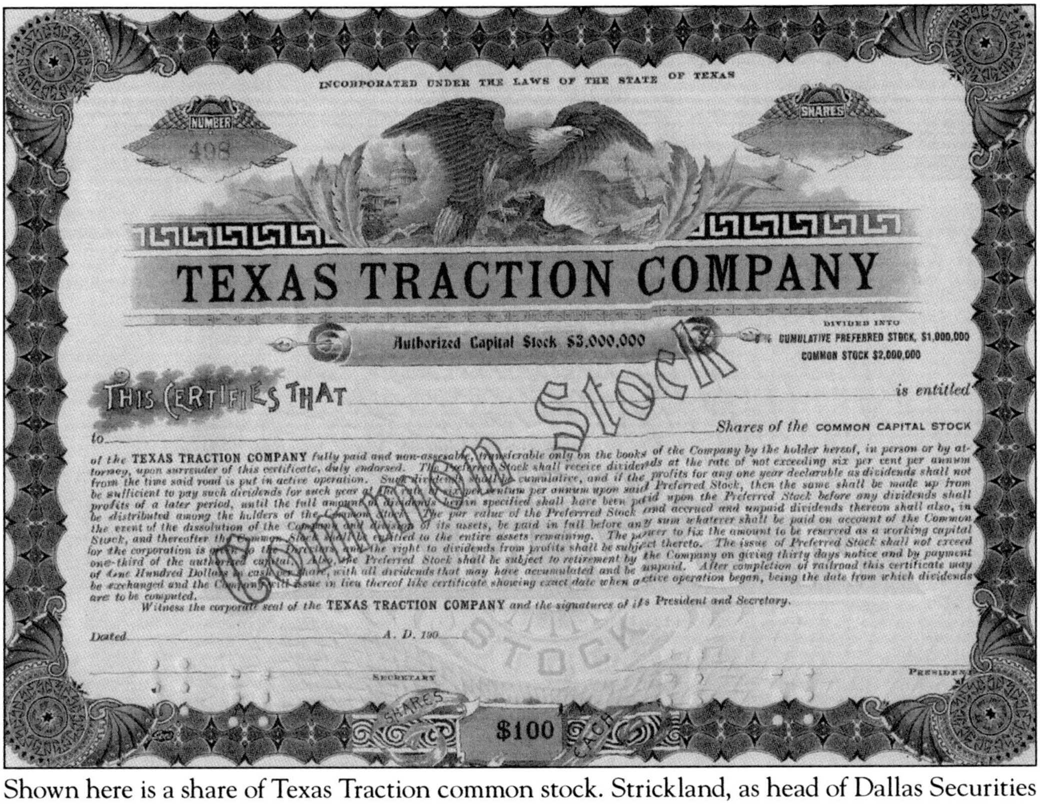

INCORPORATED UNDER THE LAWS OF THE STATE OF TEXAS

NUMBER 498

SHARES

TEXAS TRACTION COMPANY

Authorized Capital Stock $3,000,000

DIVIDED INTO 6% CUMULATIVE PREFERRED STOCK, $1,000,000
COMMON STOCK $2,000,000

Common Stock

THIS CERTIFIES THAT ______________________________ is entitled to ______________________________ Shares of the COMMON CAPITAL STOCK of the TEXAS TRACTION COMPANY fully paid and non-assessable, transferable only on the books of the Company by the holder hereof, in person or by attorney, upon surrender of this certificate, duly endorsed. The Preferred Stock shall receive dividends at the rate of not exceeding six per cent per annum from the time said road is put in active operation. Such dividends shall be cumulative, and if the profits for any one year declarable as dividends shall not be sufficient to pay such dividends for such year at the rate of six per centum per annum upon said Preferred Stock, then the same shall be made up from profits of a later period, until the full amount of dividends herein specified shall have been paid upon the Preferred Stock before any dividends shall be distributed among the holders of the Common Stock. The par value of the Preferred Stock and accrued and unpaid dividends thereon shall also, in the event of the dissolution of the Company and division of its assets, be paid in full before any sum whatever shall be paid on account of the Common Stock, and thereafter the Common Stock shall be entitled to the entire assets remaining. The power to fix the amount to be reserved as a working capital for the corporation is given to the Directors, and the right to dividends from profits shall be subject thereto. The issue of Preferred Stock shall not exceed one-third of the authorized capital. Also, the Preferred Stock shall be subject to retirement by the Company on giving thirty days notice and by payment of One Hundred Dollars in cash per share, with all dividends that may have accumulated and be unpaid. After completion of railroad this certificate may be exchanged and the Company will issue in lieu thereof like certificate showing exact date when active operation began, being the date from which dividends are to be computed.

Witness the corporate seal of the TEXAS TRACTION COMPANY and the signatures of its President and Secretary.

Dated ______________________ A. D. 190__

SECRETARY PRESIDENT

SHARES $100 EACH

Shown here is a share of Texas Traction common stock. Strickland, as head of Dallas Securities Company, packaged blocks of stocks and bonds and sold them in North Texas.

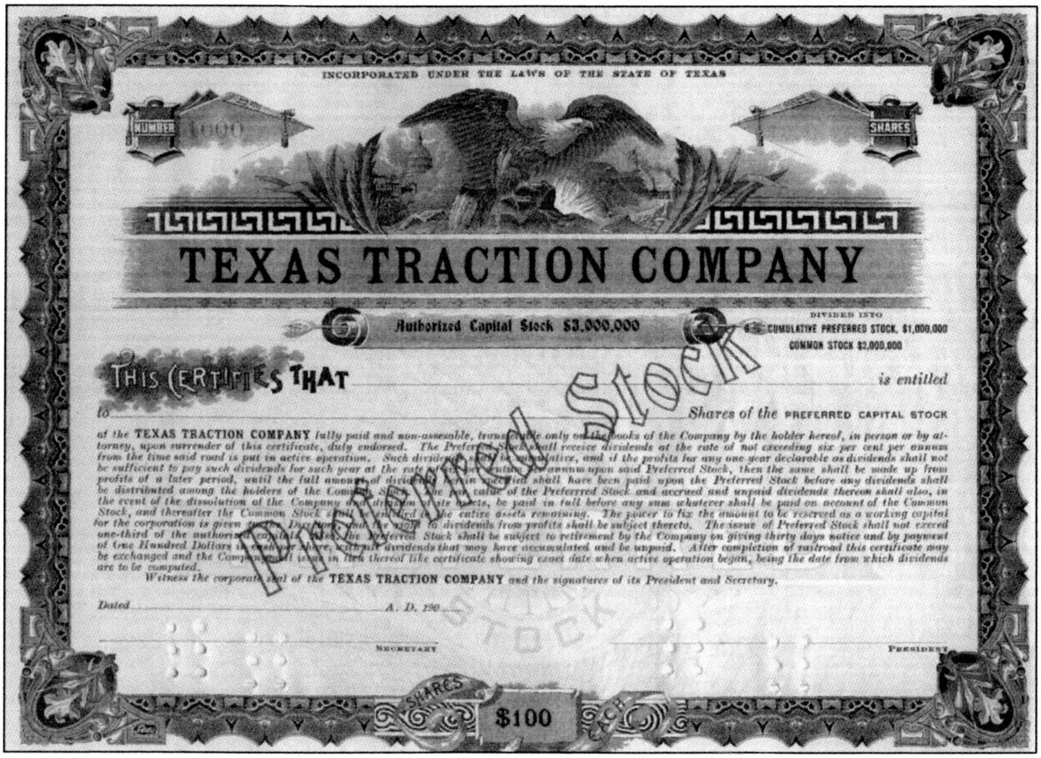

The new company had an authorized capital structure of debt and stock issues totaling $7 million. J. F. Strickland knew that by combining and merging smaller electric companies into bigger ones, he could increase efficiencies, interest other investors, and command more capital. All electric interurban systems at this time, and Texas Traction Company was no exception, were privately financed by sales of stocks and bonds. As a founder and twice president of Southwestern Electric and Gas Company, he partnered with other financiers who also saw the opportunity presented by building an electric interurban railway between the cities of Dallas and Sherman. The new company was the Texas Traction Company.

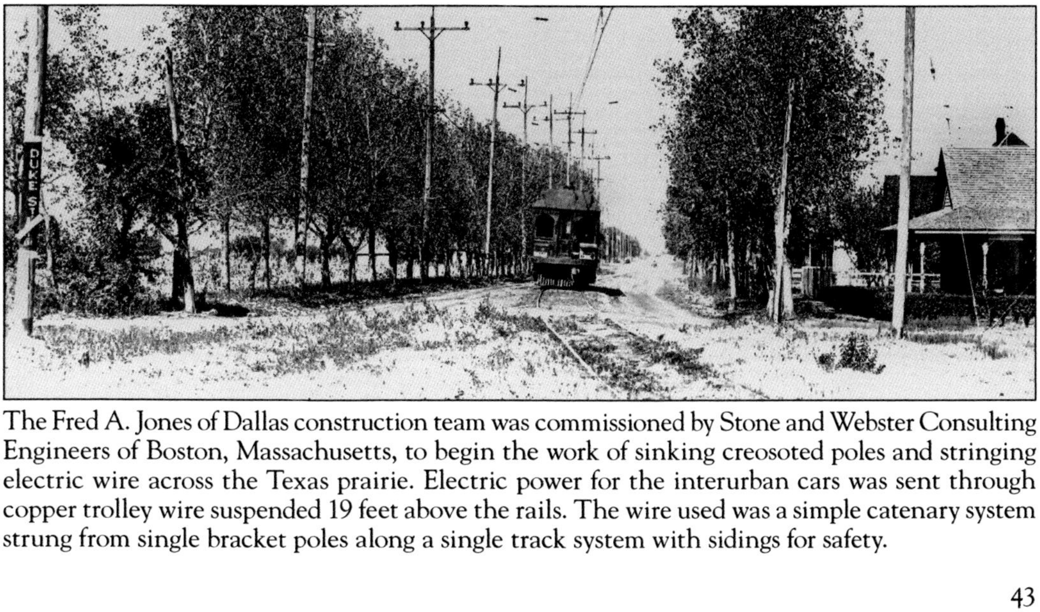

The Fred A. Jones of Dallas construction team was commissioned by Stone and Webster Consulting Engineers of Boston, Massachusetts, to begin the work of sinking creosoted poles and stringing electric wire across the Texas prairie. Electric power for the interurban cars was sent through copper trolley wire suspended 19 feet above the rails. The wire used was a simple catenary system strung from single bracket poles along a single track system with sidings for safety.

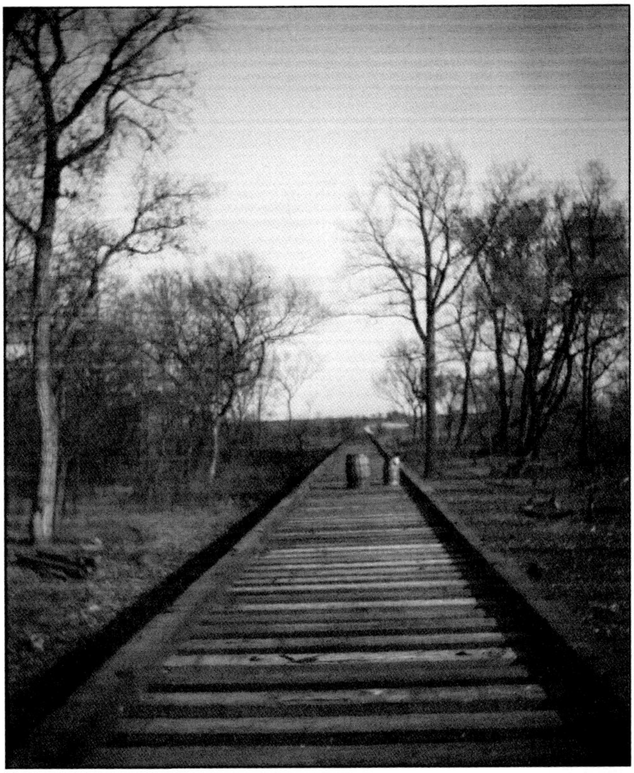

An early, *c.* 1906 construction photograph shows steel rails resting atop wooden ties and two barrels of spikes waiting to be pounded into the ties. No electric wire had been strung yet. (Courtesy of Bryan Lean/ North Texas History Center.)

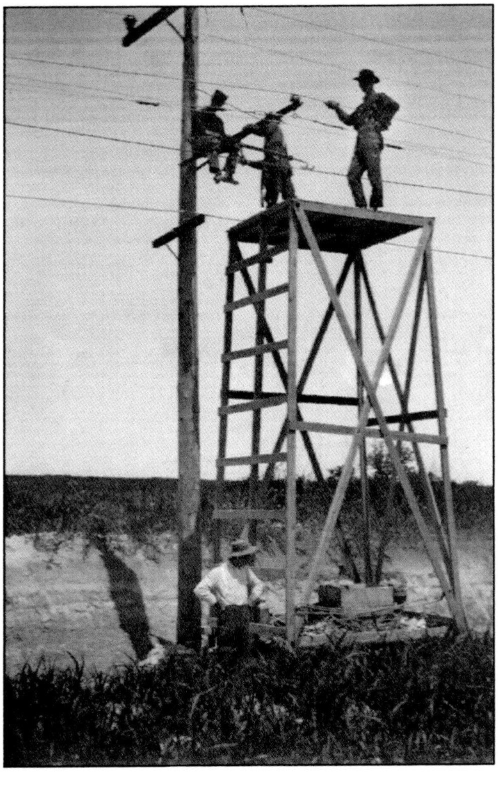

Stringing electric wire across the prairie was done from wooden scaffolding.

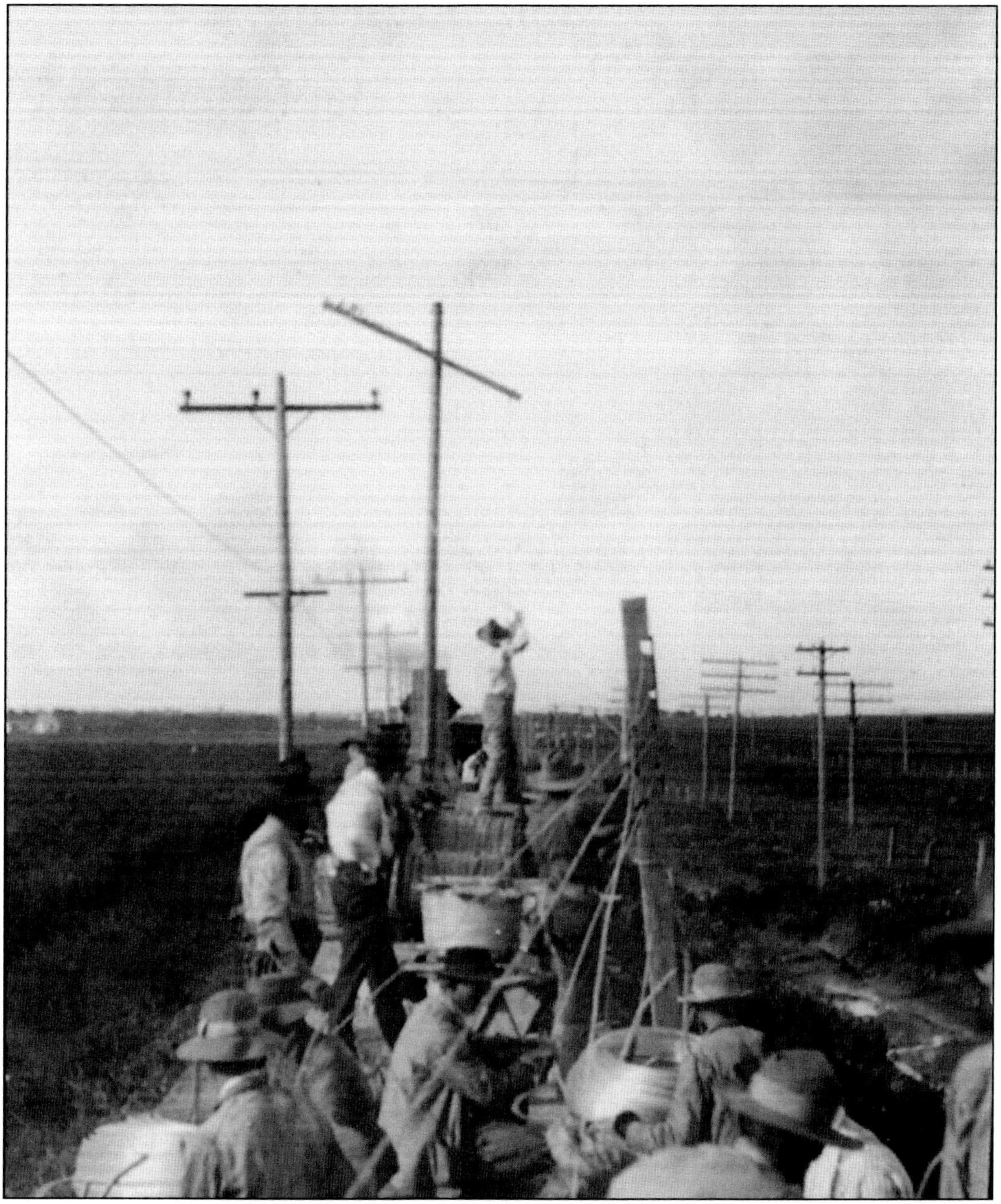

As the need for electric interurban systems expanded, a bandwagon effect developed for financiers who rushed to make "big returns" on their money by investing in electric railway construction. Often built without careful cost and feasibility analysis, some of the systems lost money before start-up and some were never even completed. Here Stone and Webster, an original consulting engineering company founded in 1888 in Boston, begins construction of the electric rail system in the Oak Cliff section of Dallas (Oak Cliff was annexed by Dallas in 1903). Stone and Webster also worked on both Fort Worth to Dallas and Dallas to Waxahachie and the Gaston and Houston Electric in South Texas. Stone and Webster normally used large crews of African Americans and European immigrants for the heavy labor. (Courtesy of City of Plano, Department of Parks and Recreation.)

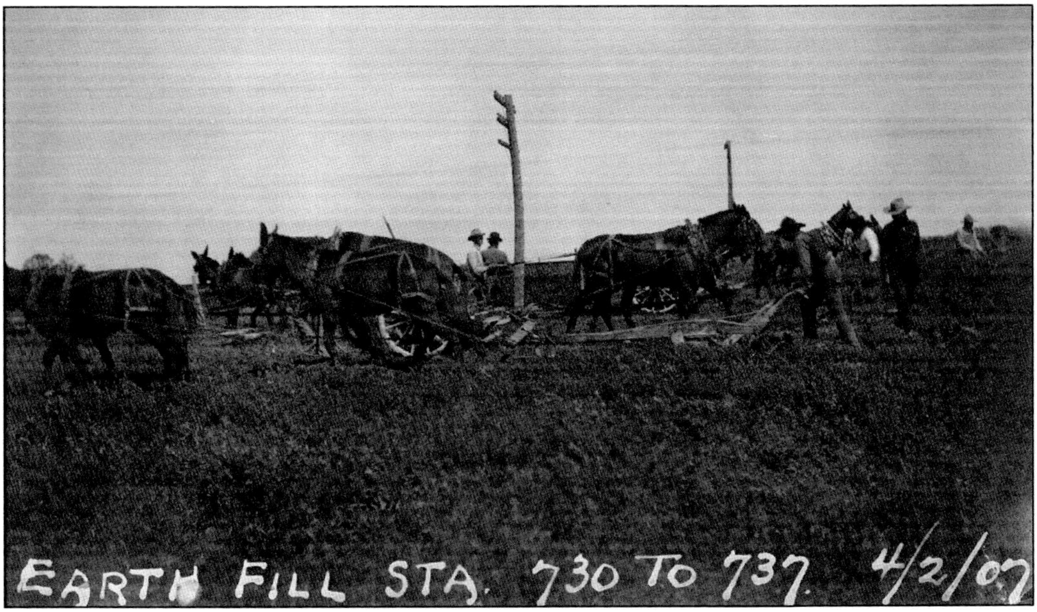

Mules were used to grade the track bed. (Courtesy of City of Plano, Department of Parks and Recreation.)

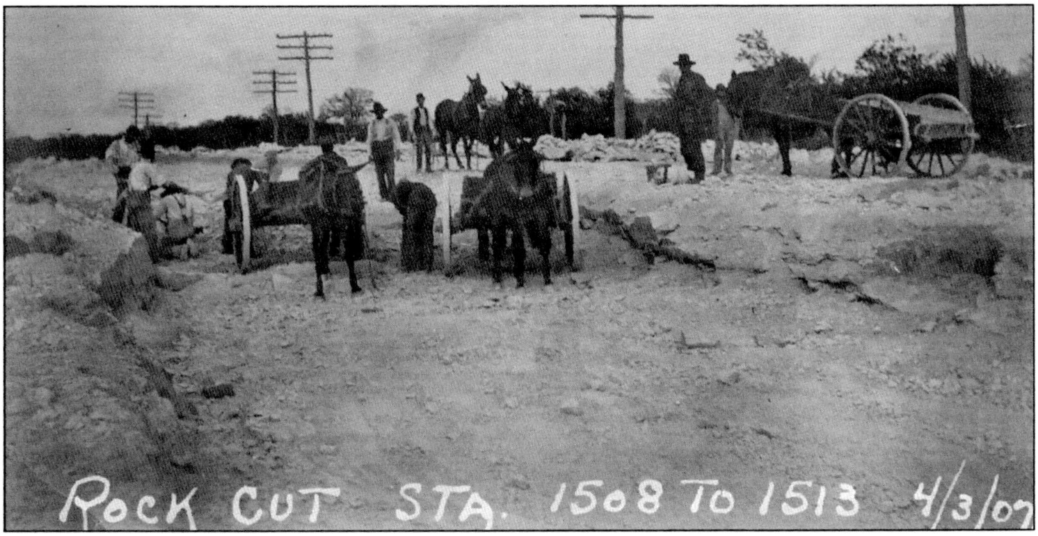

Construction begins. (Courtesy of City of Plano, Department of Parks and Recreation.)

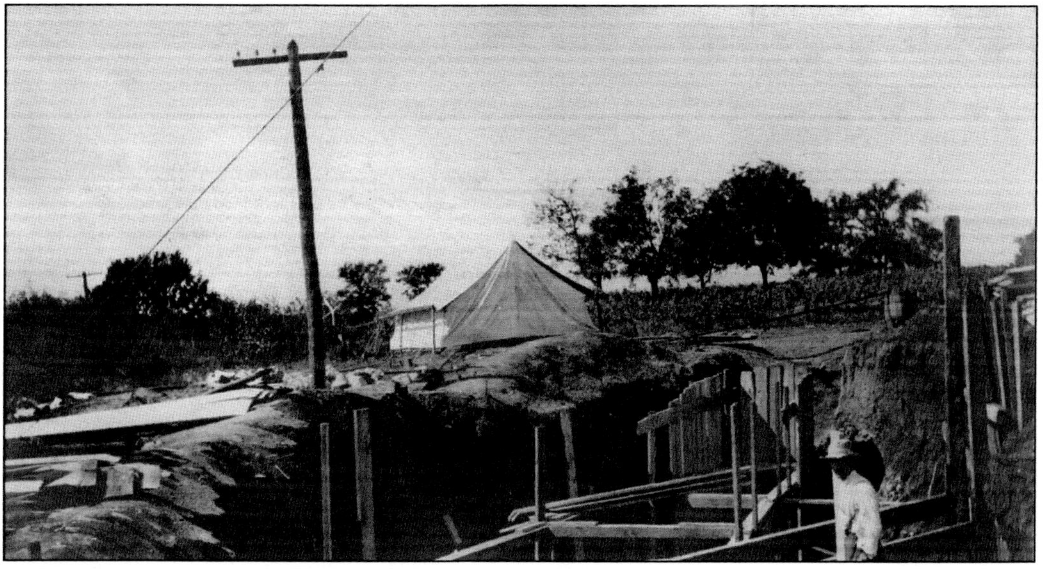

Here is the construction of concrete supports for a bridge abutment. (Courtesy of City of Plano, Department of Parks and Recreation.)

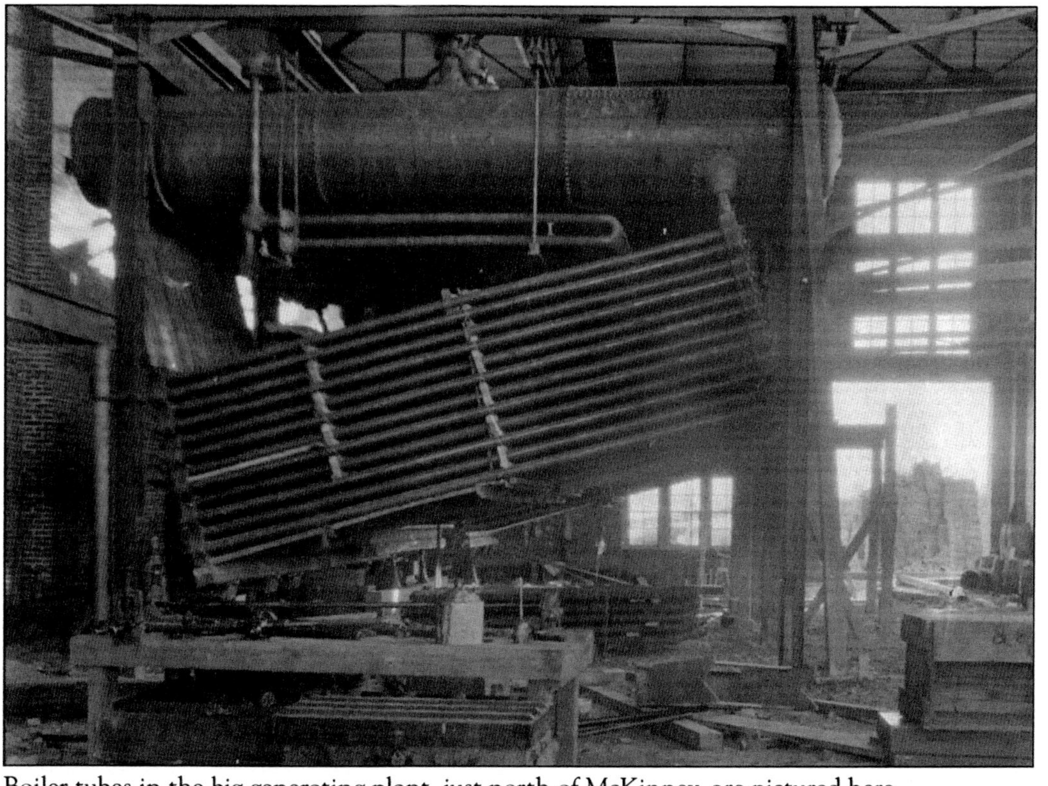

Boiler tubes in the big generating plant, just north of McKinney, are pictured here.

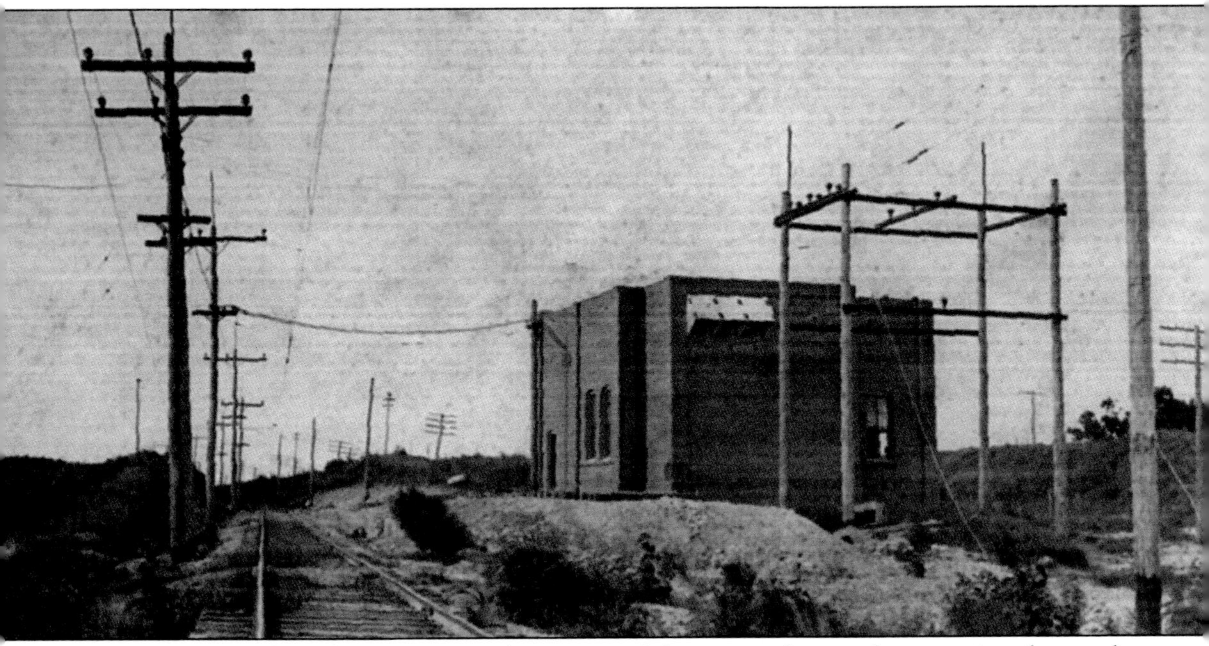

Construction of Southern Traction substations and depots was done at the same time that tracks were being laid and poles and wires were strung. Here in a 1907 photograph, looking south at the partially completed Jenkins substation just south of Walnut Hill Lane, interurban tracks stretch south toward the Dallas depot a few miles down the line.

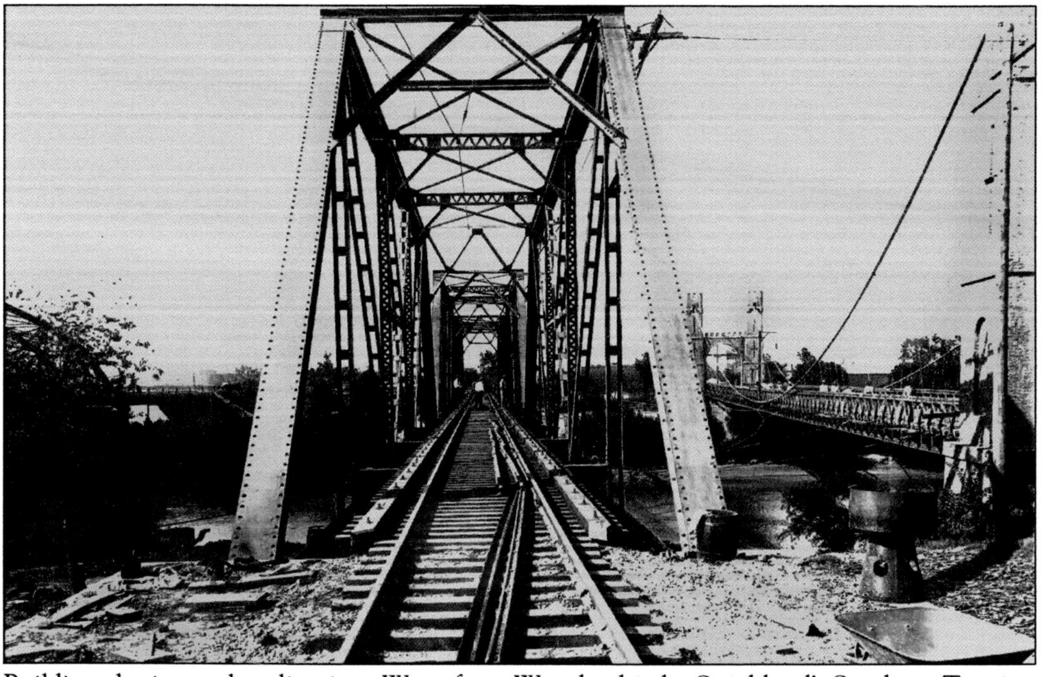

Building the interurban line into Waco from Waxahachie by Strickland's Southern Traction Company required erecting the 450-foot, three-span, steel truss bridge across the Brazos River. Engineering and survey had begun in 1911, and the charter for operation was granted by the ICC (Interstate Commerce Commission) on March 27, 1912. The bridge opened for service September 30, 1913, when the first cars, filled with stockholders and investors, rolled across the structure into Waco.

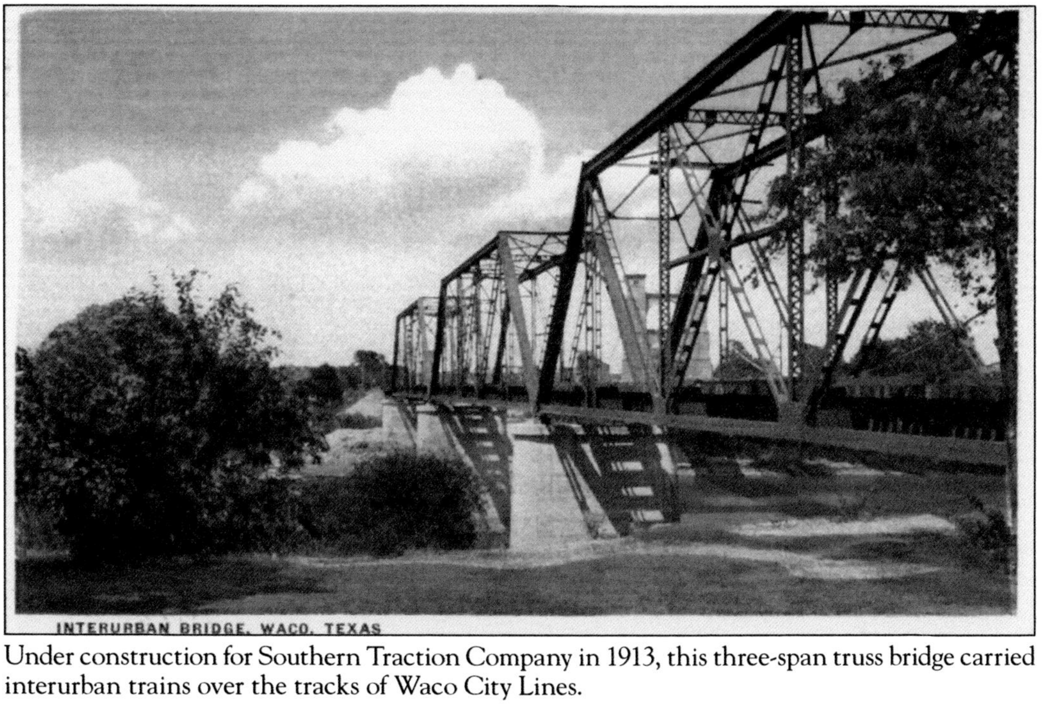

Under construction for Southern Traction Company in 1913, this three-span truss bridge carried interurban trains over the tracks of Waco City Lines.

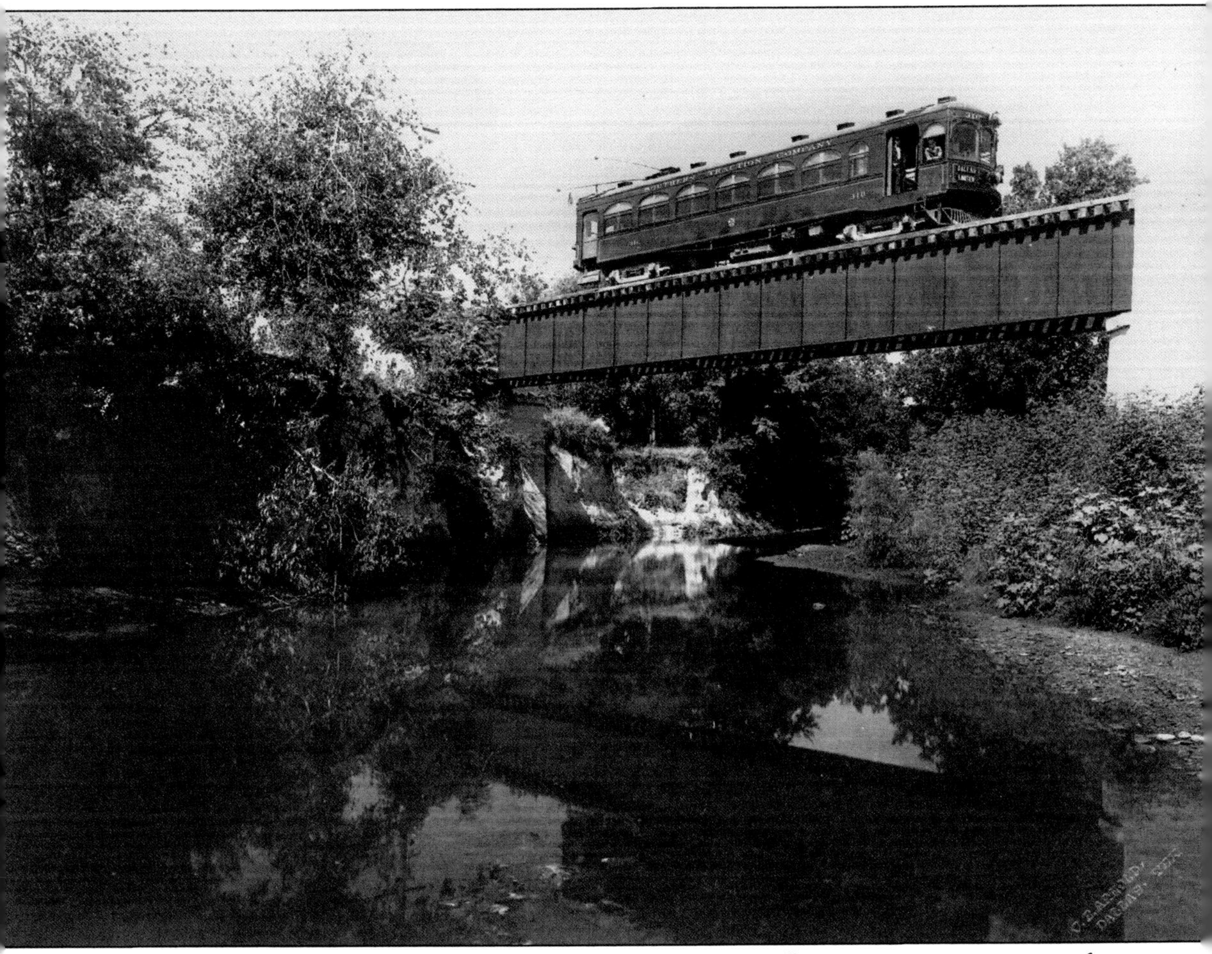

The camera catches a Southern Traction car and motorman reflecting an inspiring image from the still waters of Waxahachie Creek.

Two

Moving toward the Future at 60 Miles Per Hour

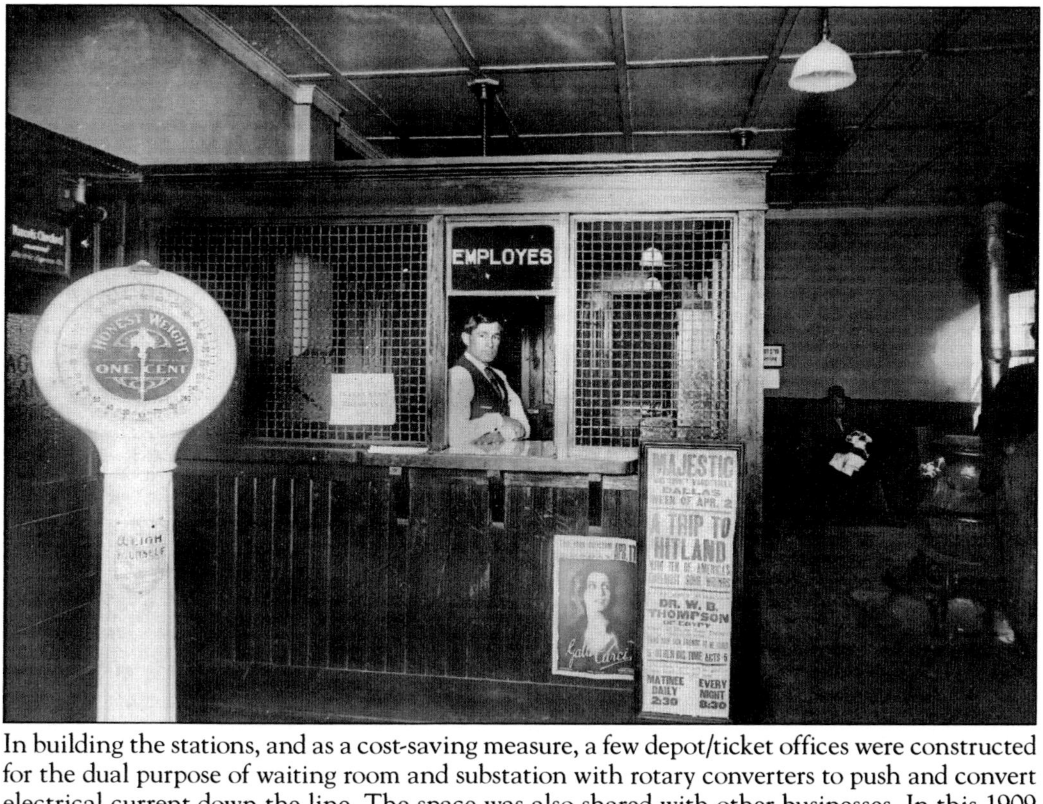

In building the stations, and as a cost-saving measure, a few depot/ticket offices were constructed for the dual purpose of waiting room and substation with rotary converters to push and convert electrical current down the line. The space was also shared with other businesses. In this 1909 photograph, the first McKinney interurban office shares quarters with a telegraph company. In many instances, interurban tickets could be purchased at drugstores, hotel lobbies, and other convenient locations. Tickets could also be purchased aboard the train. (Courtesy of Bryan Lean/ North Texas History Center.)

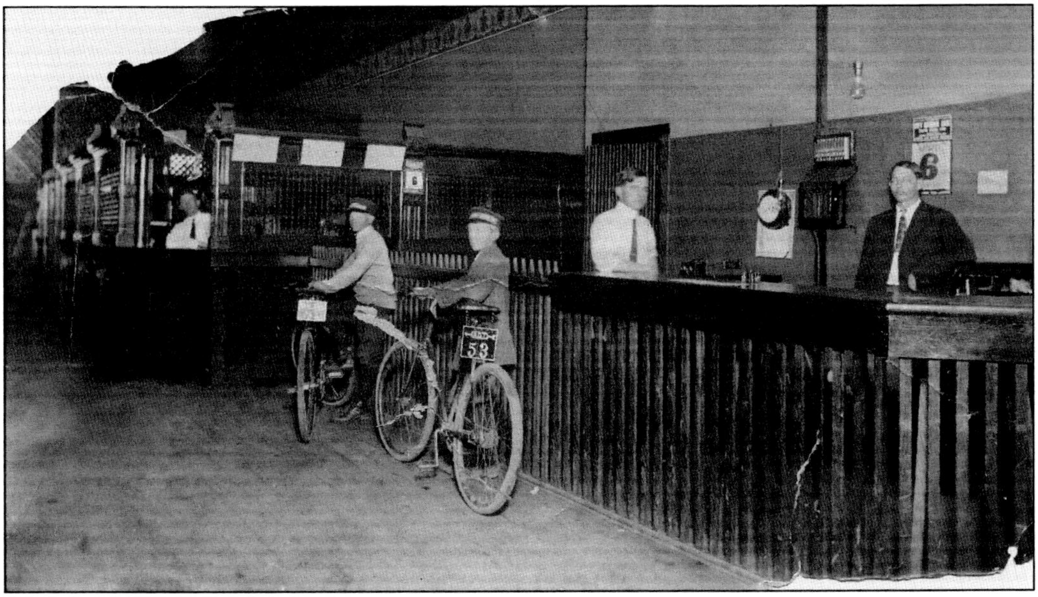

This telegraph office shared space with the McKinney interurban ticket office and depot.

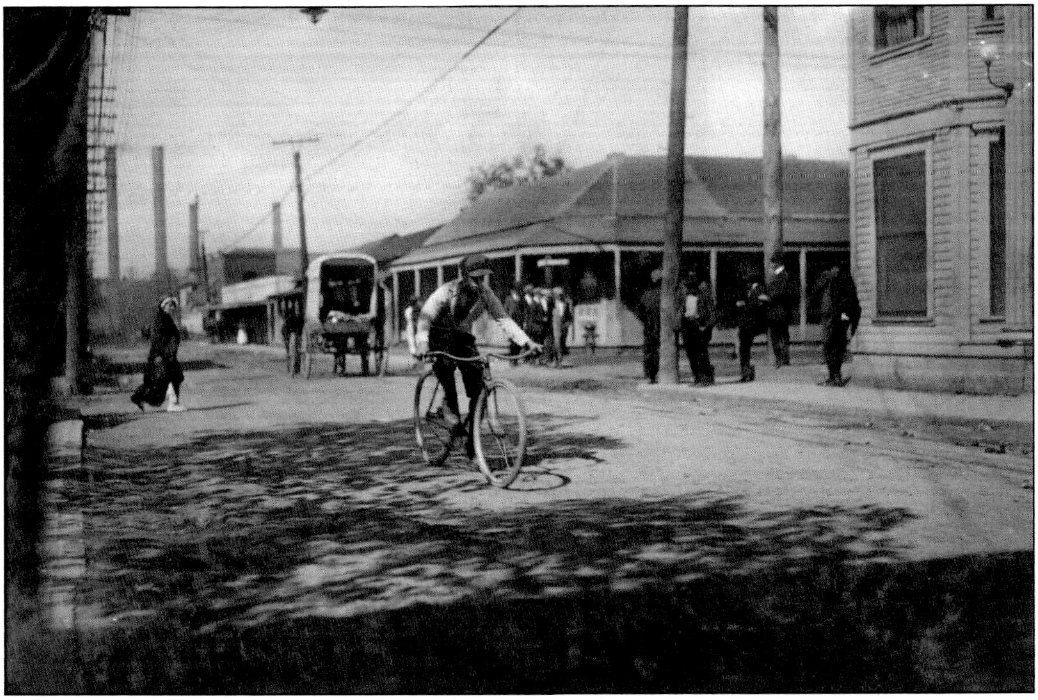

Delivery boys on bicycles were a common sight on town and city streets at the time, delivering messages, the news, and gossip. They delivered for grocery stores, pharmacies, and newspapers and generally ran errands around town. (Courtesy of the Library of Congress.)

The delivery boy at right is from the Waco station. These youths grew up quickly to help support their families and took on adult behaviors such as smoking at an early age. (Courtesy of the Library of Congress.)

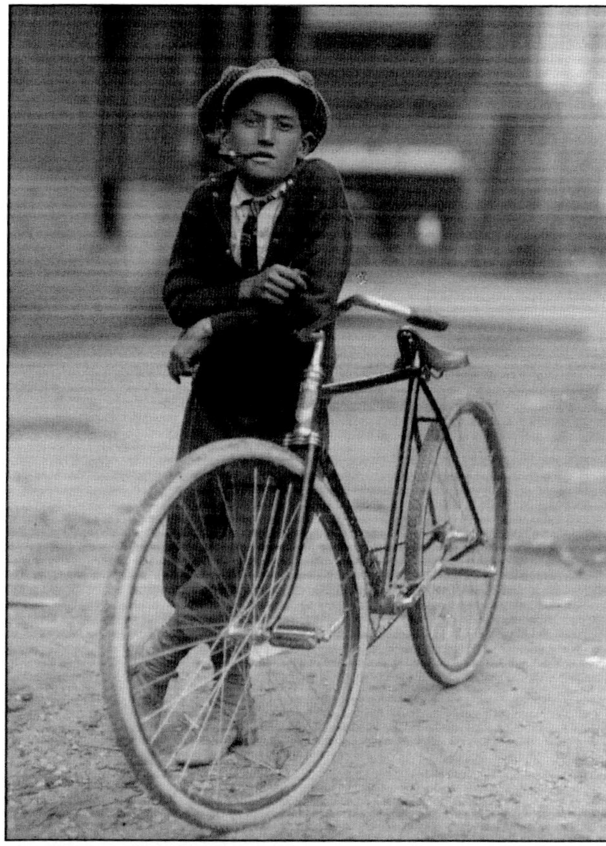

The new Plano substation and depot opened in June 1908. Taking a trip on the interurban often meant wearing your Sunday best. In order to sweeten the deal to bring an interurban depot and substation to town, the City of Plano granted Texas Traction Company 10.5 miles of right-of-way, 60 feet in width, 100 feet if necessary where there were cuts or fills to be made. The Plano substation housed an ingenious electromechanical device known as a rotary converter that changed incoming alternating current to direct current, providing electricity to the overhead line that powered railcars on the tracks. (Courtesy of the Al and Charlene Sparman Postcard Collection.)

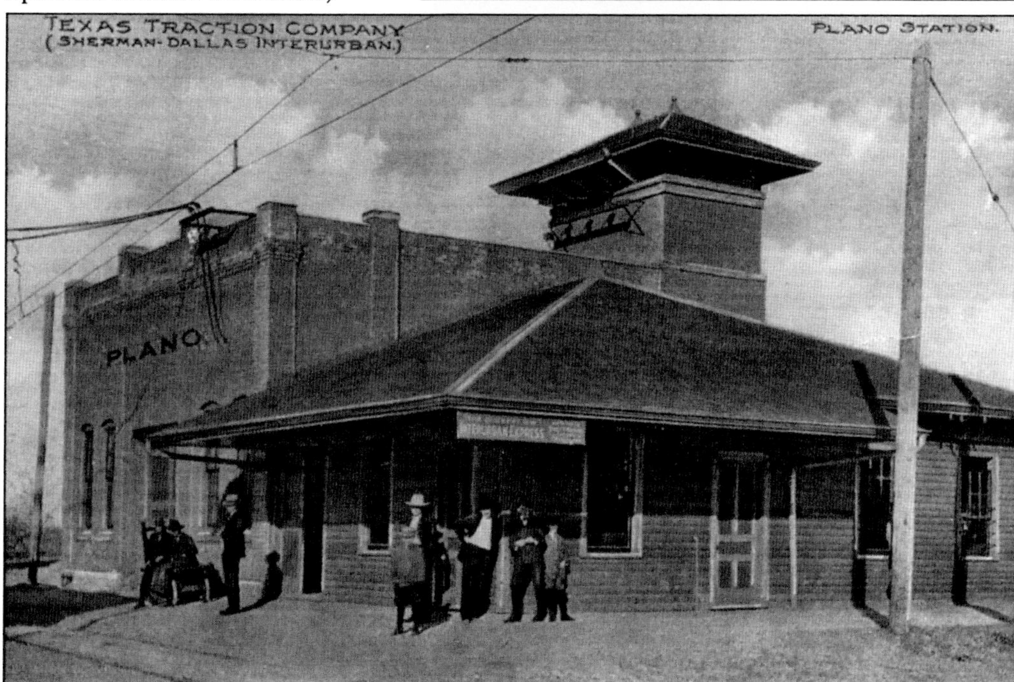

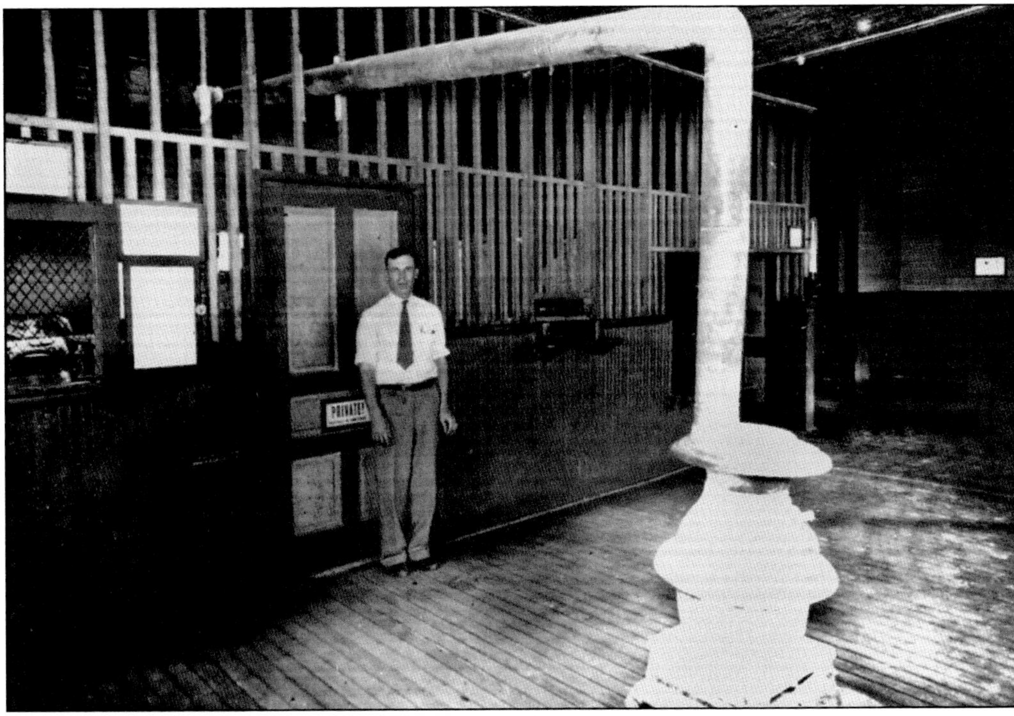

Dick Sheridan, ticket agent of the Plano Texas Electric station, stands in front of the wooden ticket cage in this 1933 photograph taken by his proud parents.

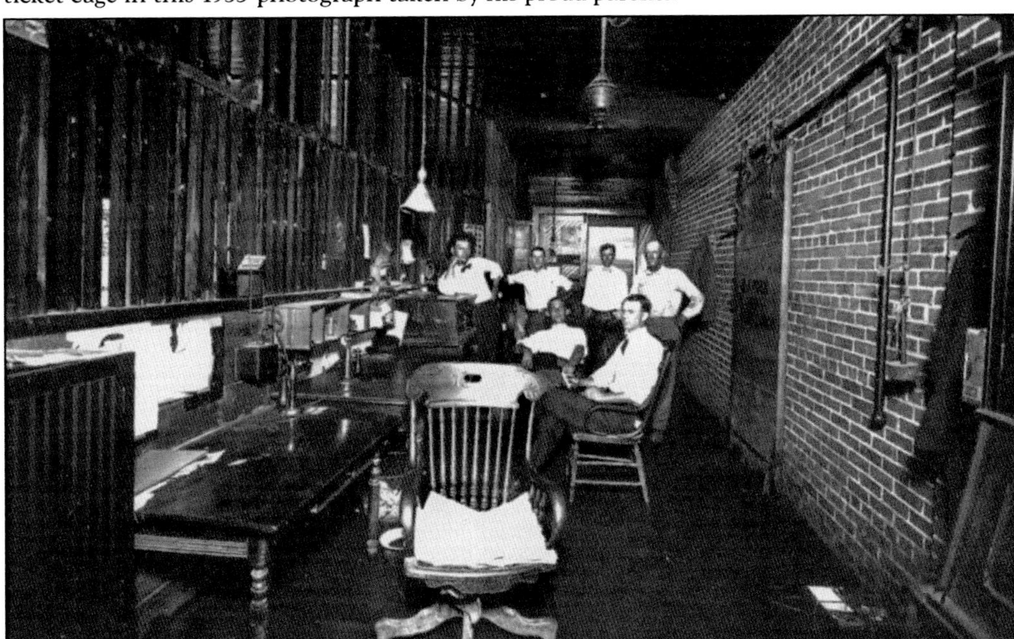

A glimpse behind the counter and cage of the Texas Traction Company depot and substation in this 1916 photograph shows a larger crew than required to sell tickets. Harvey F. "Dad" Brown was supervisor of the Freight and Express Department of the station. Brown stands in the back row closest to the brick wall. (Courtesy of the Wells Collection, Plano Public Library.)

This is the interior of the substation behind the door of a cage at Plano substation, built by Fred A. Jones Company in 1907. (Courtesy of Bryan Lean/ North Texas History Center.)

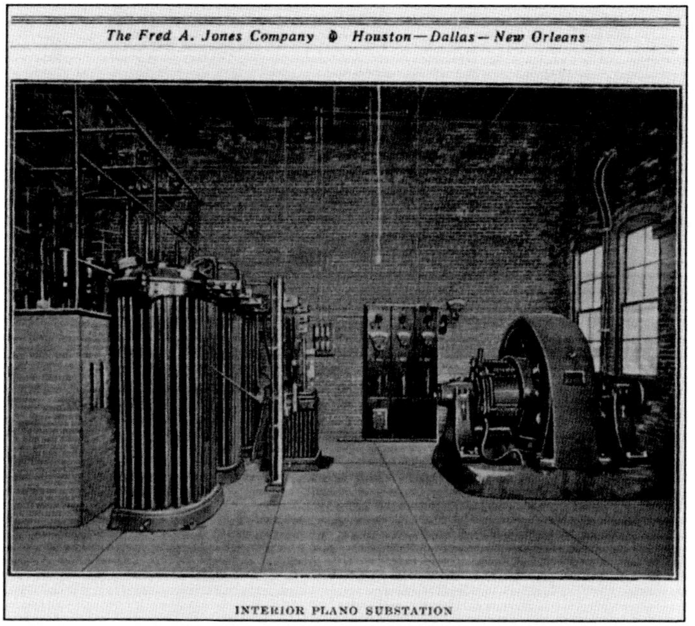

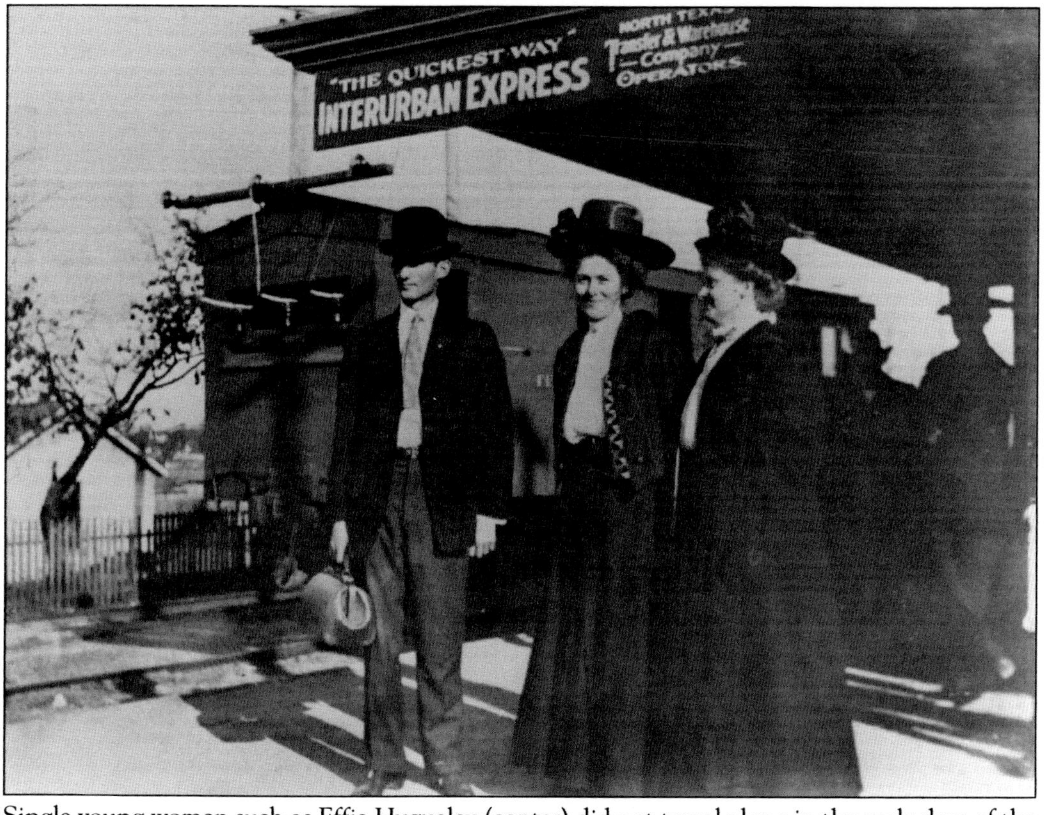

Single young women such as Effie Hugueley (center) did not travel alone in the early days of the interurban but were accompanied by a chaperone. Her beau, C. C. Allen, holds a grip possibly containing lunch as they wait at the Plano station for a Texas Traction car into Dallas in 1908. (Courtesy of the Wells Collection, Plano Public Library.)

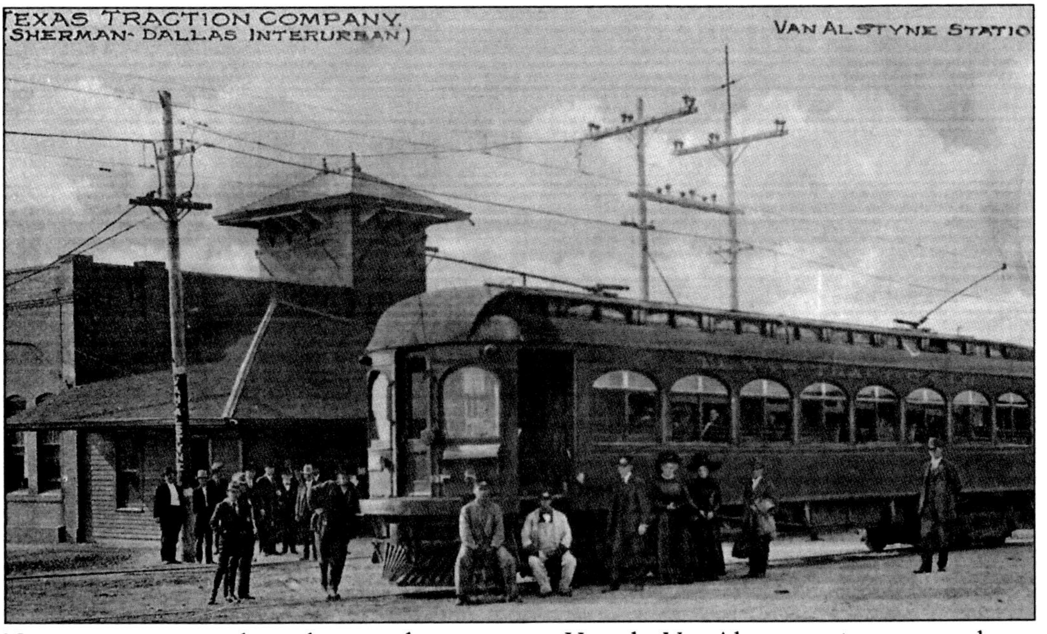

New stations were similar in design and construction. Here the Van Alstyne station appears almost exactly the same as the Plano station except the railcar runs down the middle of the street. It is unclear how women in long dresses navigated the mud to board the car in rainy weather.

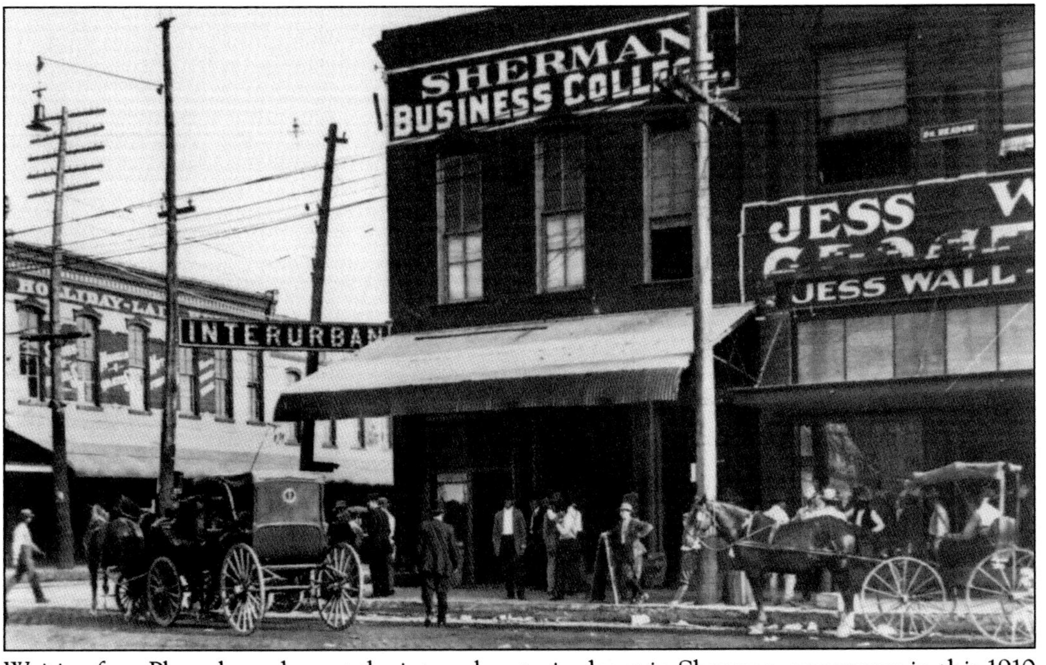

Waiting for a Plano-bound car at the interurban train depot in Sherman, passengers in this 1910 photograph are probably contemplating the dramatic technological contrast of arriving in town at the station by horse and buggy to catch an electric train that zoomed almost silently on steel tracks at speeds upwards of 60 miles per hour. The Sherman depot shared its quarters with the Sherman Business College, on the second story. The business college moved out in 1913 to a stand-alone location that also included a dormitory on the same property.

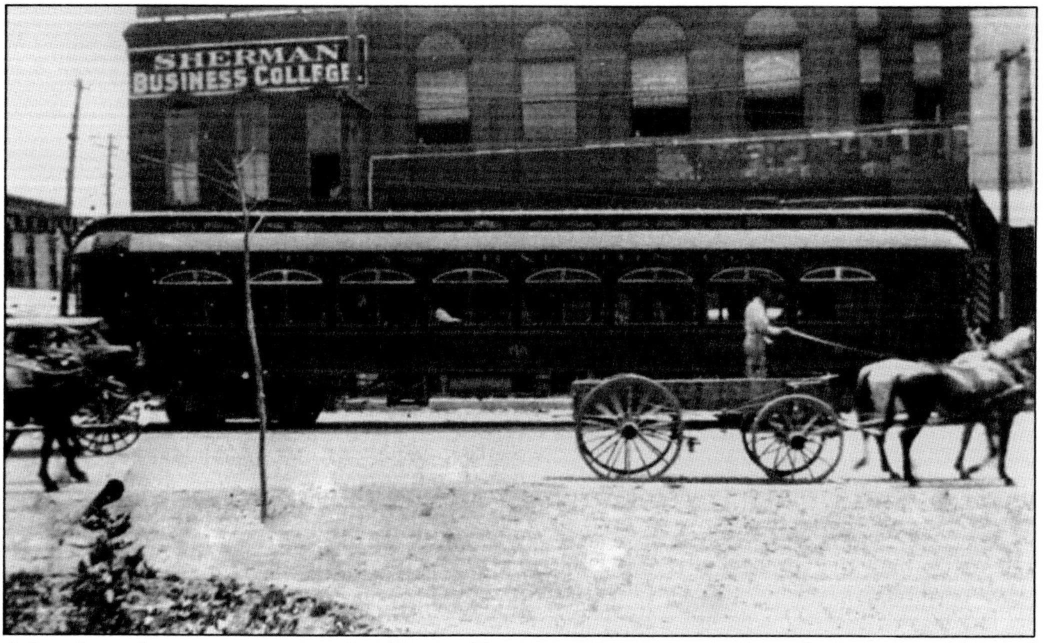

After boarding passengers, the Texas Traction Company railcar departs southbound toward Plano.

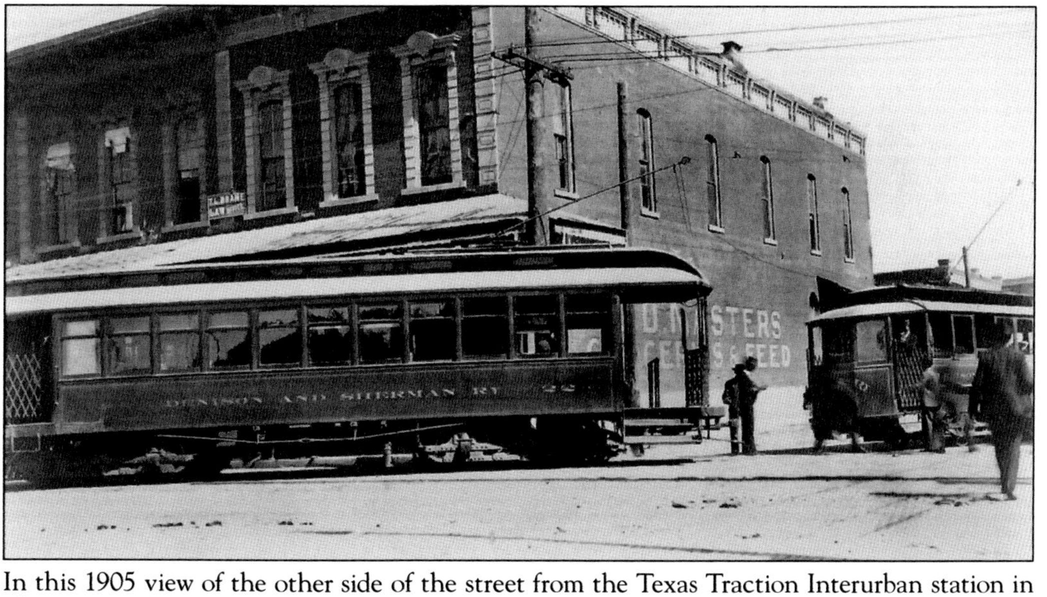

In this 1905 view of the other side of the street from the Texas Traction Interurban station in Sherman, at the rail intersection of Travis and Lamar Streets, was a rail crossroads where streetcars, railroads, and the interurban cars came together in a busy hub of motion and human activity. The Interurban Café stayed open all night as an oasis for travelers passing through. The opposite side of the street from the interurban station completed the busy spot in town.

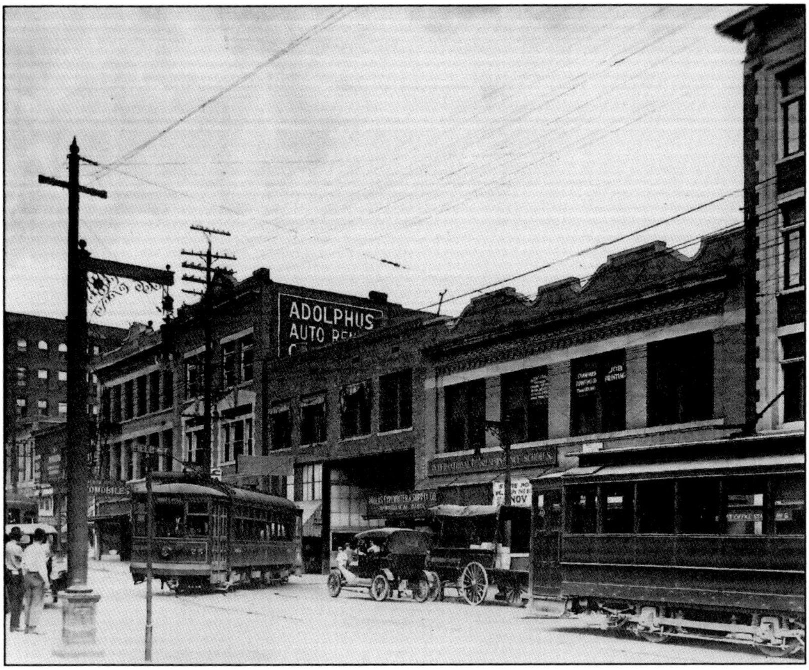

A 1915 photograph shows a Dallas streetcar leaving the station and depot shared with the Sherman-to-Dallas interurban.

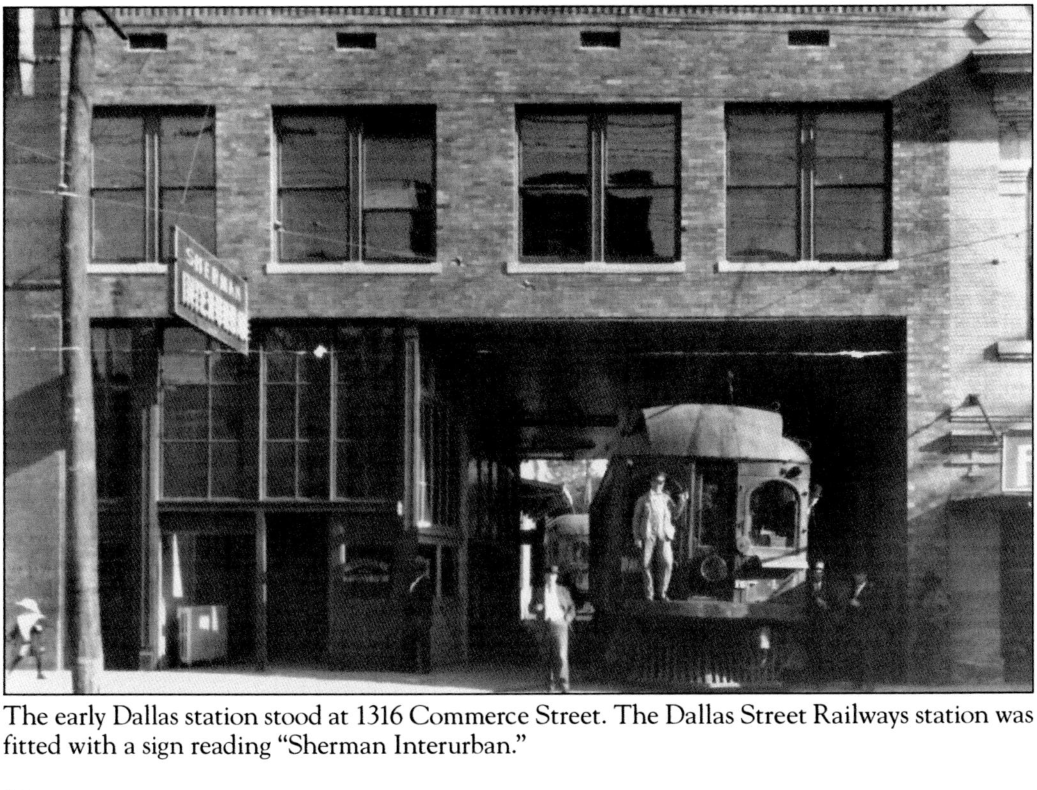

The early Dallas station stood at 1316 Commerce Street. The Dallas Street Railways station was fitted with a sign reading "Sherman Interurban."

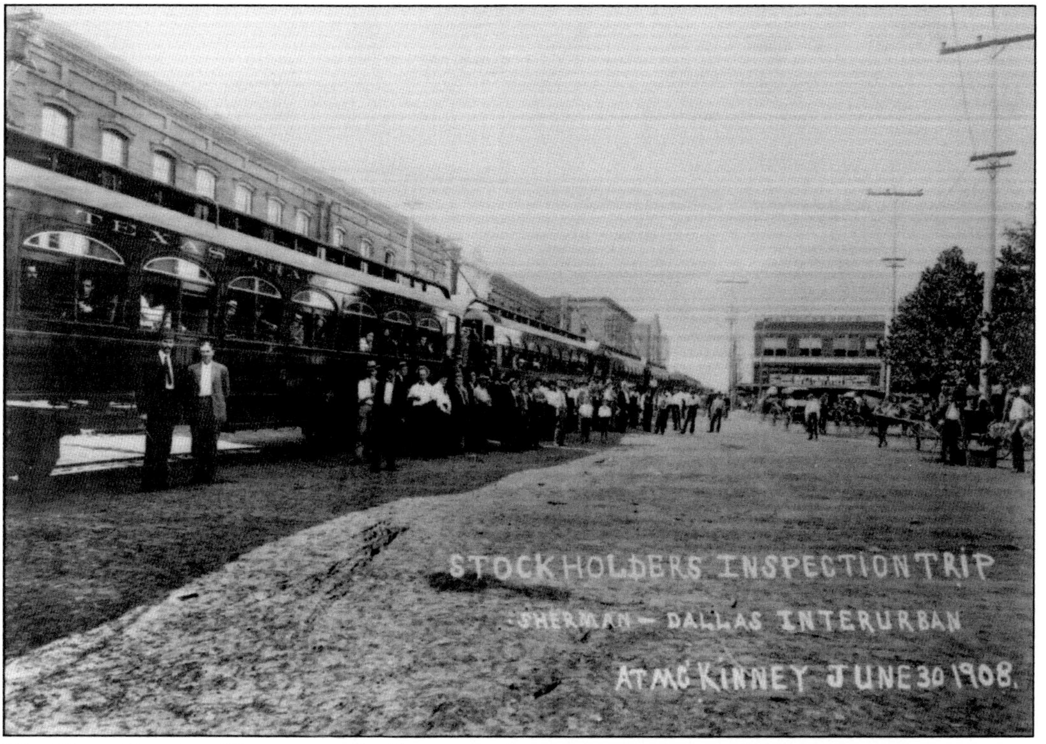

The Texas Traction Sherman to Dallas interurban opens with a stockholders inspection run.

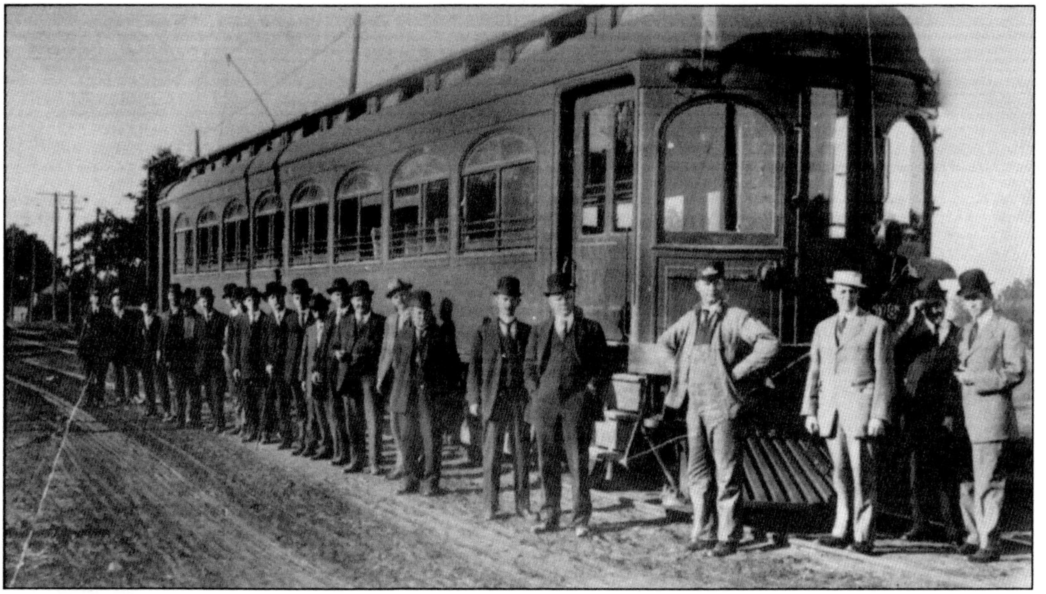

The stockholders inspection trip was a common and important event. Investors who owned stock in the electric rail company would take a ride in the cars over the line to a specific destination, inspecting the new cars and the newly constructed depots. The president of the company, trustees, and the executive staff would also be on board to answer questions. It was always a festive occasion attended by marching bands, photographers, and grand speeches. John F. Strickland stands fifth from right.

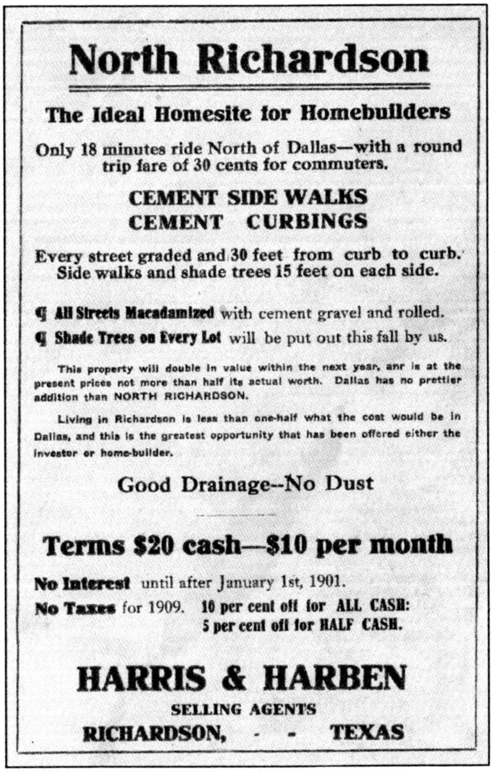

Completion of the interurban system encouraged the sale of suburban home sites.

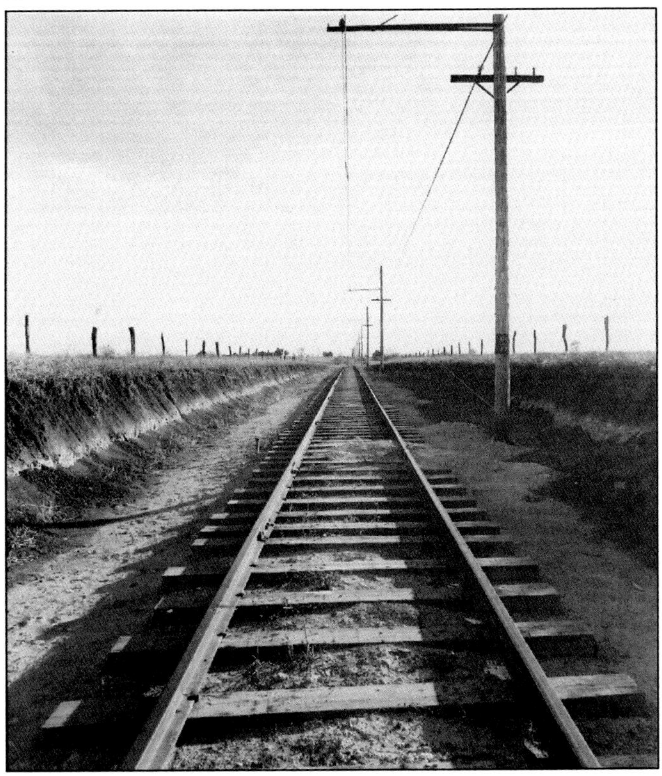

New track, poles, and wire stretch endlessly into the horizon of the North Texas prairie awaiting the first new interurban railcar. The interurban rail lines brought Texans together from distant farms, small towns, and settlements to the big cities for commerce, culture, and socialization, thus ending the feeling of isolation associated with a rural way of life.

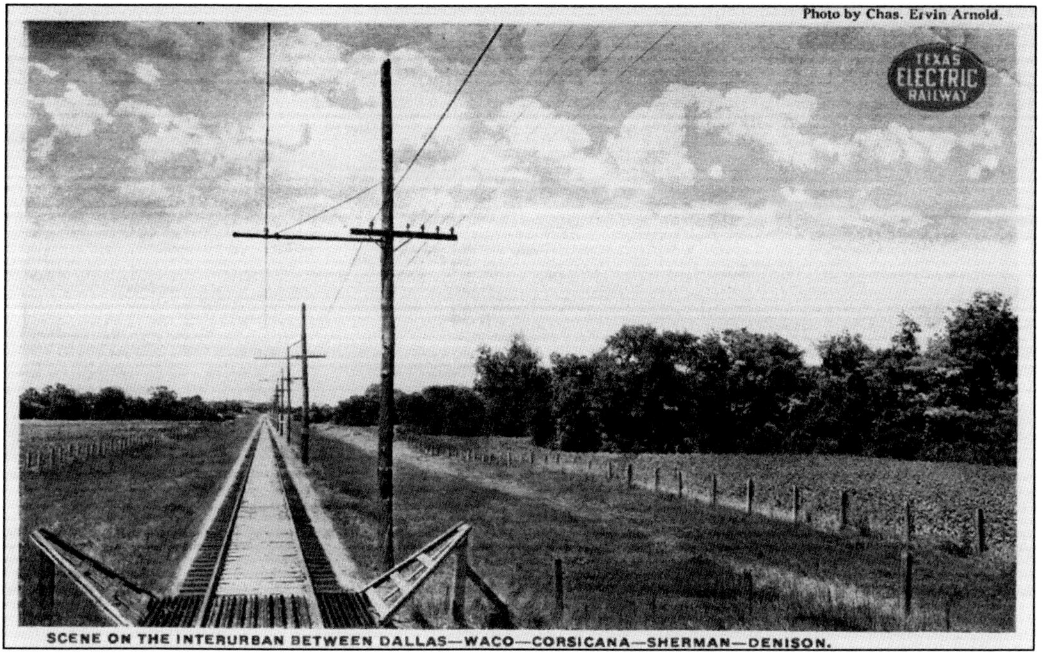

Cattle catchers were contrivances set at railway crossings to prevent cattle from wandering onto the tracks. Steel spikes are set in a grid beneath the two rails of the track stretching between the two wooden wedges on either side of the track. Any animal stepping onto the grid experienced sharp pain from the spikes and avoided being run down by the railcar.

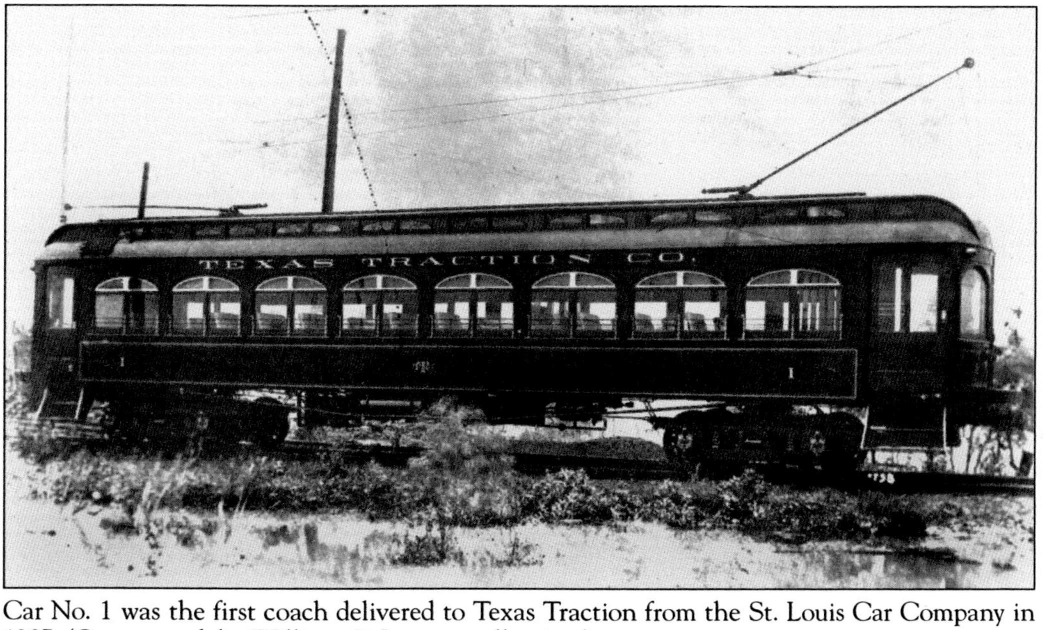

Car No. 1 was the first coach delivered to Texas Traction from the St. Louis Car Company in 1907. (Courtesy of the William C. Janssen collection.)

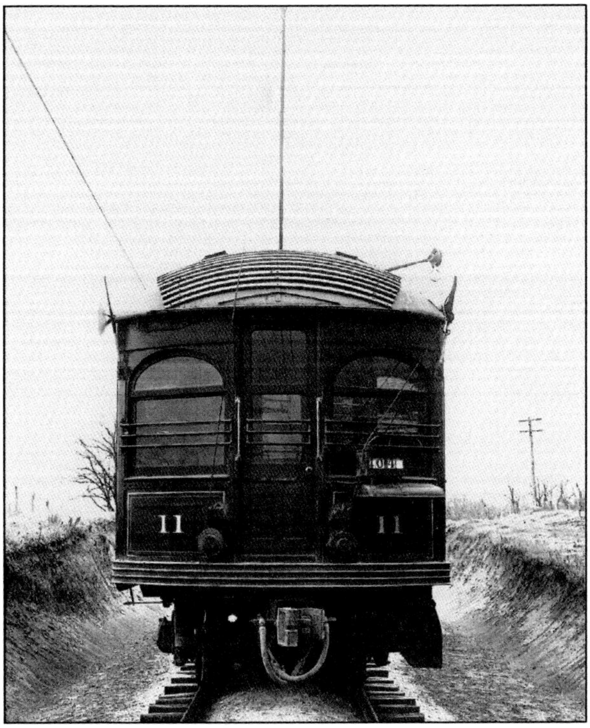

The new cars (on this page and at the top of the next) bought from the American Car Company, numbered 11 and 14 for John Strickland's Southern Traction Company, were beautiful to behold and had a look of wonder to the 1909 eyes, which may have never seen anything so impressive as an electric interurban railcar.

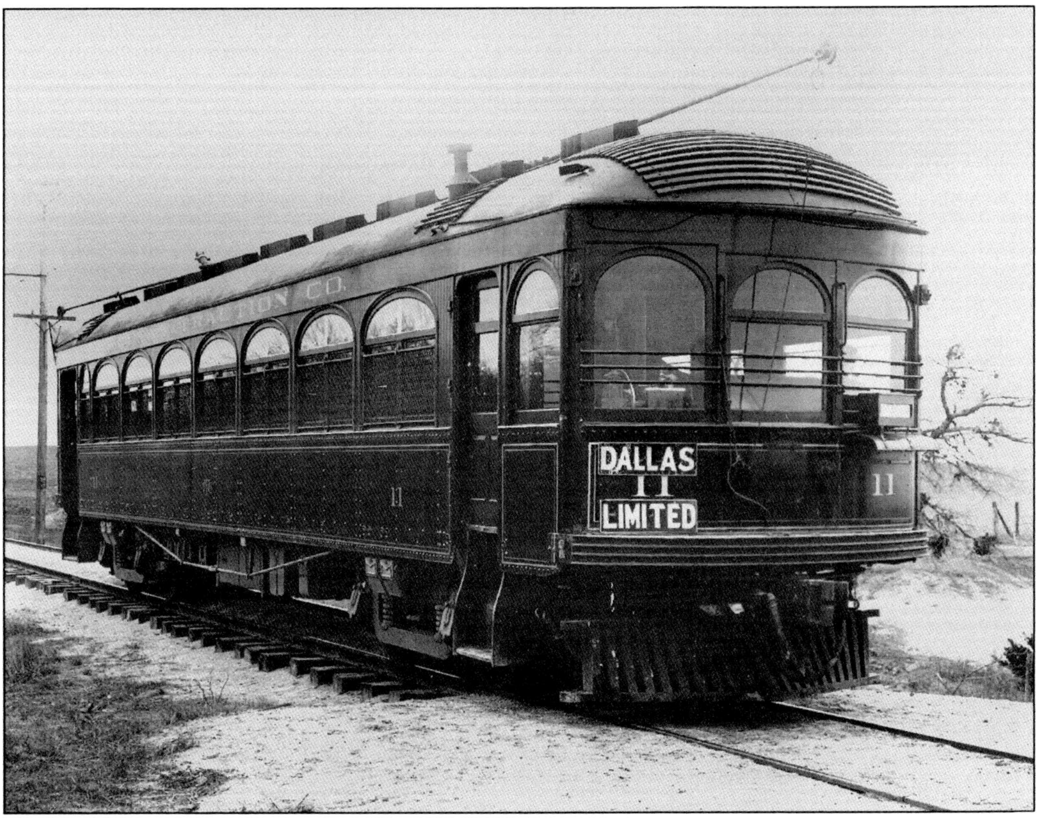

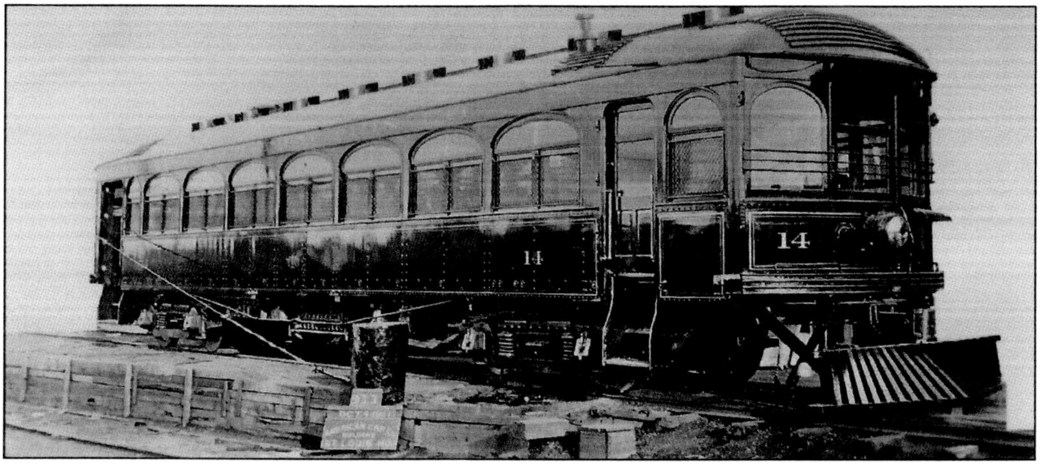

Painted Pullman Green with a brown roof and red windowsills, the cars moved in majestic quiet through the towns and cities, picking up their well-dressed passengers.

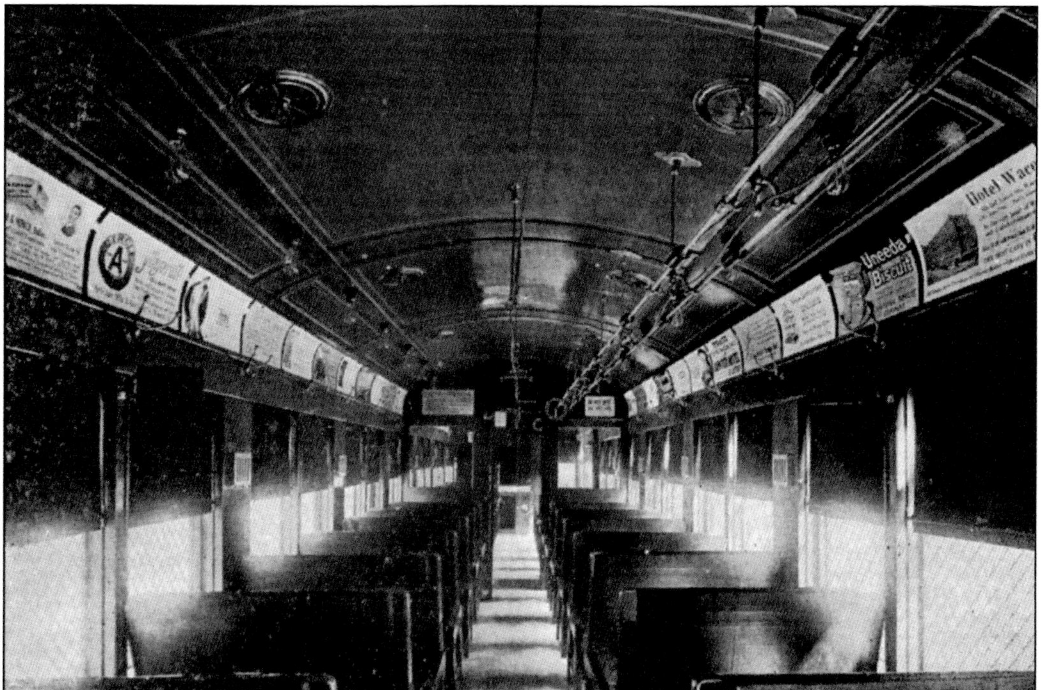

This was the standard delivery seating configuration for Southern Traction cars when they arrived from the factory.

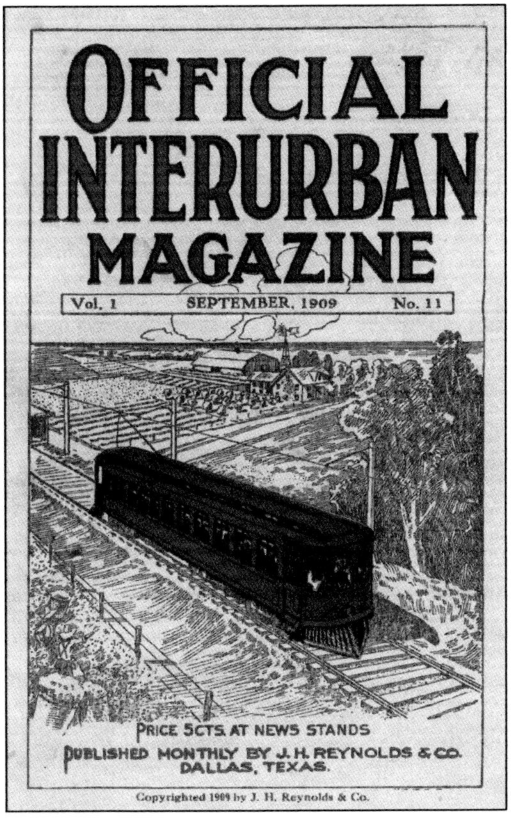

To pass the time while riding the Southern Traction Interurban train, the company provided a free monthly magazine. It contained local advertising, promoted interurban travel, and carried humorous and informative articles. The magazine was also sold on newsstands and was available inside the stations.

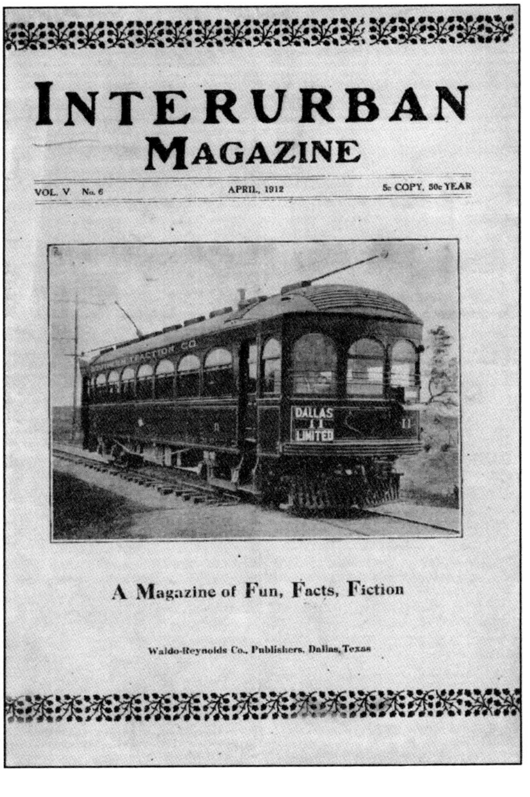

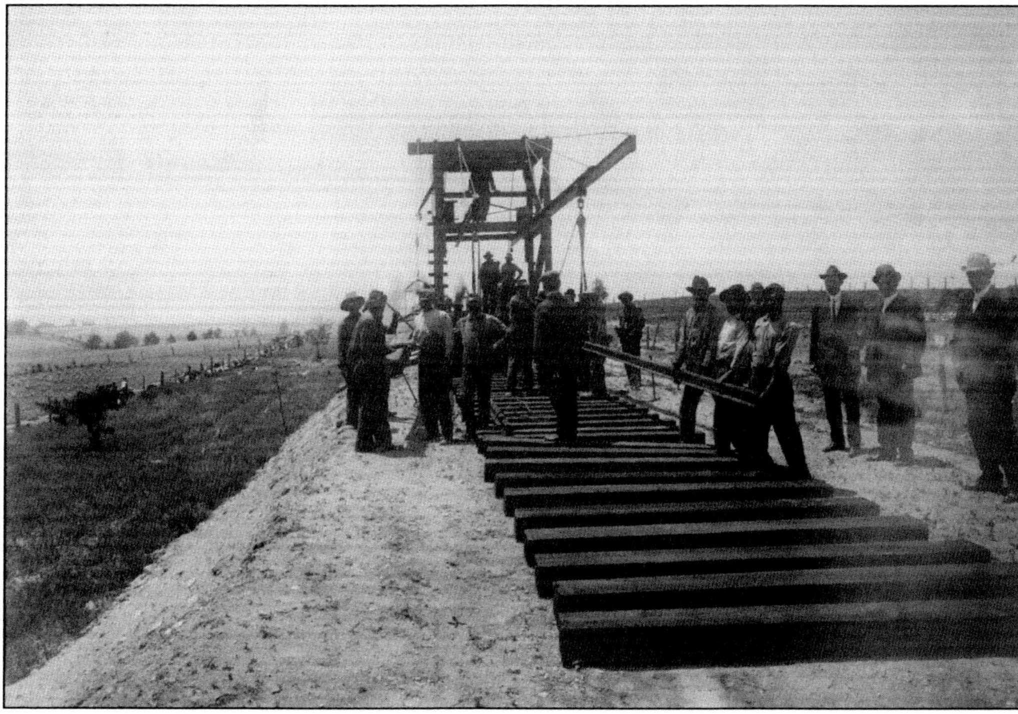

Racing to build the line south from Dallas, the Stone and Webster construction crew used a windlass track-laying machine to lay track in Oak Cliff going toward Waxahachie.

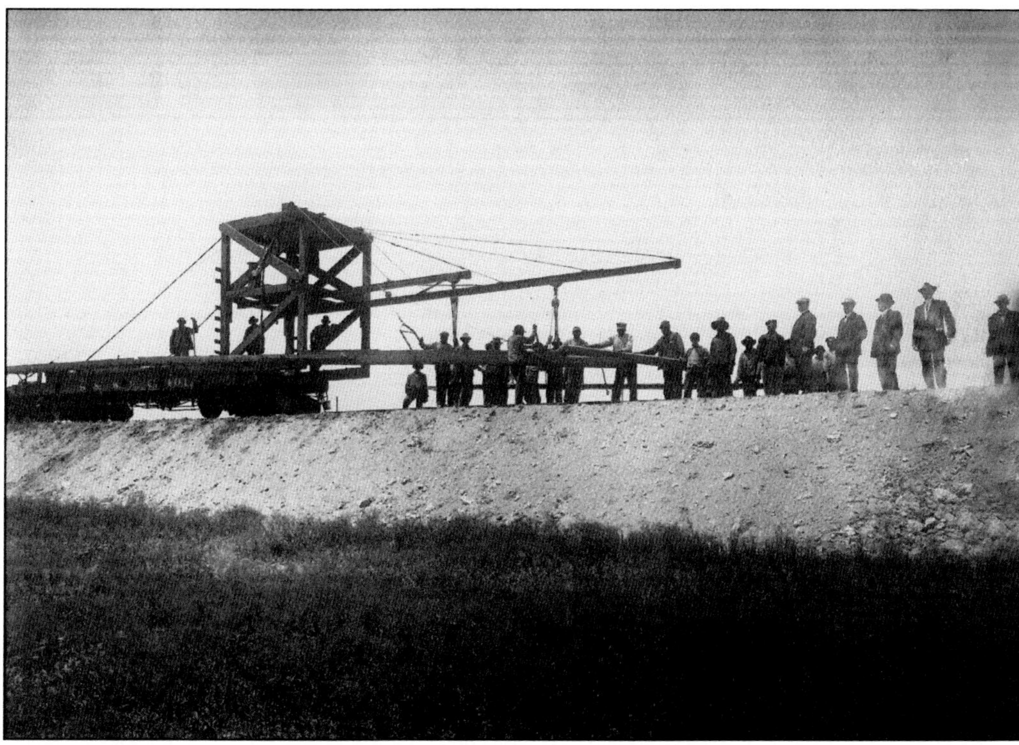

This is a side view of a windlass track-laying machine in operation.

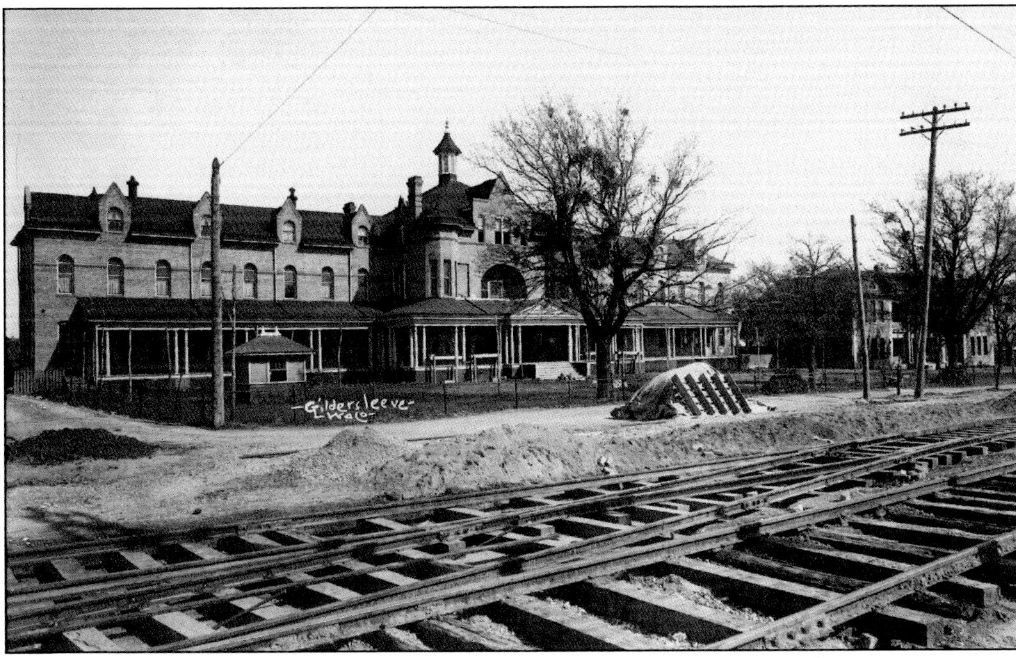

Construction of the line through Waco takes place in front of the local orphanage.

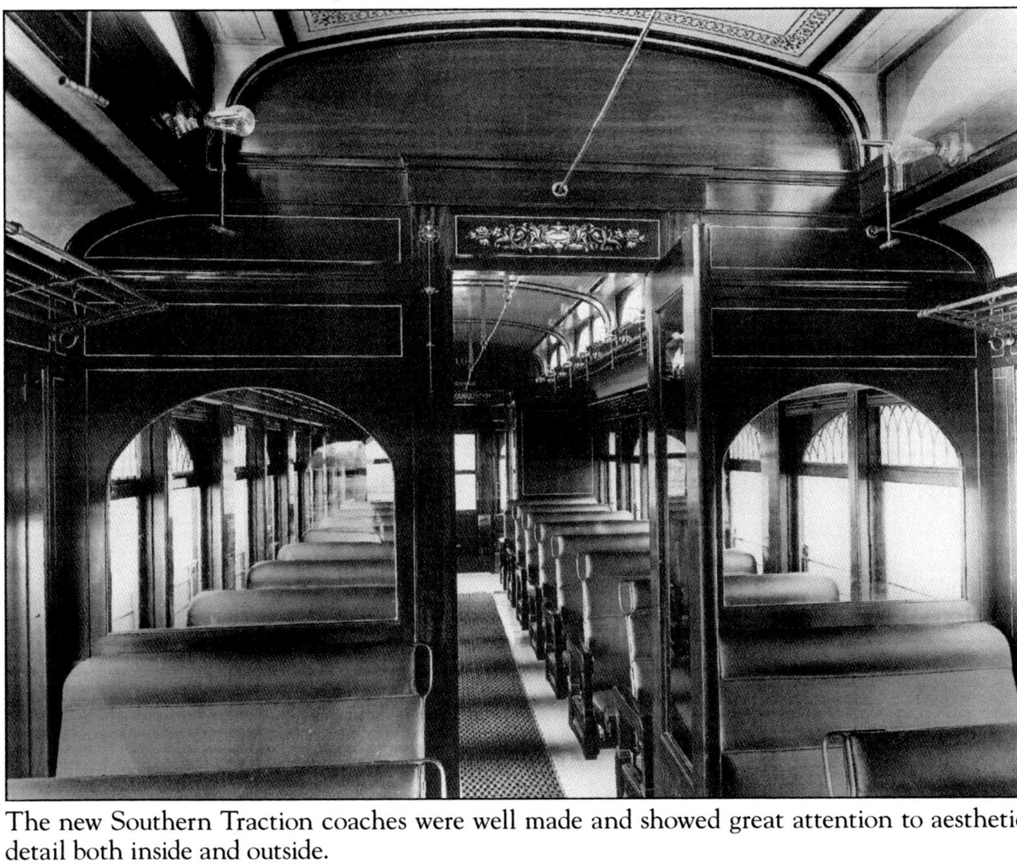

The new Southern Traction coaches were well made and showed great attention to aesthetic detail both inside and outside.

Here is a view looking toward the front of the Southern Traction car.

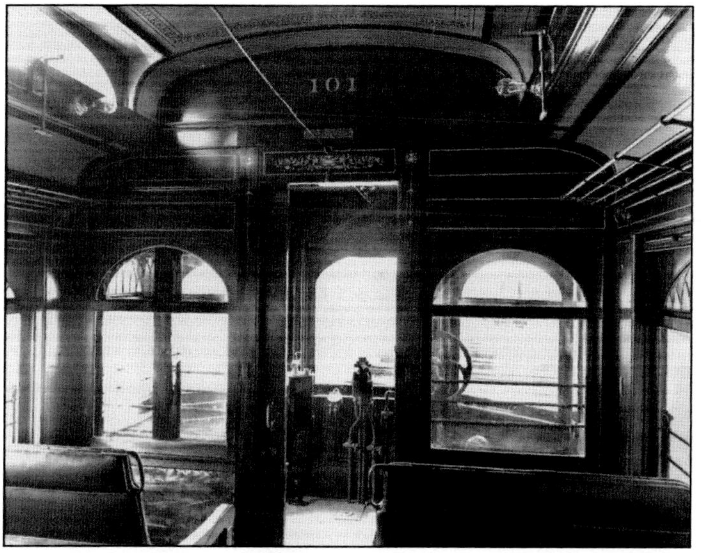

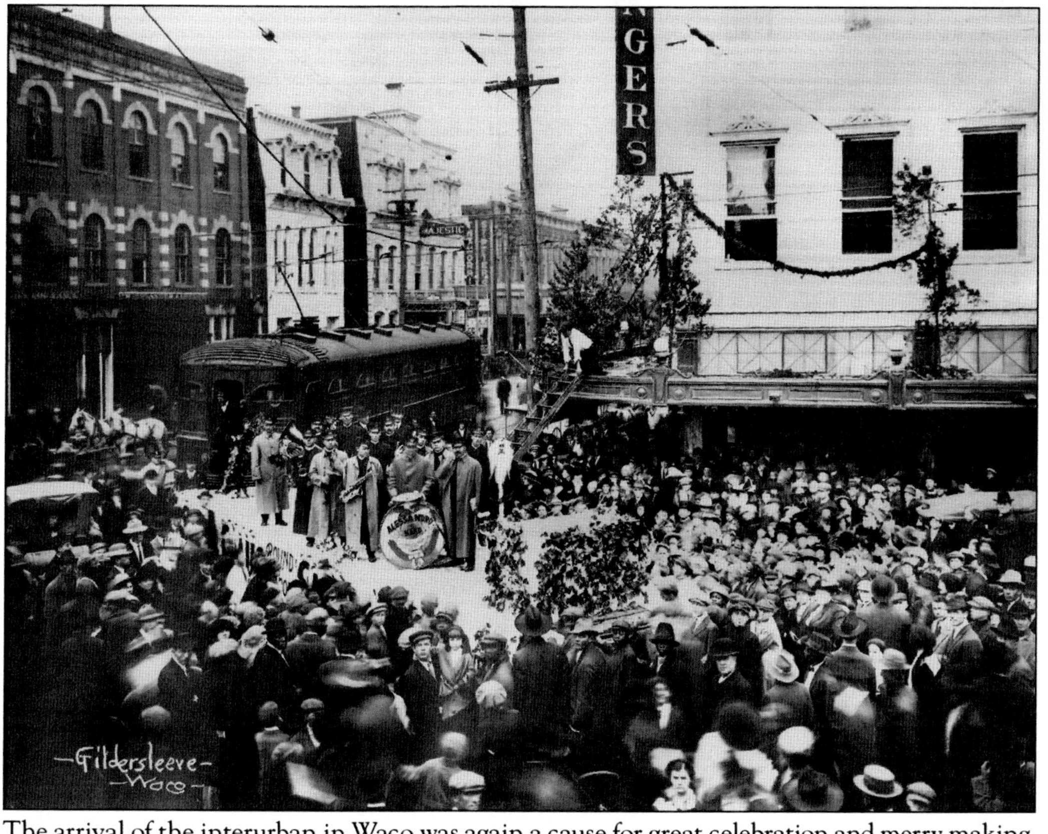

The arrival of the interurban in Waco was again a cause for great celebration and merry making. Everybody who was anybody wanted to ride the interurban. So how else would Santa Claus travel? This photograph, by famous local photographer Fred R. Gildersleeve, shows Santa arriving in Waco for the holidays. Yet many people in the crowd are more fascinated by the fact that a photograph is being taken as they turn toward the camera. (Courtesy of Baylor University Library, Gildersleeve Collection.)

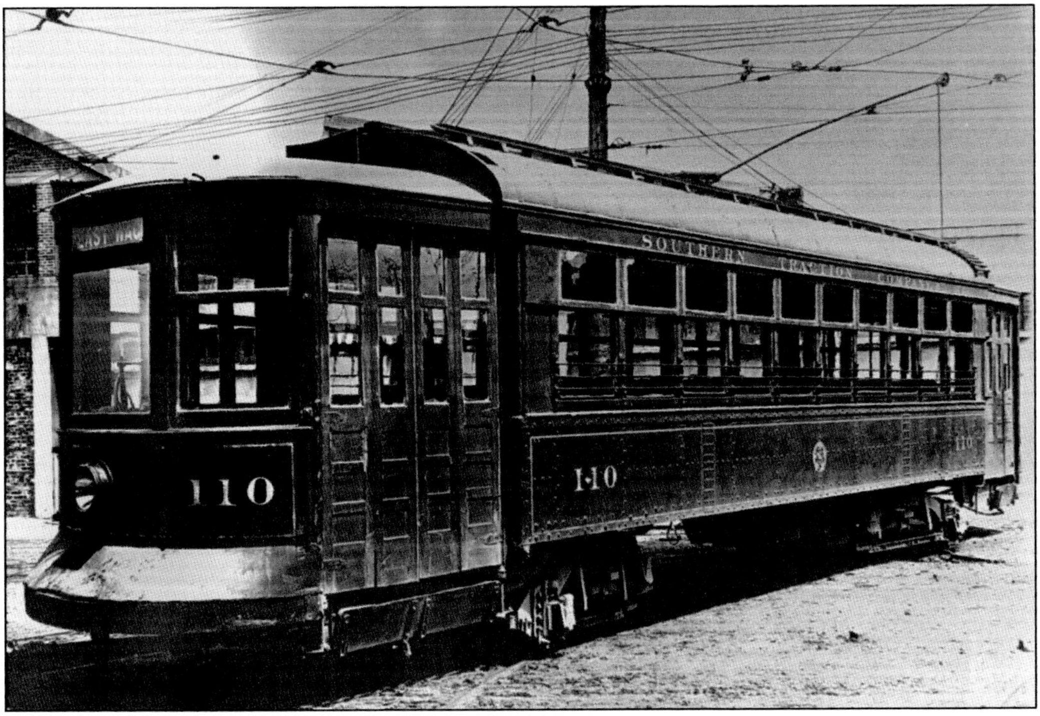

Waco City Lines were well established when consolidated with the Texas Electric Railway System.

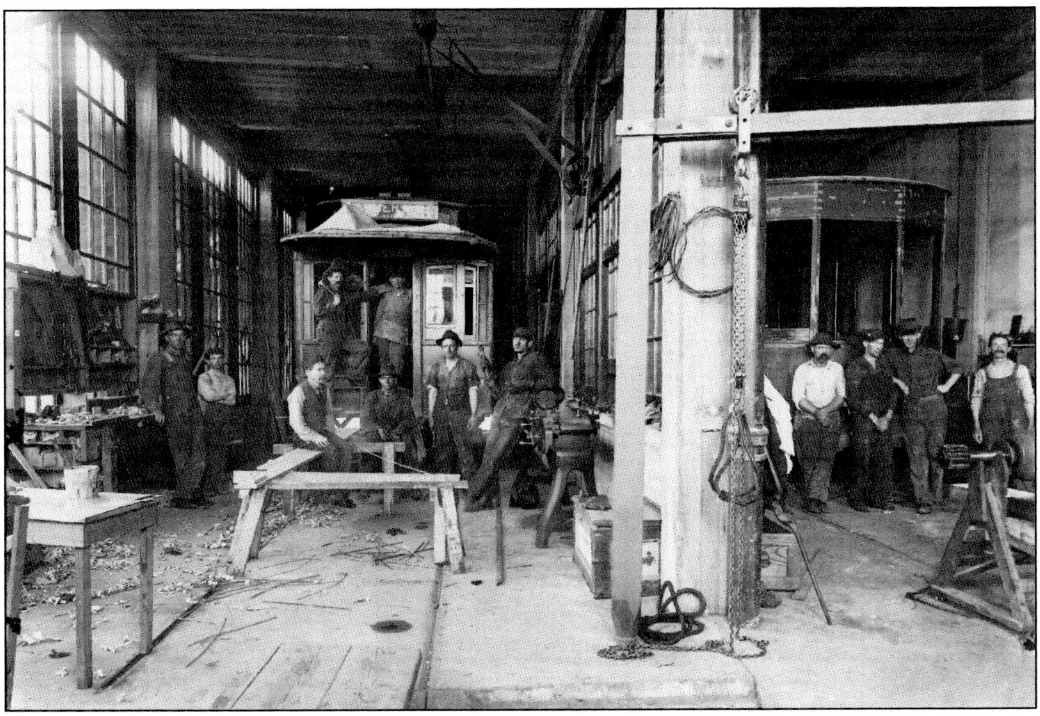

Even before becoming a part of the interurban system, Waco had a modern and complete electric streetcar barn, pictured here around 1905. (Courtesy of Baylor University Library.)

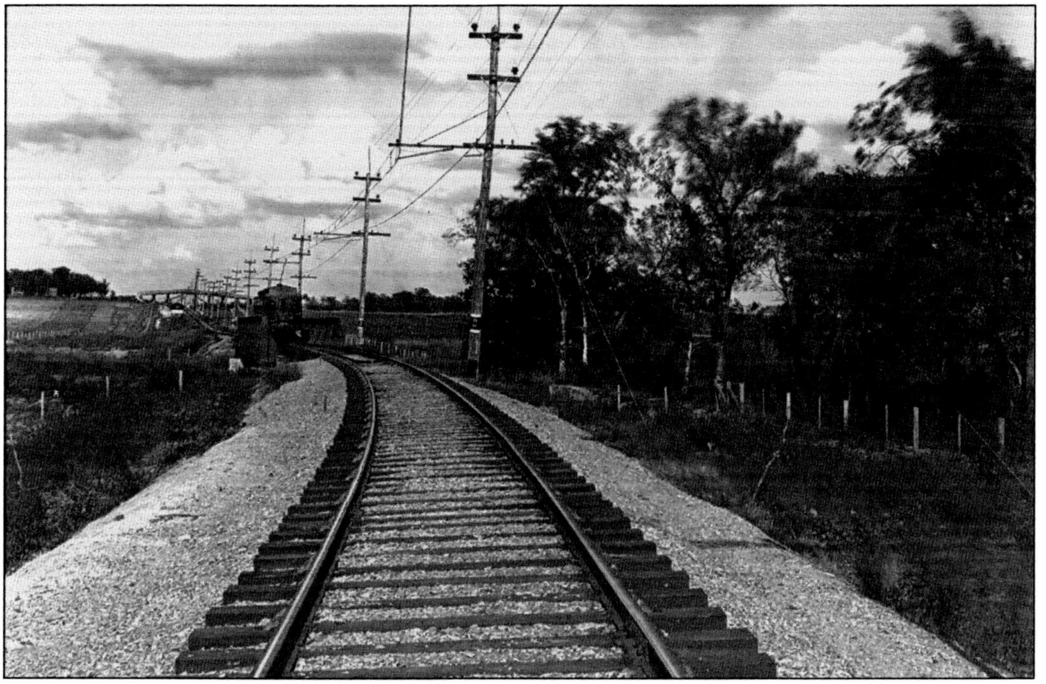

The countryside between Dallas and Fort Worth was a beautiful sight to behold in 1912.

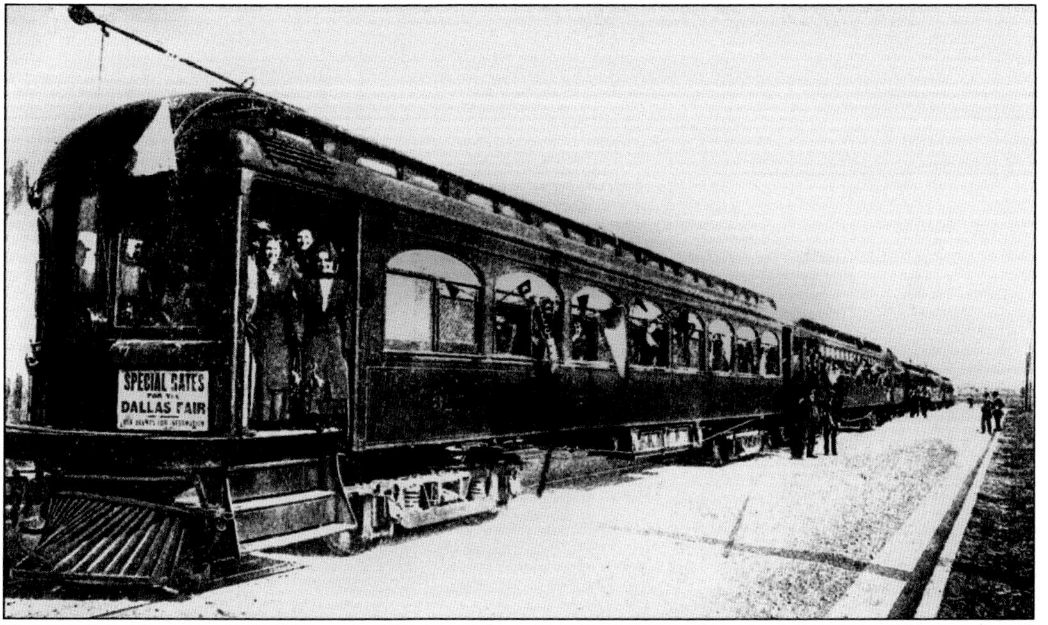

Founded in the 1860s, Kidd-Key College in Sherman was originally a coeducational high school. It later became a music conservatory and was administered under a very strict moral discipline. It was also known as the North Texas Female College and Conservatory of Music. It reached its heyday at the turn of the century, and by 1915, the strict regulations regarding dress and chaperonage passed out of favor. An annual event was the Kidd-Key Day at the Texas State Fair. For the occasion, they always chartered several railcars to take them from Sherman to Dallas. It was the custom for Kidd-Key alumnae to meet them at the fair and enjoy a day of merriment.

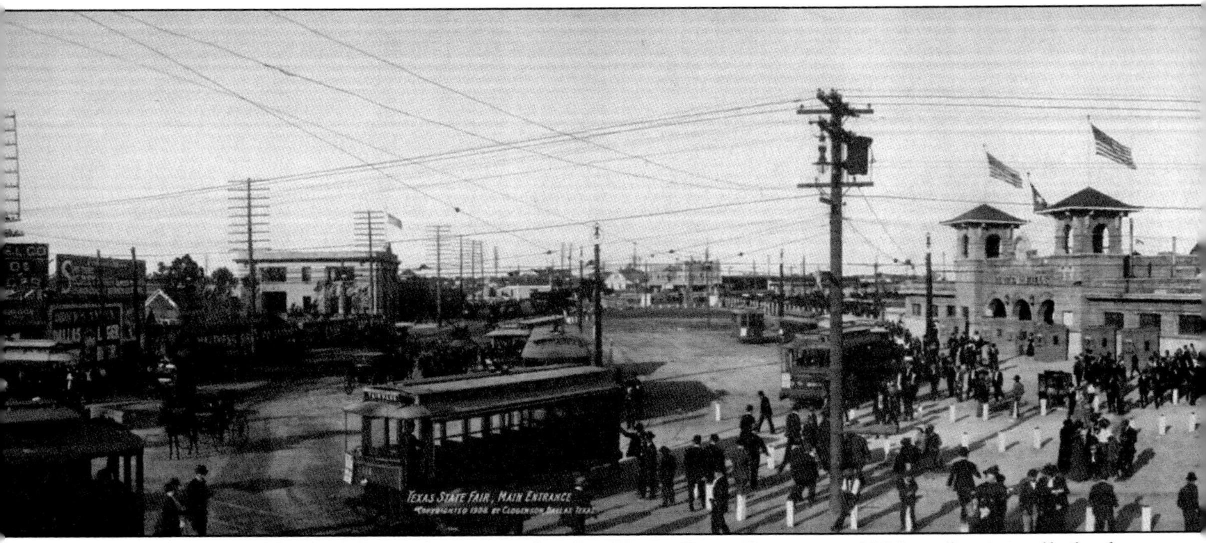

Fair Park in Dallas had been the venue for the Texas State Fair since 1888 and originally had a racetrack that ran its own season. A small village of shotgun houses surrounded the Fair Park area,

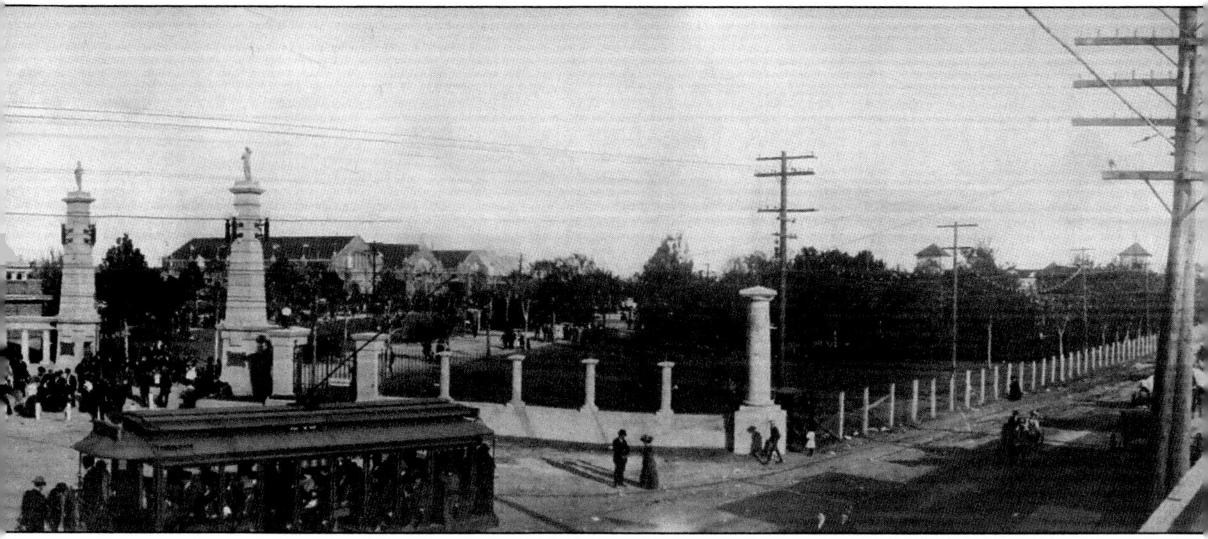

where workers cared for the horses and tended the park. (Courtesy of the Library of Congress.)

54 OFFICIAL INTERURBAN MAGAZINE

TEXAS TRACTION COMPANY

DENISON-SHERMAN RAILWAY CO.

"THE CONVENIENT WAY"
TO THE

DALLAS FAIR

Reduced Rates — Special Schedules

GOING---A Car Every Hour.
RETURNING---Last Car Leaves Dallas for Denison and intermediate Points at 10:00 p. m.; for McKinney and Intermediate points, 11:30 p. m.
Call up Agents for Information.

COMFORTABLE — CLEAN — CONVENIENT

BAGGAGE CARRIED ON REGULAR PASSENGER CARS

Through Tickets for Sale to Ft. Worth and Intermediate Points

M. R. FEWELL	**JAS. P. GRIFFIN**
Ass't General Passenger Agent	General Passenger Agent
Dallas, Texas	Dallas, Texas

Charter coaches to the State Fair were an annual revenue stream for the interurban.

Three

The Golden Age

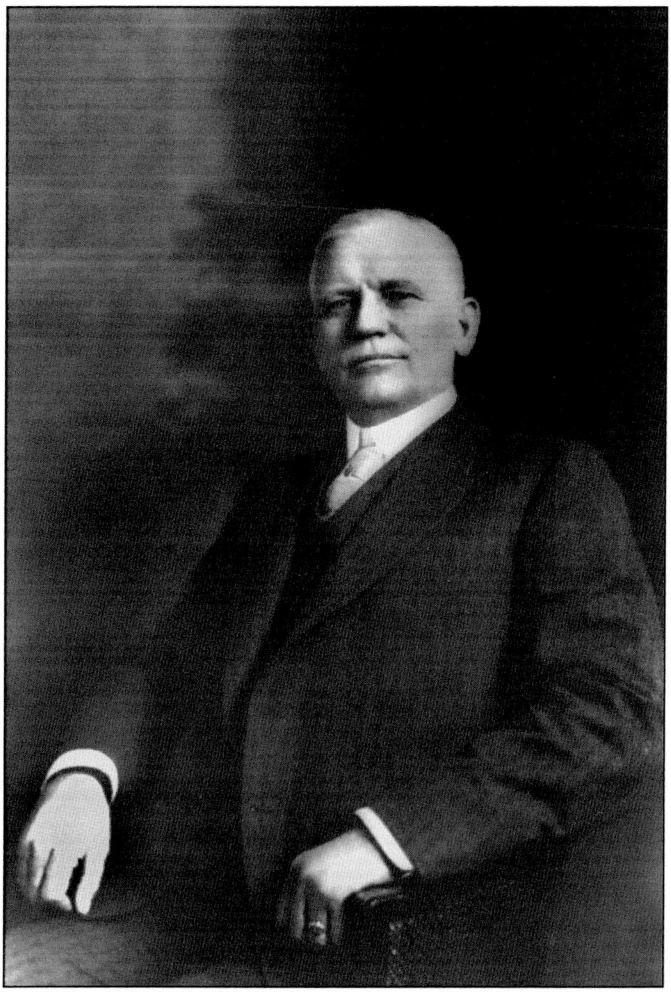

John Frank Strickland, president of the Texas Electric Railway, Dallas Light and Power, and Dallas Securities Company, wrote in the 1919 Annual Report, "Gross earnings from operations have increased over those for 1918 by $570,036.18, or 23.9%, making the earnings for the current year $2,951,511.27, the largest in the history of the Company." This statement launched the Golden Age of the Texas Electric Railway. Always the visionary who foresaw the benefit to North Texas of a consolidated rail transportation system that would give residents freedom to move about the region at will, John Strickland died suddenly of a heart attack on May 21, 1921. He lived to see his vision become an impressive reality. Strickland was honored many times over for his outstanding contributions to the development of North Texas transportation.

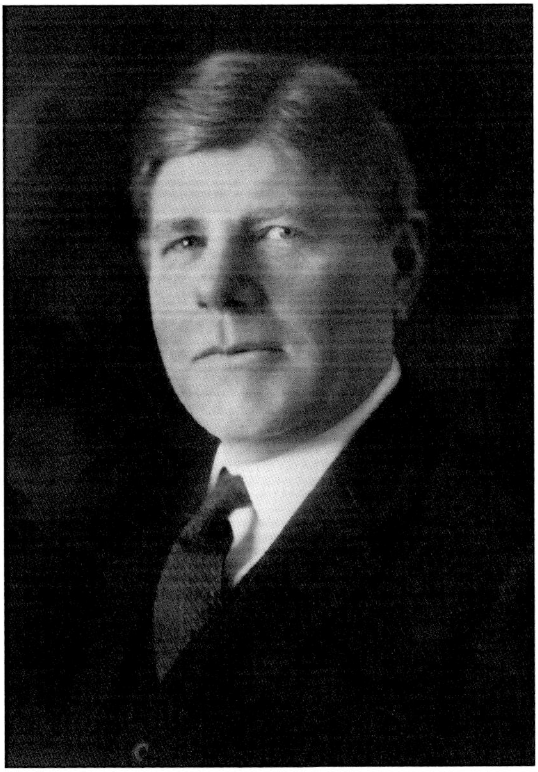

James Andrew Beall (left), U.S. Congressman from 1903 to 1915 and president of Texas Electric 1921–1929, succeeded John Strickland as president of Texas Electric. Beall was a longtime friend and associate and a member of Strickland's inner circle.

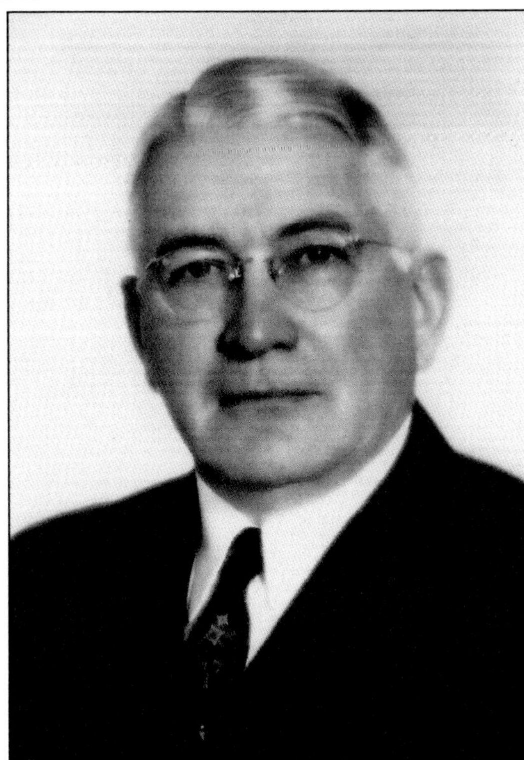

James P. Griffin (right) was the last president of Texas Electric, succeeding Jack Beall, who was his uncle. He, too, was a member of Strickland's inner circle.

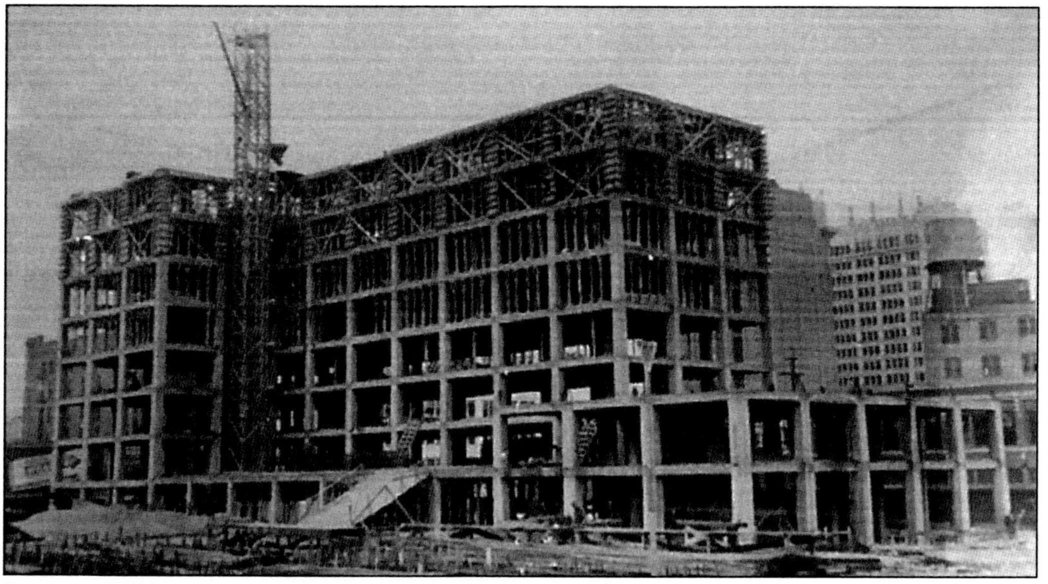

Stone and Webster managed construction projects, building the new Texas Electric Headquarters in 1915.

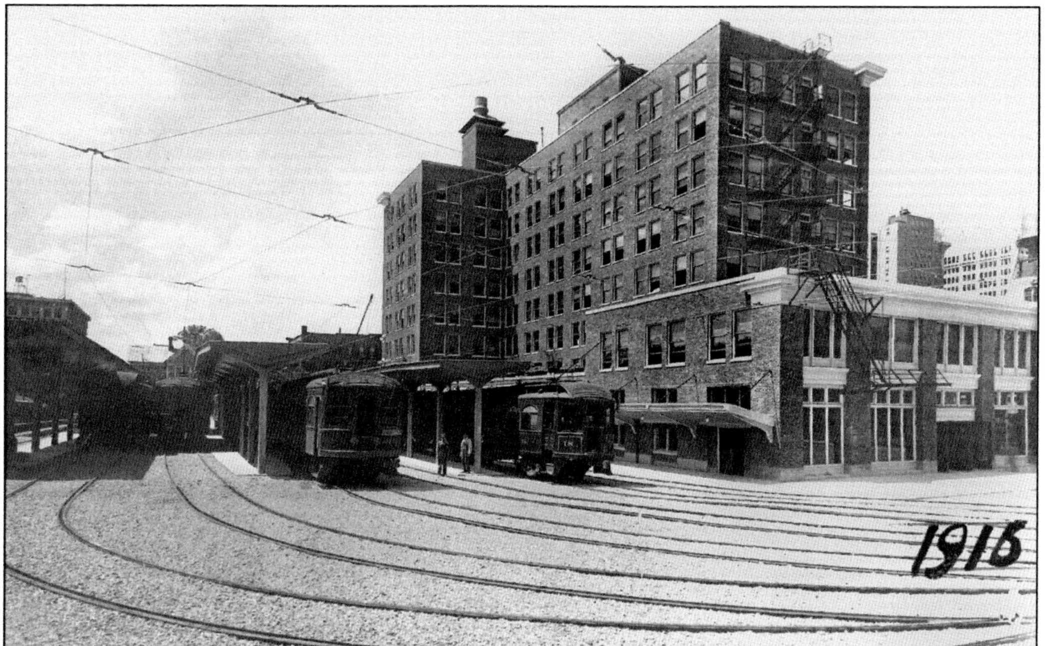

A new interurban headquarters building was constructed in downtown Dallas under the oversight of Stone and Webster Consulting Engineers. Considered one of the finest of its kind in the country, the building opened to the public on September 1, 1916, two months after the new Texas Electric Railway charter was filed with the Texas Secretary of State. The eight-story structure was modern in every detail and compared favorably with other fine interurban buildings in the country, such as Los Angeles, Akron, Milwaukee, and Indianapolis. A seven-track yard was behind the building that could accommodate an astonishing 24 interurban cars at a time. The 1904 Indianapolis building had nine tracks.

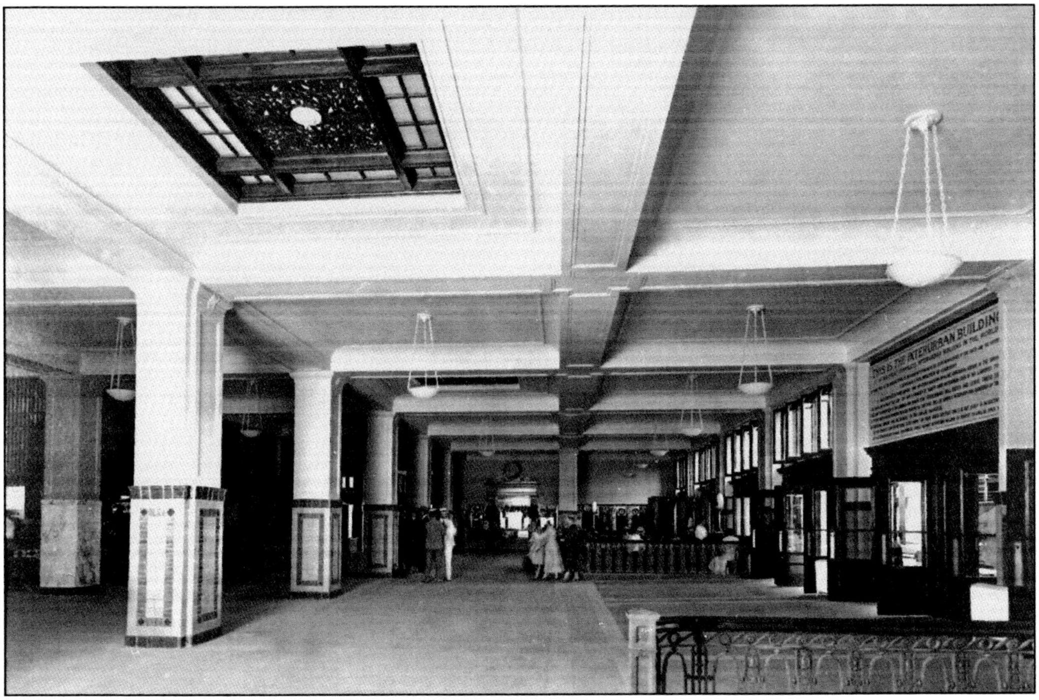

The interior of the new interurban station is pictured here around 1919.

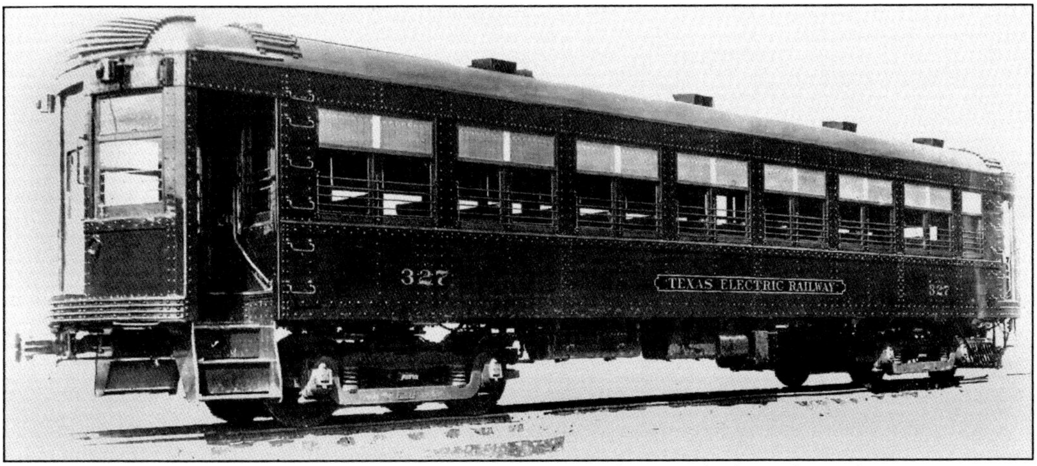

The Texas Electric railcars received a new system of numbers and a brand-new logo.

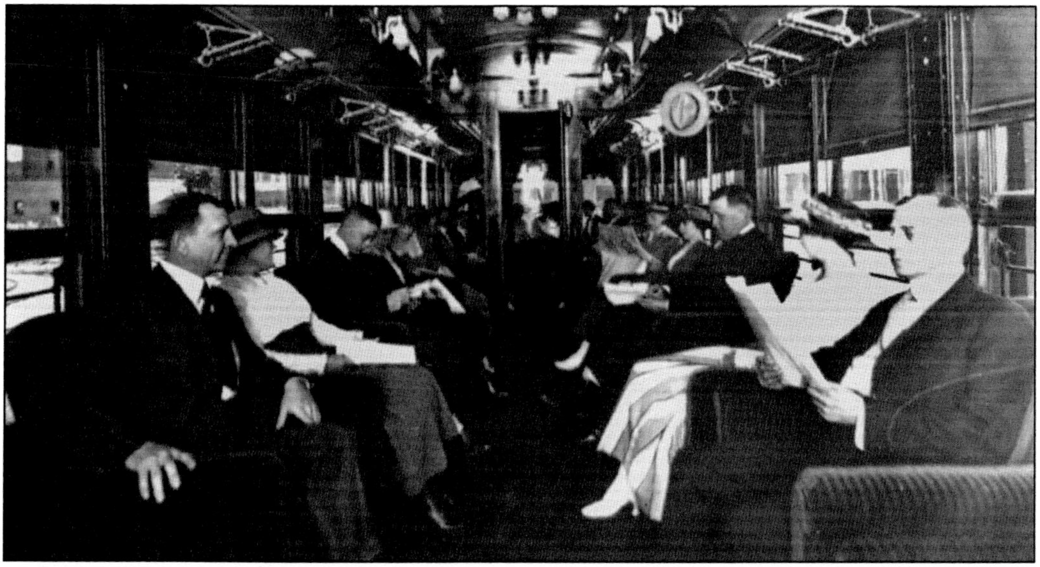

A promotional campaign to persuade passengers to leave their automobiles at home and ride the Texas Electric Railway included advertisements showing affluent and fashionably dressed passengers riding in ease and comfort aboard luxuriously appointed railcars. Such upgrades were a direct result of competition to interurban trains created by jitney cars, which became fashionable beginning in 1915. Texas Electric Parlor Car Service was available at slightly higher rates than regular service.

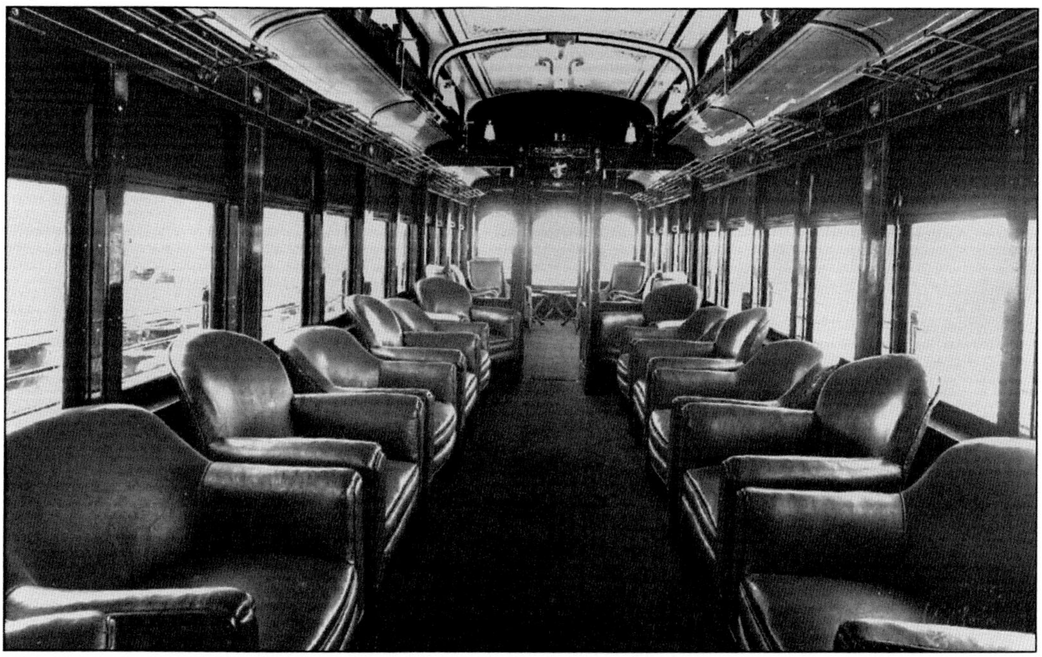

The parlor cars were outfitted with 22 large and comfortable leather chairs, an observation area, and smoking section at the end. A porter attended the passengers by helping ladies to board and providing soft drinks and the latest magazines for their reading pleasure. The parlor car rate from Dallas to Waco was 35¢ above the regular fare of $1.50 and 25¢ more to Denison above the regular $1.35 regular fare.

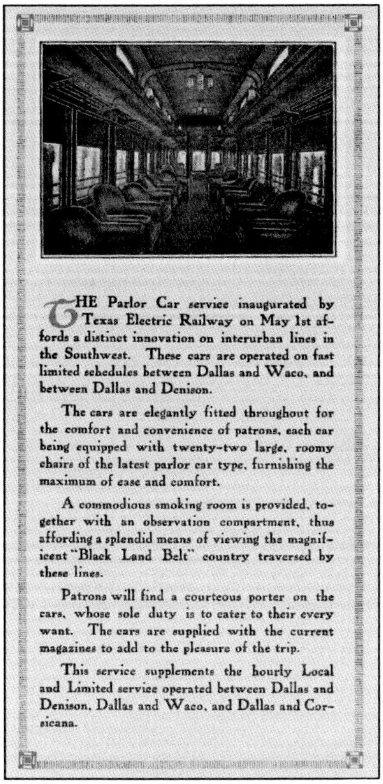

THE Parlor Car service inaugurated by Texas Electric Railway on May 1st affords a distinct innovation on interurban lines in the Southwest. These cars are operated on fast limited schedules between Dallas and Waco, and between Dallas and Denison.

The cars are elegantly fitted throughout for the comfort and convenience of patrons, each car being equipped with twenty-two large, roomy chairs of the latest parlor car type, furnishing the maximum of ease and comfort.

A commodious smoking room is provided, together with an observation compartment, thus affording a splendid means of viewing the magnificent "Black Land Belt" country traversed by these lines.

Patrons will find a courteous porter on the cars, whose sole duty is to cater to their every want. The cars are supplied with the current magazines to add to the pleasure of the trip.

This service supplements the hourly Local and Limited service operated between Dallas and Denison, Dallas and Waco, and Dallas and Corsicana.

This advertising brochure is for the new Service DeLuxe Parlor Car.

Texas Electric routinely advertised in a variety of magazines and newspapers to persuade readers to ride the interurban.

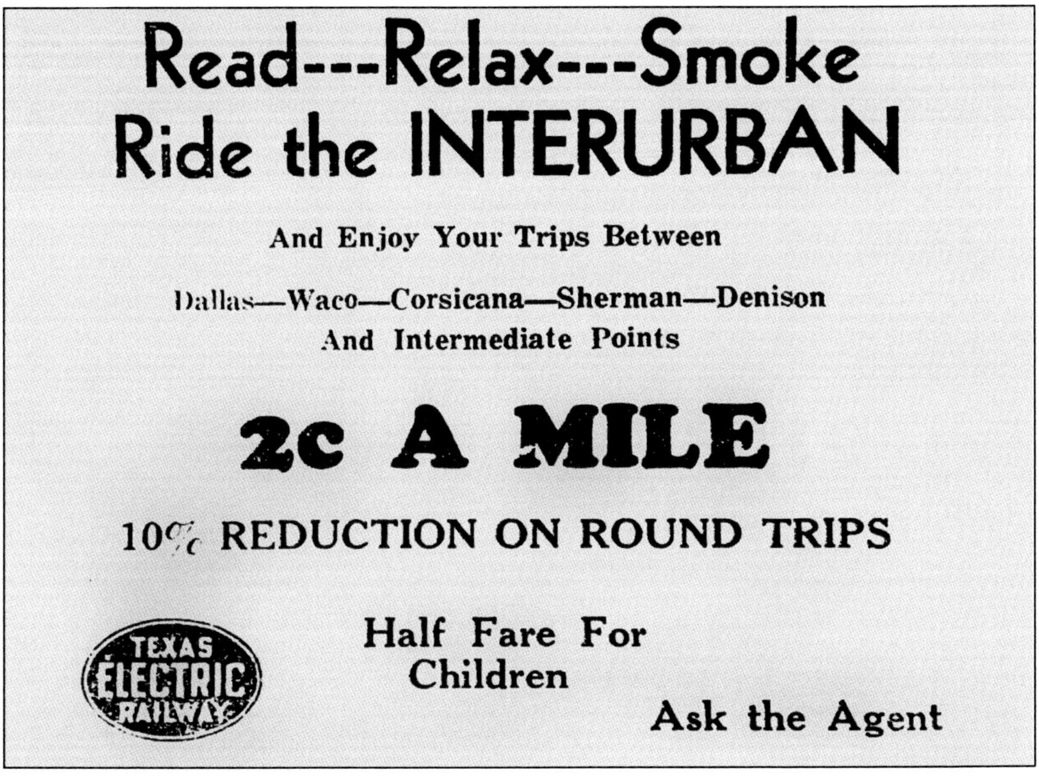

Although segregated seating was the policy on interurban travel, there was only one non-segregated toilet aboard the railcars. The headquarters building in Dallas had two waiting rooms and other segregated facilities. The rear door of the railcar, leading to the Railway Post Office, was always kept locked when the car was in motion and armed postal employees were aboard.

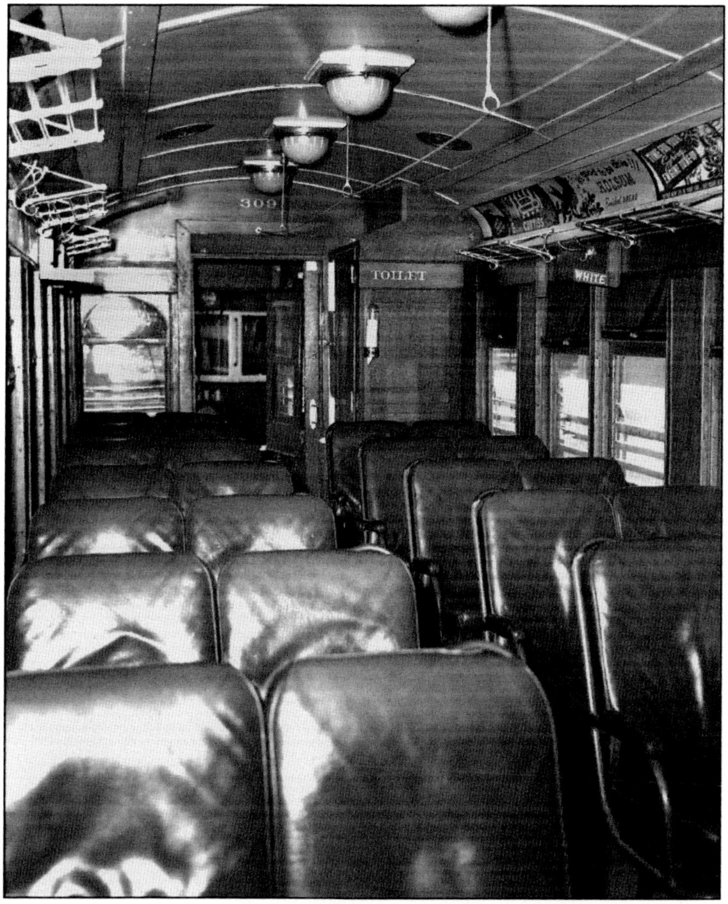

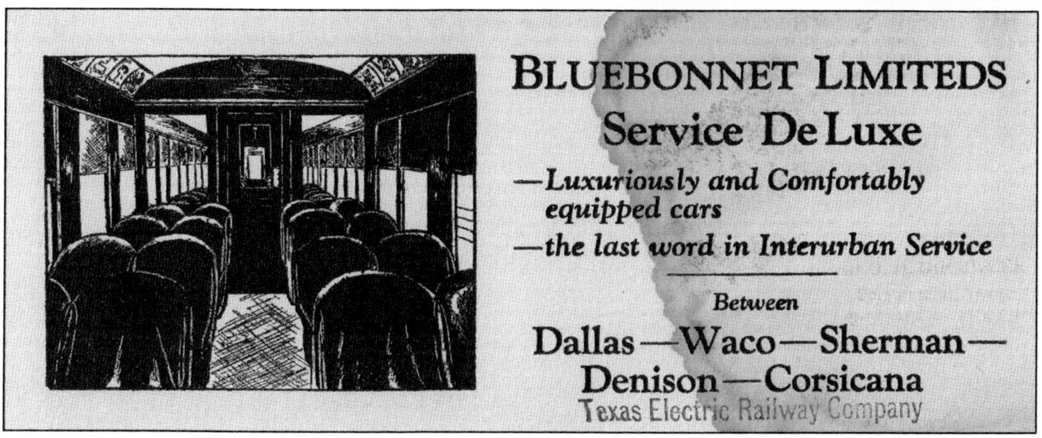

As part of the promotional campaign to persuade passengers to use the *Bluebonnet Limited* coaches, Texas Electric Railway gave away these special ink blotters on the assumption that anyone using the *Bluebonnet Limited* would be inclined to use a fountain pen and not a pencil. *Bluebonnet* cars offered limited-stop service, mainly in the principal cities along the lines. The cars were painted the brilliant blue of the Texas state flower of the same name. Advertising promotions called it "The transportation service SUPREME!" During the Roaring Twenties, when money was plentiful, extra services were welcomed by passengers who had the means to pay.

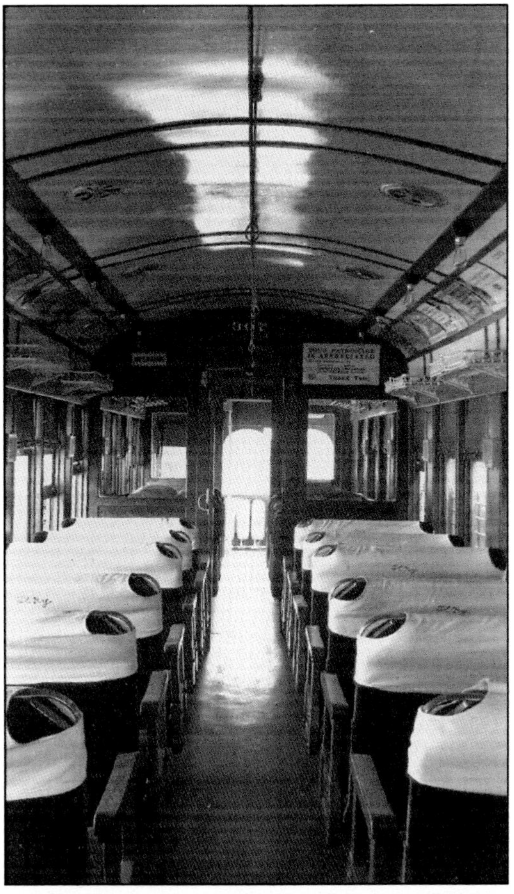

The white covers on the back of the seats, pictured here, gave *Bluebonnet* coaches a special touch.

Northern Texas Traction Company and the Fort Worth *Crimson Limited* were introduced in 1925. First-class cars included a "Salounge" with wicker chairs. The forward part had rotating individual chairs. The *Crimson Limited* was particularly noted for its distinctive touches of luxury and convenience. (Courtesy of the DeGolyer Library, Southern Methodist University/John J. Myers.)

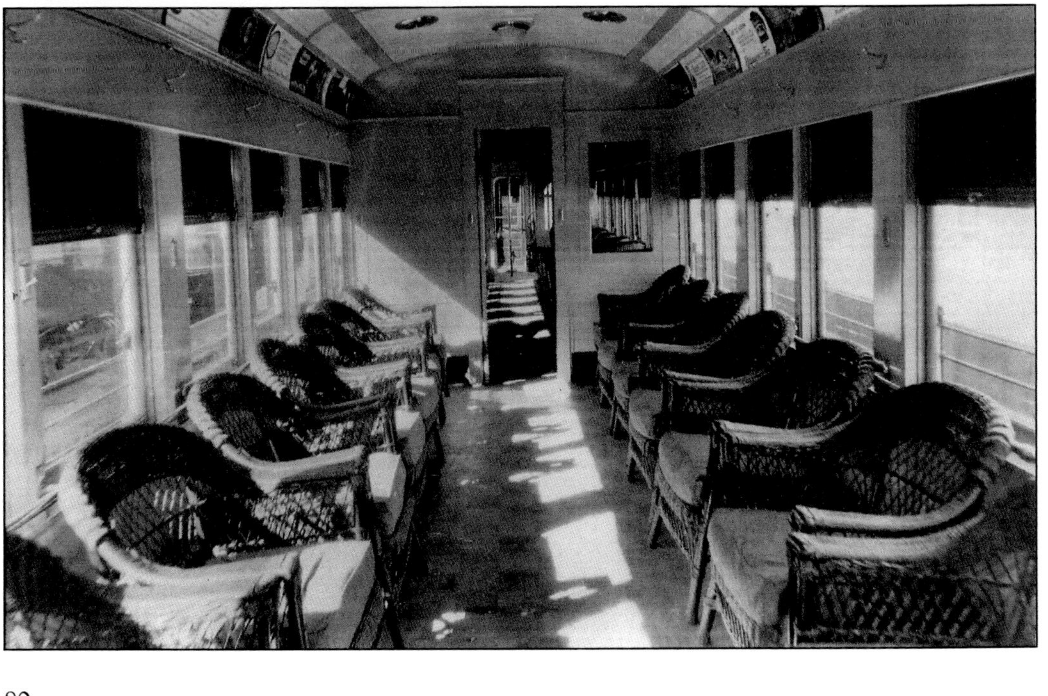

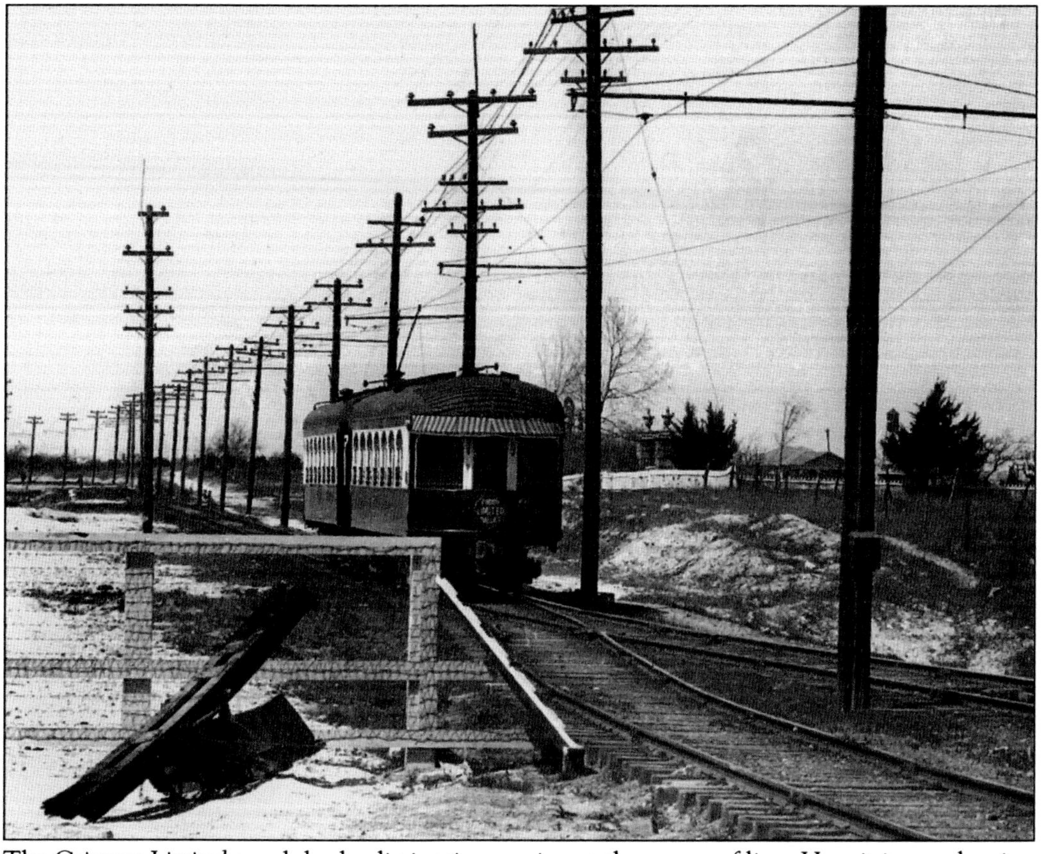

The *Crimson Limited* coach had a distinctive awning at the rear roof line. Here it is seen leaving Dallas for Fort Worth. There were five *Crimson Limited* coaches that traveled between Dallas and Fort Worth. Luxury service to other destinations was provided by the Pioneer Local cars that were painted maroon. (Courtesy of John J. Myers.)

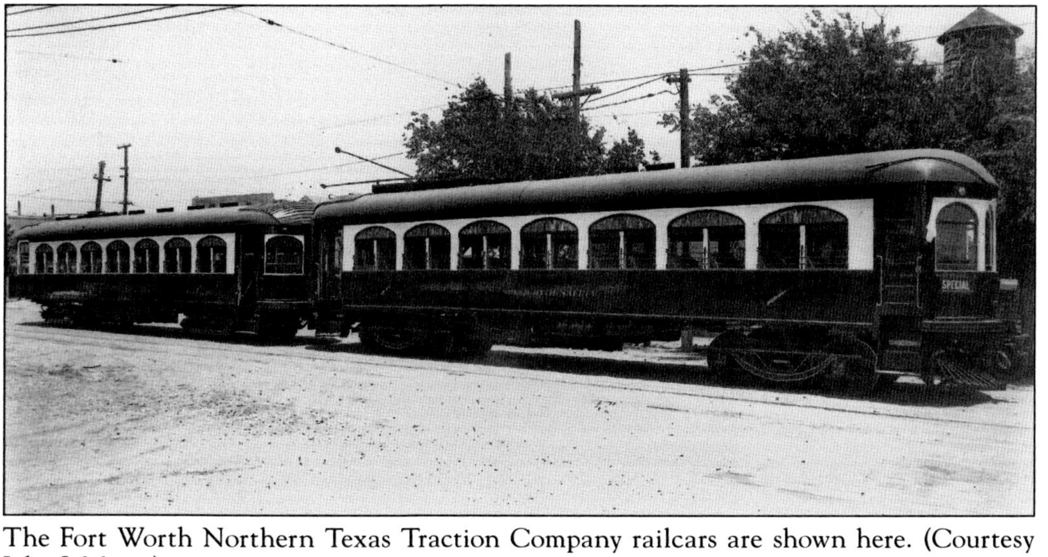

The Fort Worth Northern Texas Traction Company railcars are shown here. (Courtesy John J. Myers.)

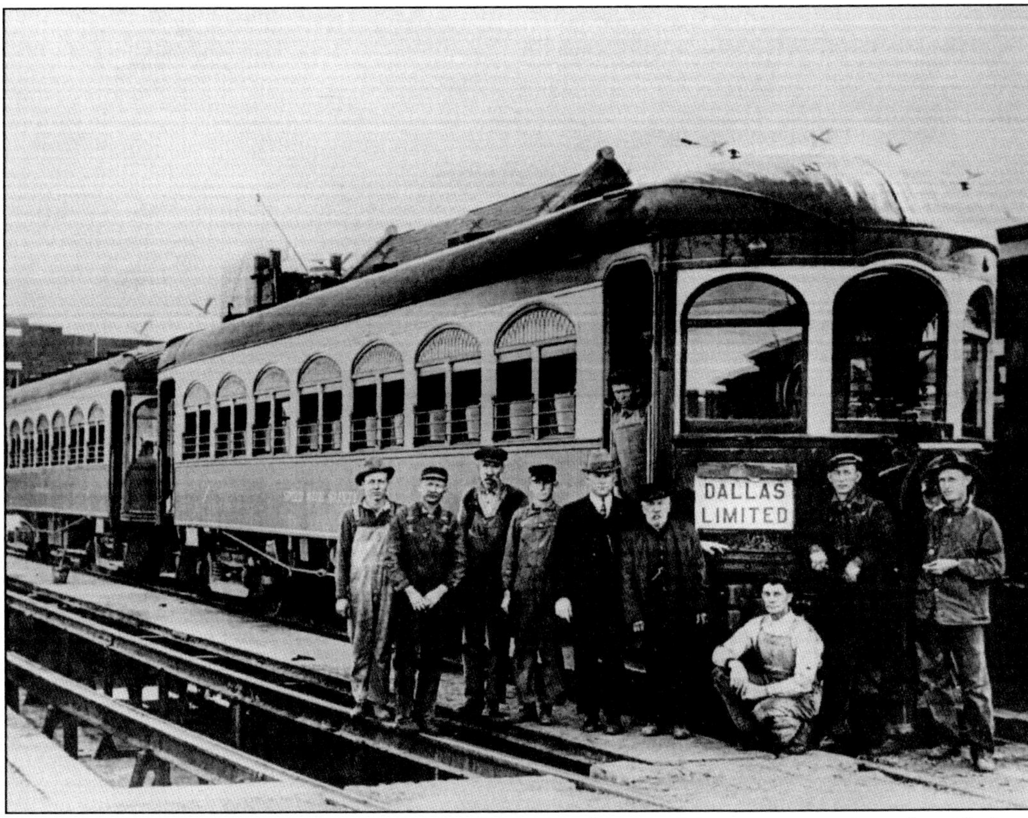

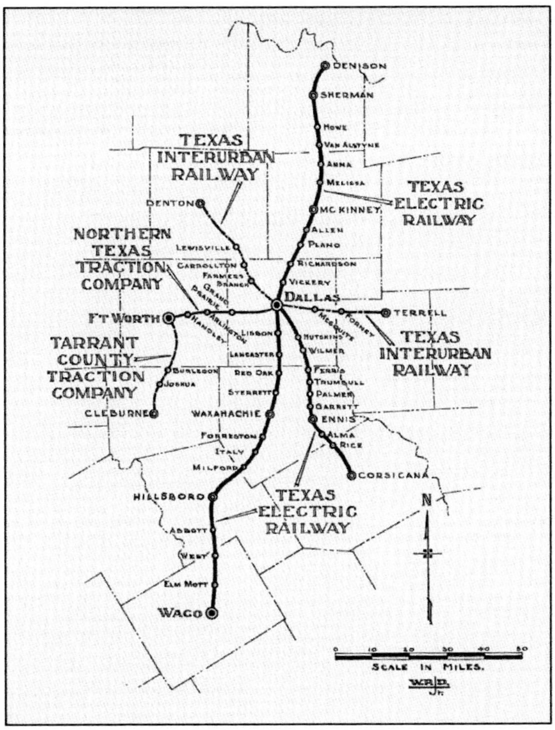

A maintenance crew and unidentified management representatives posed beside the Fort Worth *Crimson Limited* in a layover in downtown Fort Worth's Belknap Yard, just north of the Tarrant County Courthouse, around 1927. (Courtesy of John J. Myers.)

Texas Electric Railway routes offered service from Denison to Dallas and from Dallas to Waco and Corsicana. Other interurban companies were Texas Interurban Railway, which extended from Dallas to Terrell and Dallas to Denton; the Northern Texas Traction Company, which serviced Dallas to Fort Worth; and the Tarrant County Traction Company from Fort Worth to Cleburne. (Map by W. P. Donalson Jr.)

Texas Electric Railway Car No. 360 makes a night run to Denison. During the golden age, it was a two-man car with a conductor and a motorman who operated the car. The Fresnel lens, created from 19th-century lighthouse technology and mounted on the front of the car, provided an extremely bright beam of light that lit up the tracks for several hundred feet at night. (Photograph by Frank Rogers.)

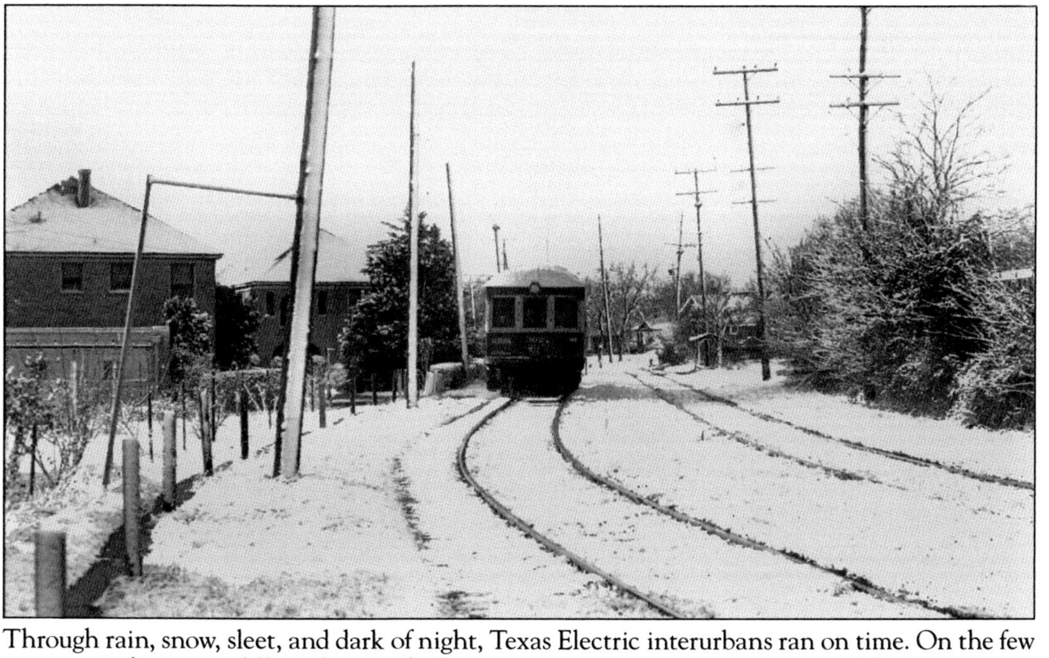

Through rain, snow, sleet, and dark of night, Texas Electric interurbans ran on time. On the few occasions when snow fell on the North Texas prairie, Texas Electric cars carried their passengers through a wonderland of snow, creating a very different scenic travel experience. Each railcar was heated inside, and passengers rode along in total comfort past trees and prairie grasses transformed in appearance by freshly fallen snow.

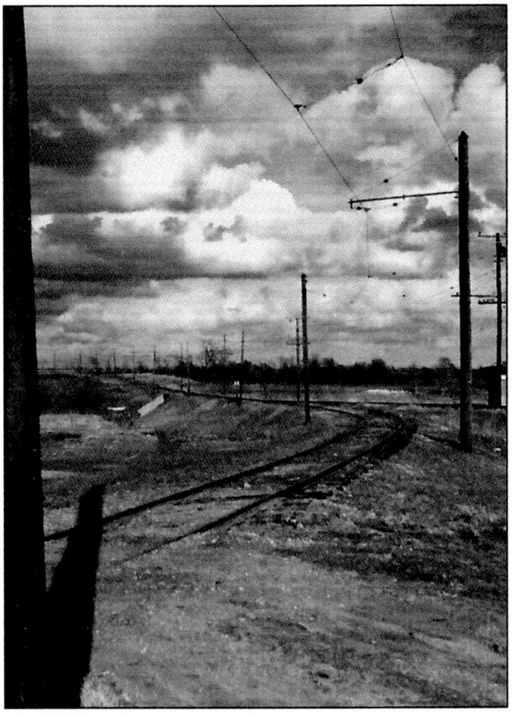

Riding the Texas Electric Railway under the spacious skies of the North Texas prairie was always enjoyable and gave Texans a deep feeling of reverence for the wide-open spaces of the West. (Photograph by C. E. DeWoody.)

Buses became an integral part of the Texas Electric Railway transportation system by being used on feeder lines and short routes when neither streetcars nor interurban electric railcars would serve the purpose. They were used to stem the competition against the interurban lines and local streetcar lines. They served to complete the transportation system that the company had promised to deliver when it was chartered. Although not as comfortable as the electric streetcars and railway cars, they were economical to operate and cost less to purchase at $3,815 apiece rather than the $10,000 plus for a railcar. Bus routes could be changed quickly, and neither tracks nor electrical wires needed to be laid or strung.

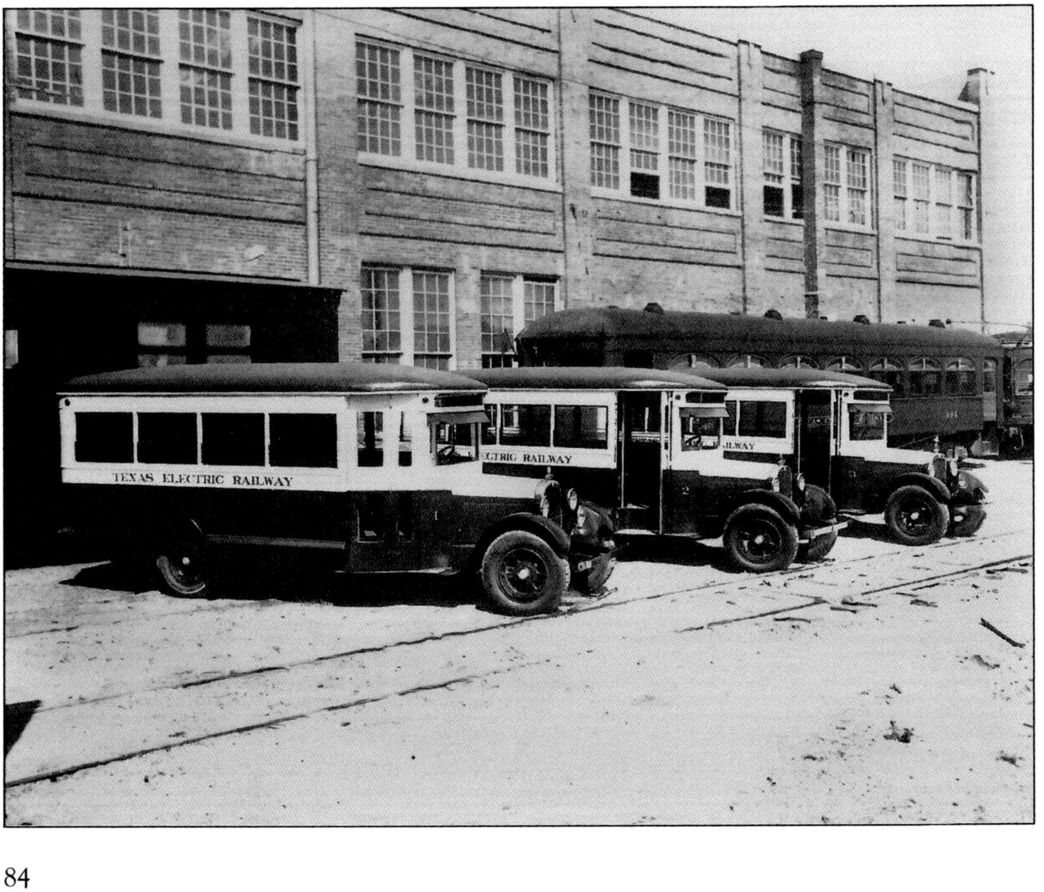

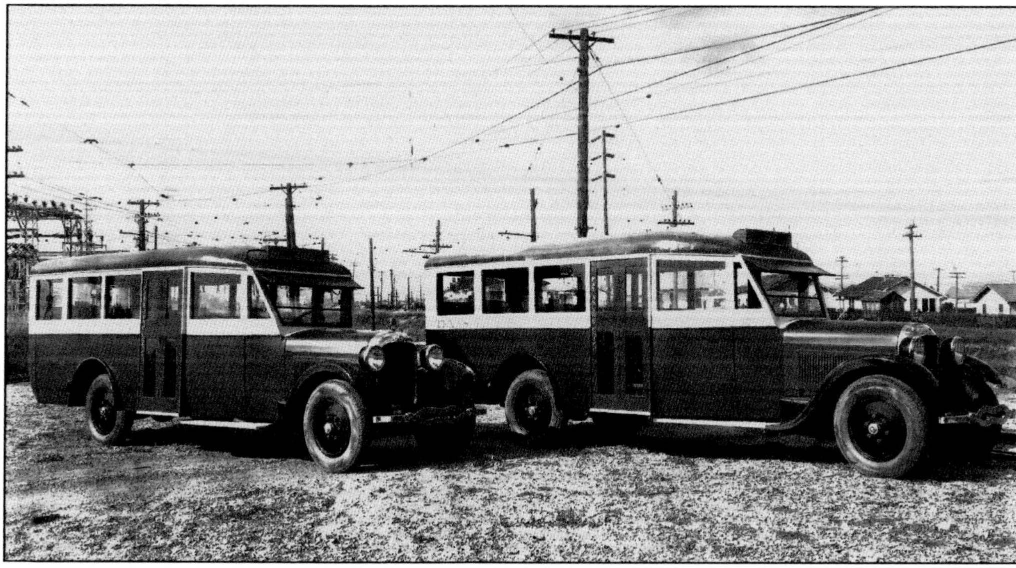

Beginning in 1925, Texas Electric Railway purchased five Studebaker motor buses to replace city streetcars in Sherman and Denison. Use of buses, with varied routes, also slowed competition from jitneys and automobiles by providing increased flexibility for riders.

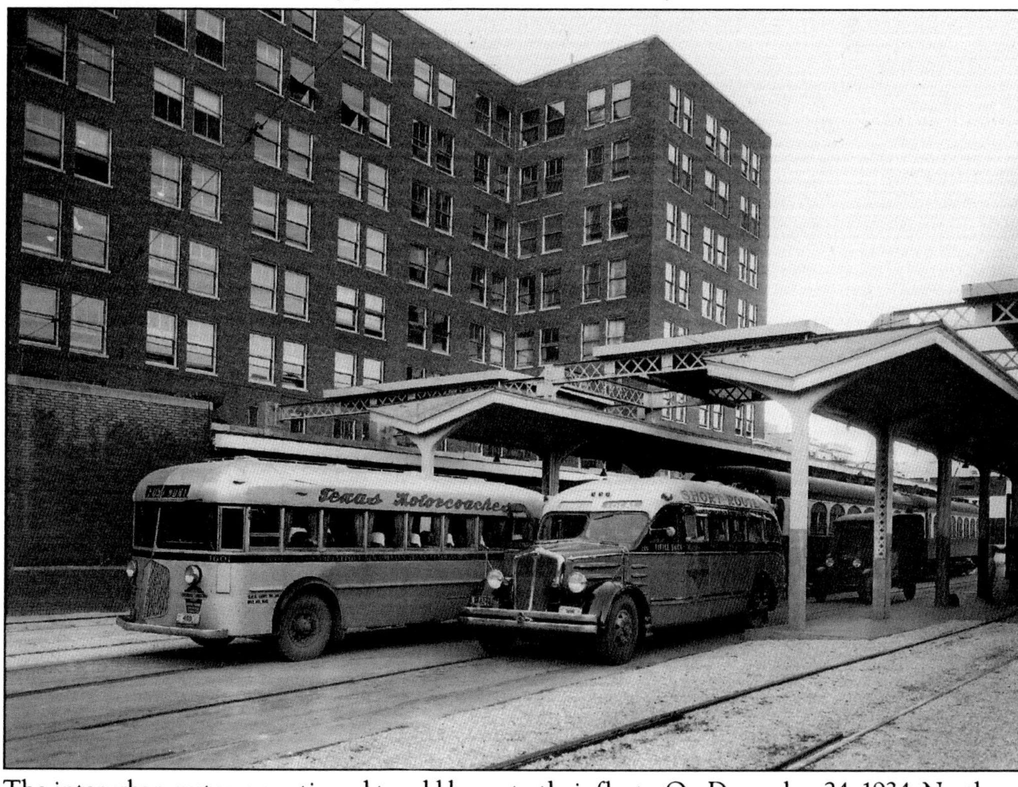

The interurban systems continued to add buses to their fleets. On December 24, 1934, Northern Texas Traction discontinued its *Crimson Limited* service between Fort Worth and Dallas and added Texas Motor Coaches, Model 30A, as shown above. The coaches retained the special seat covers that were a part of *Crimson Limited* service.

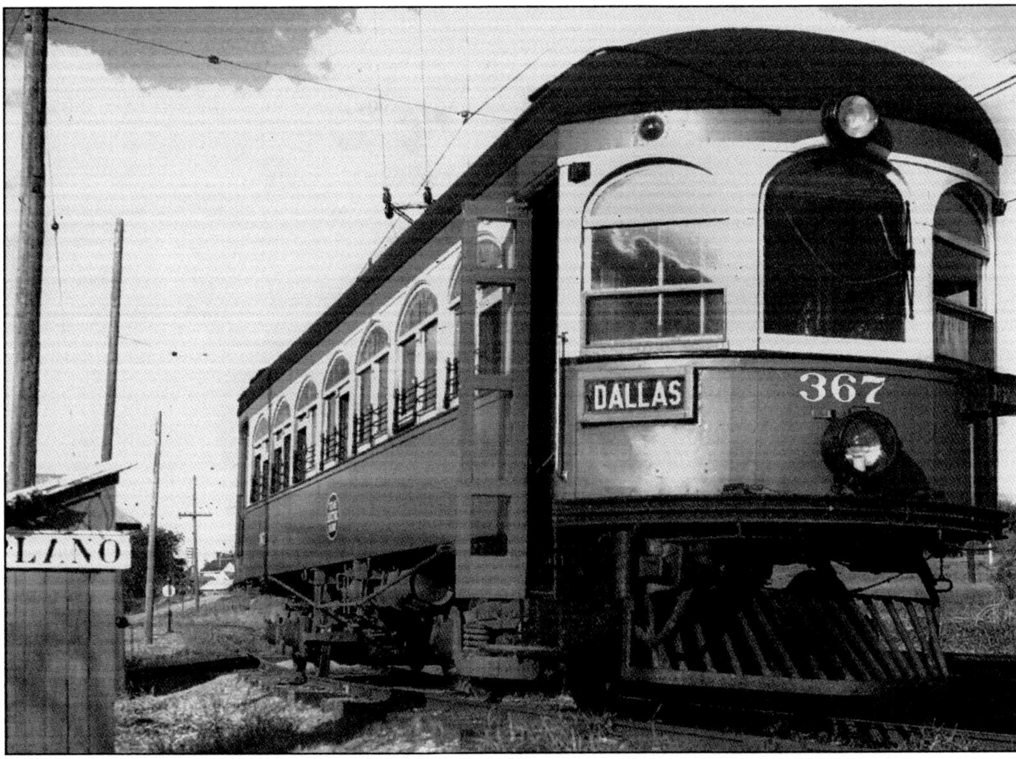

Car No. 367 stopped at the Plano station around 1935 beside the telephone call box used to phone ahead to Monroe Shops. (Photograph by John Humiston; courtesy of Richard Humiston.)

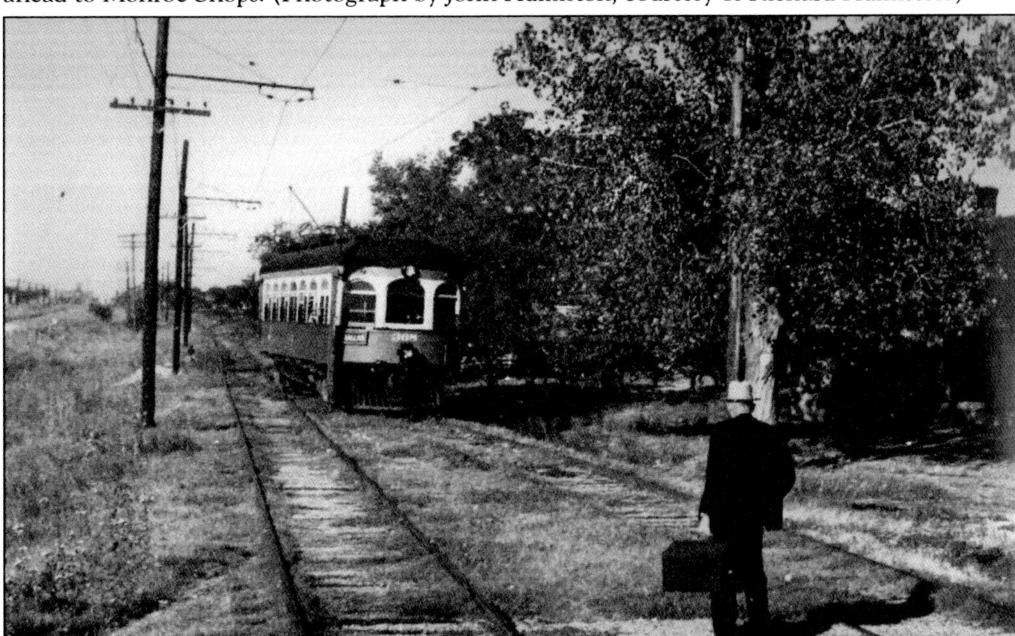

Just south of Plano, this salesman flags down the interurban train to board for a trip. (Photograph by William C. Janssen; courtesy of John J. Myers.)

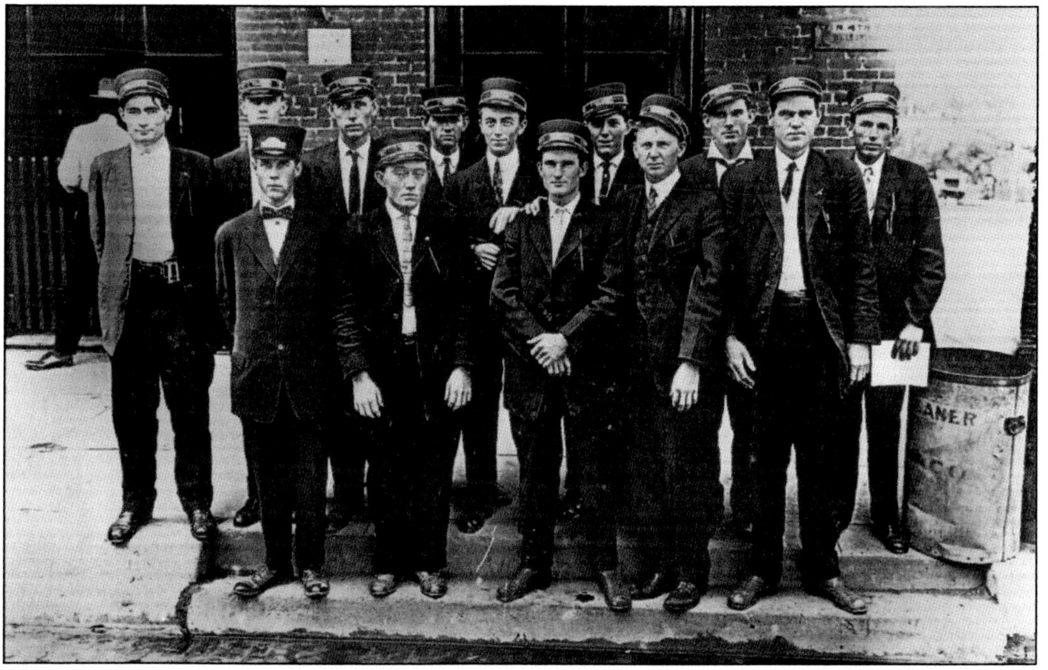

The Waco motormen posed on the sidewalk for this 1913 photograph were elite in their own right. Their status would have been above anyone who drove horses or mules. They represented the latest in transportation technology, and young boys looked up to them as heroes. (Courtesy of Baylor University Library.)

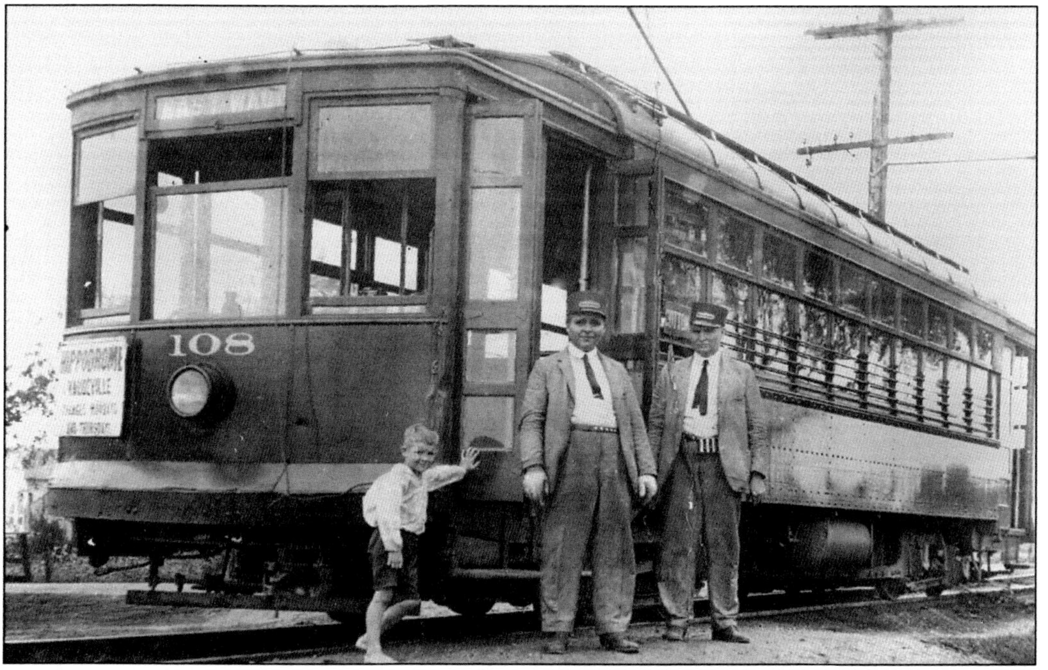

Motormen were held in high esteem. It was a pleasure and delight for a young boy to be photographed beside this Waco streetcar with a motorman and conductor around 1925. (Photograph by Ona I. Davis; courtesy of C. T. Dickinson.)

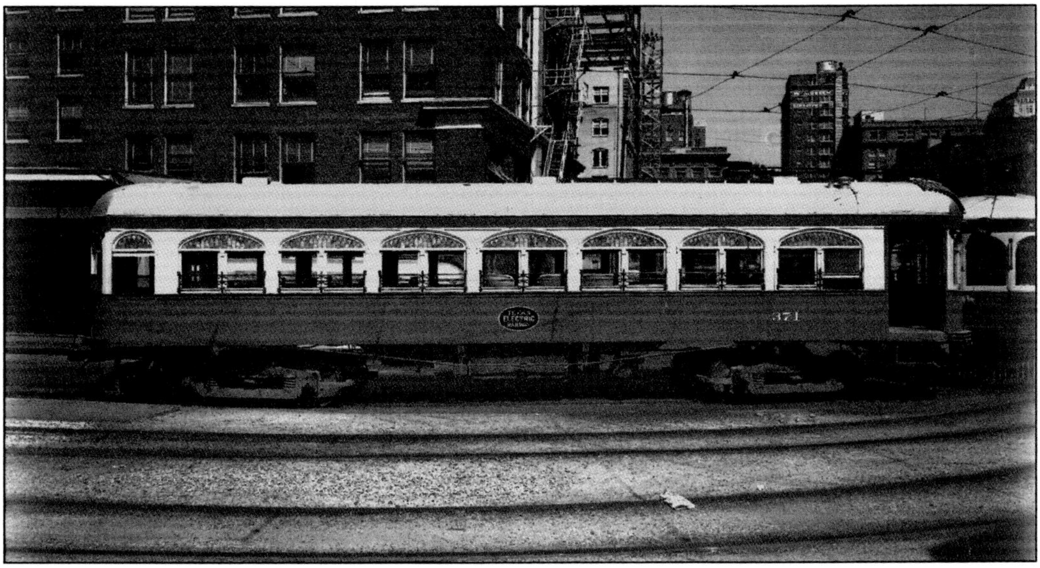

Demise came first to the Dallas–Fort Worth line of the Northern Texas Traction Company, and Texas Electric purchased six of their newest cars at a good price.

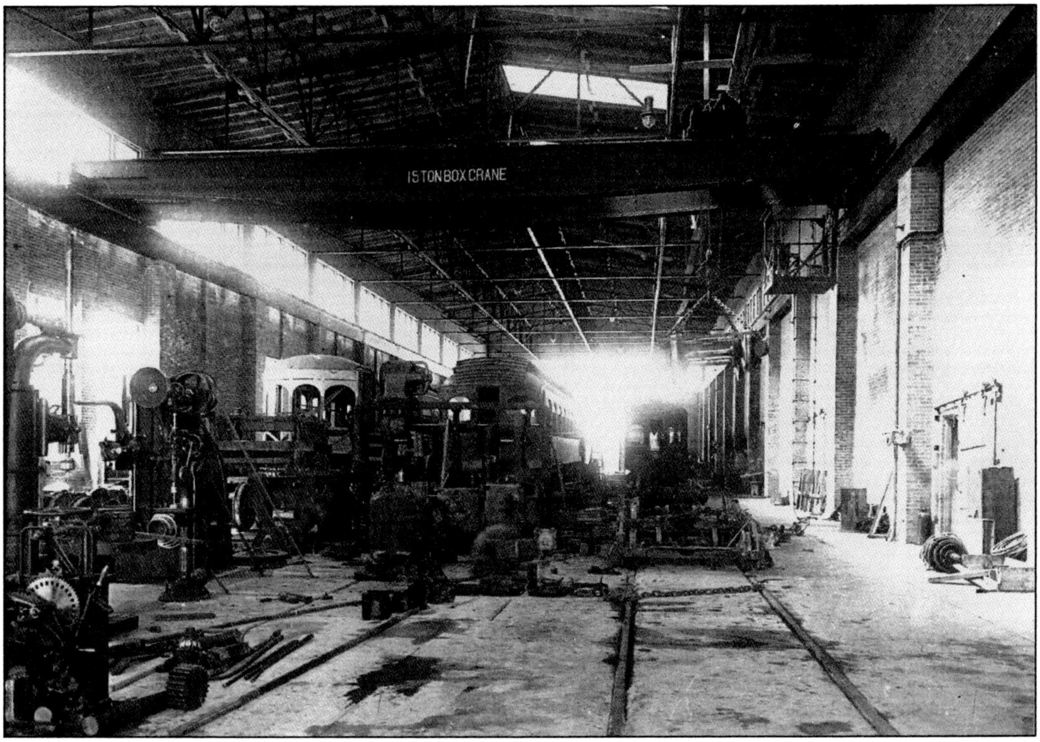

Built in 1915, the Monroe Shops housed the maintenance for repair, refurbishing, and rebuilding of interurban cars. Located in Dallas, the shop performed a myriad of operations to keep the interurban system in top form. The shops, located 4 miles south of downtown Dallas, were the largest in the South. They were completed in June 1914, and both Southern Traction and Texas Traction used the facilities. A 15-ton box crane operated in the shops to move the cars from place to place inside the building.

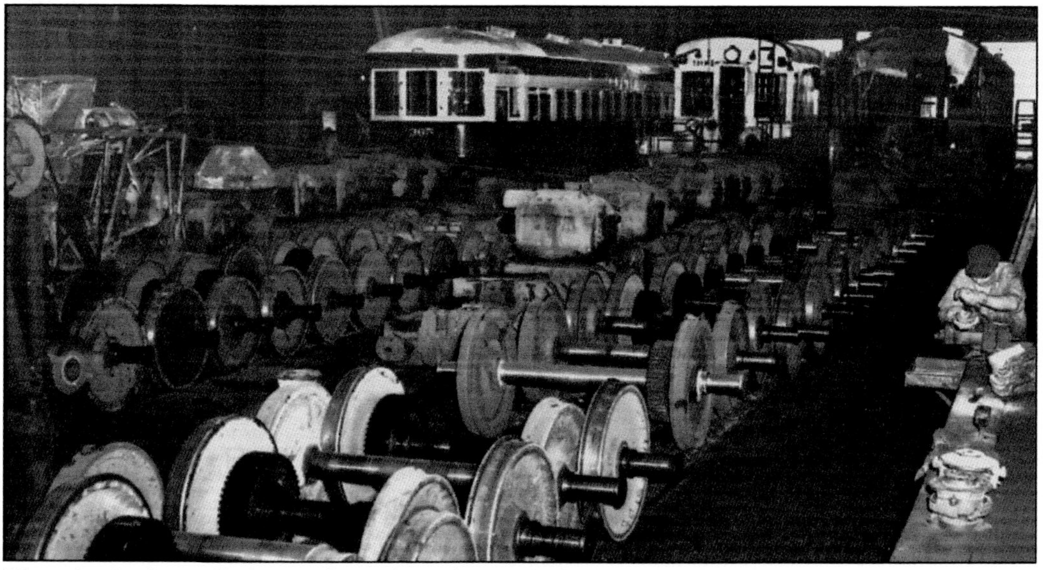

The wheels that rolled over the rails underneath the railcars were maintained at the Monroe Shops. Note the gear on the axles that connected to the electric motors, which are stacked double high and lined up between the two rows of axles. The car was driven by the motor that turned the gear on the axle. The shop was located in Dallas so that it could service the Fort Worth cars of Northern Texas Traction Company and the Dallas cars of Southern Traction Company before the consolidation created Texas Electric Railway.

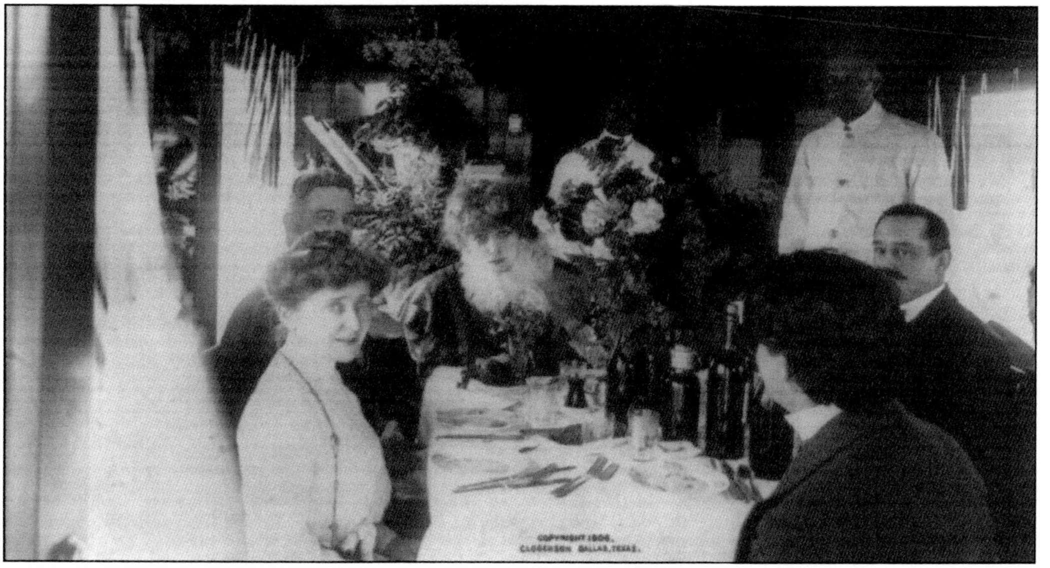

A 1906 reception is hosted to honor Sarah Bernhardt in Dallas. Before the popularity of silent films, Sarah Bernhardt and other great actors epitomized the legitimate theater and set a style for the times. However, few people could see these performances because of cost, limited appearances, and the difficulty of traveling from rural area to theaters in the cities. The popularity of silent films and the rise of Hollywood stars such as Rudolph Valentino, Greta Garbo, William S. Hart, Dorothy and Lillian Gish, Charlie Chaplin, Tom Mix, and Jack Hoxie inspired new levels of personal style and quickened the spirit of urbanization in North Texas. (Courtesy of the Library of Congress.)

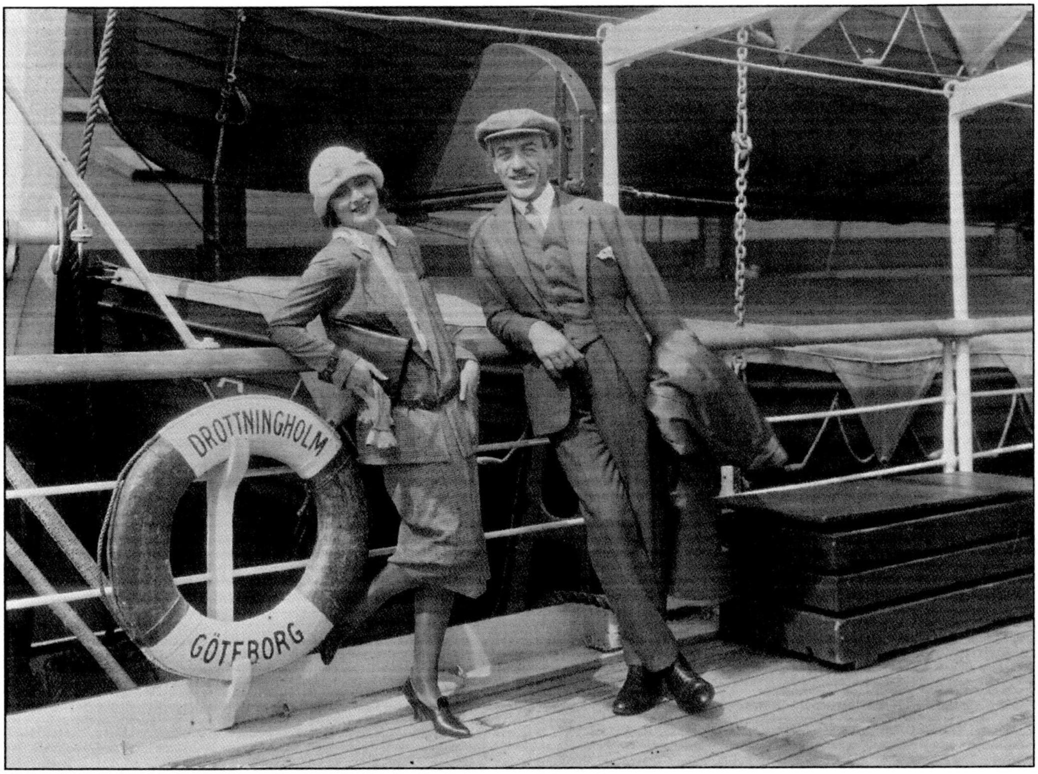

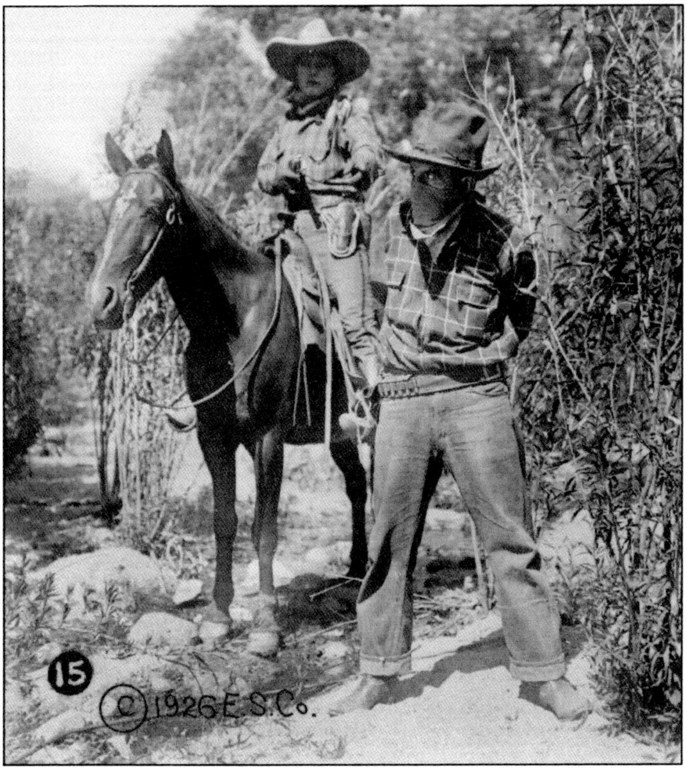

Silent film star Greta Garbo and director Mauritz Stiller sail aboard the SS *Drotingholm* en route to the United States. The lives and experiences of the silent movie greats were of keen interest to many Texans, who made an effort to see their every film. (Courtesy of the Library of Congress.)

Silent Western film stars such as William S. Hart, Tom Mix, and Jack Hoxie fired the imagination of Texans who came to see the romantic adventurous side of the Texas experience. The good guy always winning and upholding the law set behavior standards for many a young audience. (Courtesy of the Library of Congress.)

There were many silent film comedy stars who brought laughter and enjoyment to North Texas silent moviegoers. Film greats such as Fatty Arbuckle, Mabel Normand, Harold Lloyd, Charlie Chaplin, and Buster Keaton were favorites who not only entertained but led very interesting lives that generated good publicity to keep fans interested. (Courtesy of the Library of Congress.)

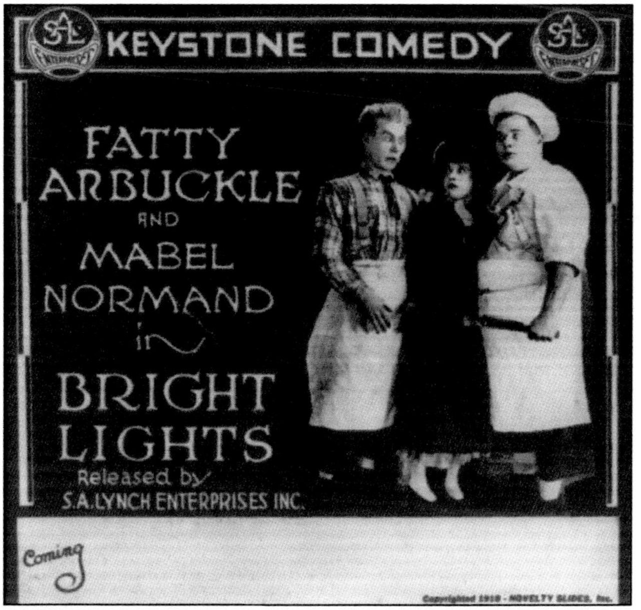

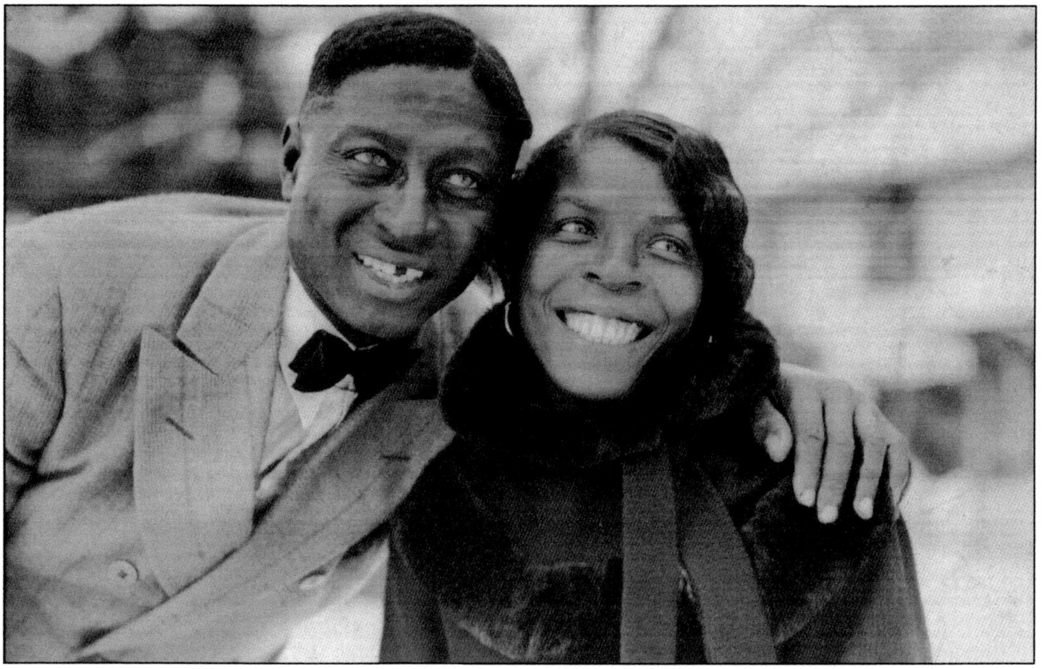

From the 1920s into the 1930s, the Deep Ellum section of Dallas developed a Harlem Renaissance type of blues and jazz for the South. Huddie "Lead Belly" Leadbetter (shown above with an unidentified woman), Blind Lemon Jefferson, and Robert Johnson performed at such Dallas spots as the Harlem and the Palace. Rural North Texas African Americans, including those from Plano, boarded Texas Electric Railway cars to spend a weekend or a Saturday night listening to blues and jazz in the Deep Ellum section. Some came by train from as far away as Oklahoma to enjoy a larger urbanized black population with a unique culture of blues and jazz. Deep Ellum was the only place where blacks and whites could come together on a limited social basis in a de facto integrated audience for entertainment. (Courtesy of the Library of Congress.)

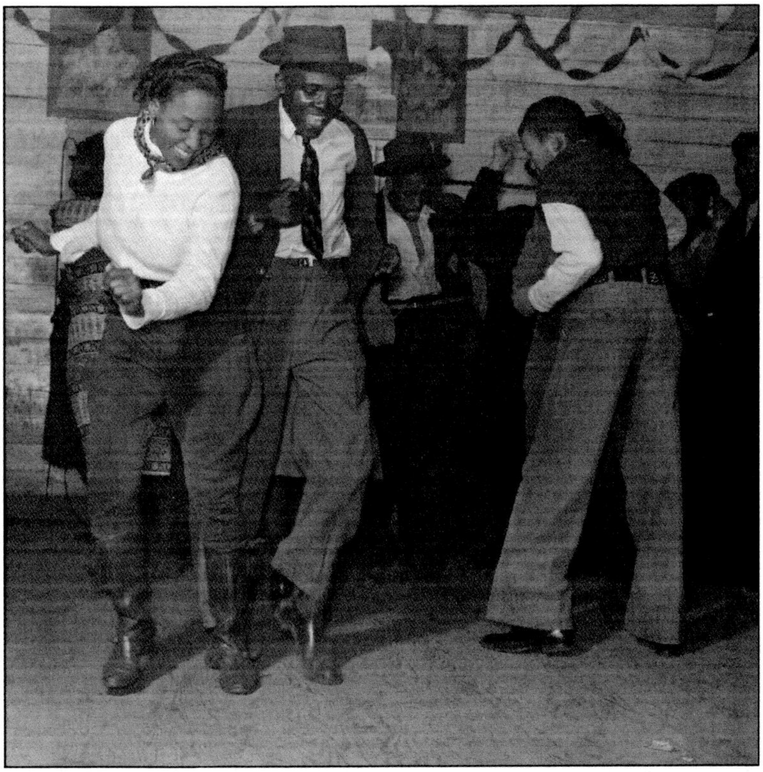

Juke joints were fun spots for dancing and drinking on Friday and Saturday nights. During the golden age, Leadbetter, Blind Lemon Jefferson, and other artists began to write folk tunes with Dallas often in the lyrics. In 1927, Billiken Johnson wrote the song "Interurban Blues": "Standing here a-wondering will that car pass my way / I'm going back to my baby: going back there to stay / I know my baby: is bound to love me some / She throws her arms around me: like the circle of the sun." (Courtesy of the Library of Congress.)

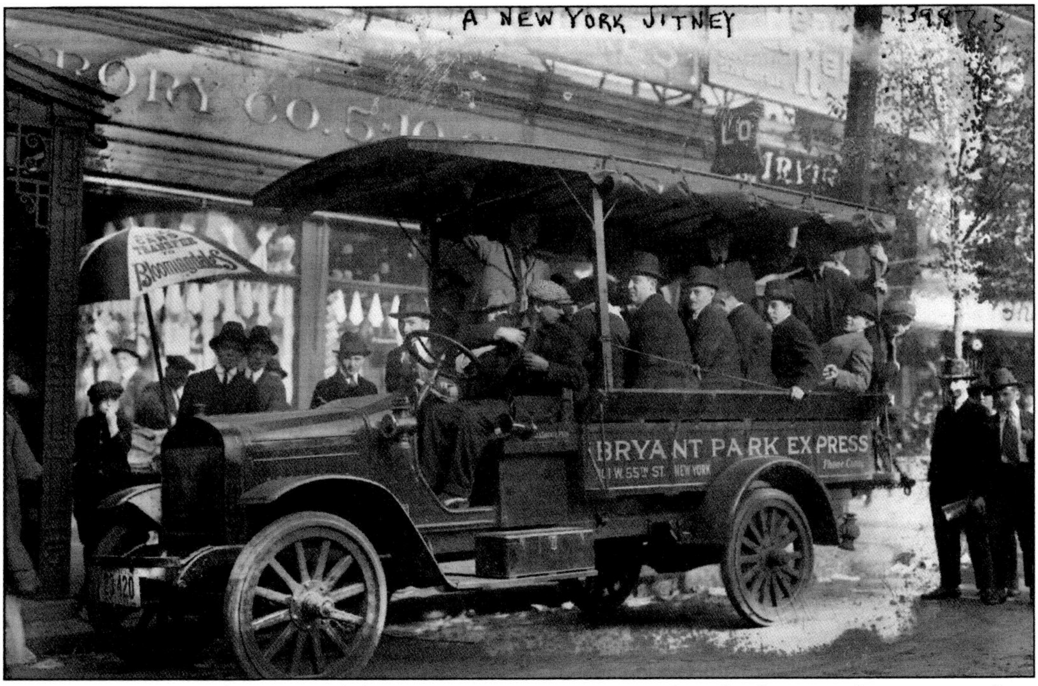

Competition from the automobile grew stronger as jitneys played a larger role in interurban transportation from coast to coast. The word "jitney" was a turn-of-the-20th-century word meaning nickel, the price paid for the ride. (Courtesy of the Library of Congress.)

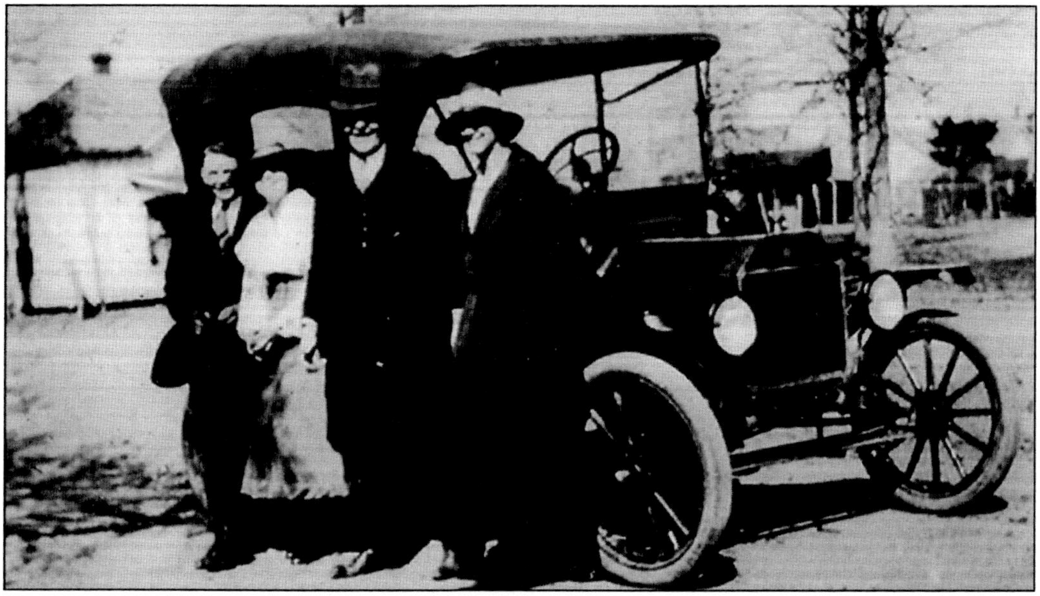

The above jitney service was operated around 1918 by Mrs. B. M. Pierce, who made regular morning and afternoon runs from Irving to Dallas. Jitneys were very popular in Dallas and the surrounding towns. At first, for the interurbans, automobiles were never thought to be serious competition. When jitneys began to pick up riders at interurban stops, interurban company managers chose to seek legislation to regulate and minimize the jitneys' financial impact on electric rail service. (Courtesy of the City of Irving Archives.)

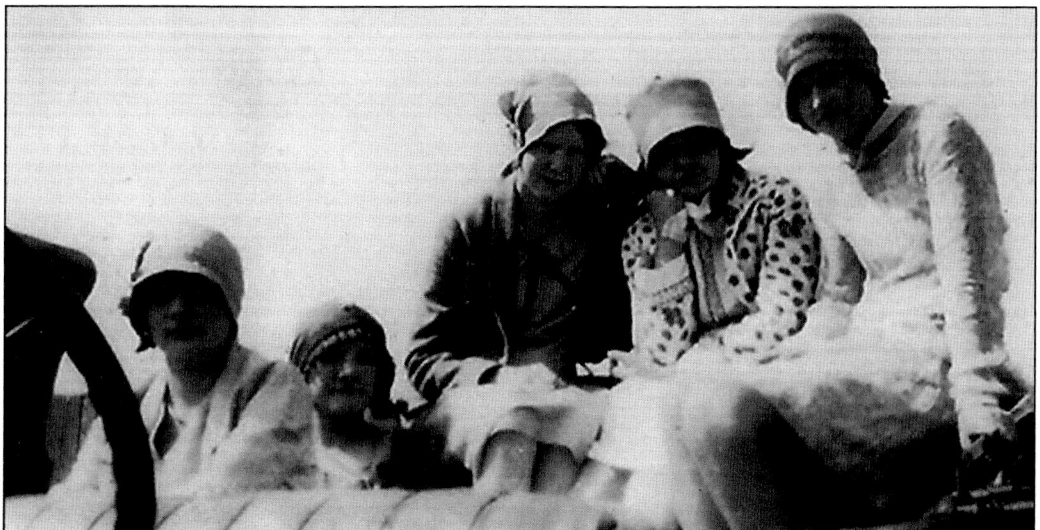

These Texas "flappers" from Irving pose for a photograph on the boot of a convertible. Young women of the golden age no longer required chaperones to accompany them when they took rides on the interurban trains. They could ride alone and take care of themselves without fear of loss of reputation. The golden age of the 1920s brought about a change in the way young women looked at themselves. The flapper image saw "racy" young women drinking liquor from flasks in public and listening to the new jazz music that was called "'jungle rhythms." (Courtesy of the City of Irving Archives.)

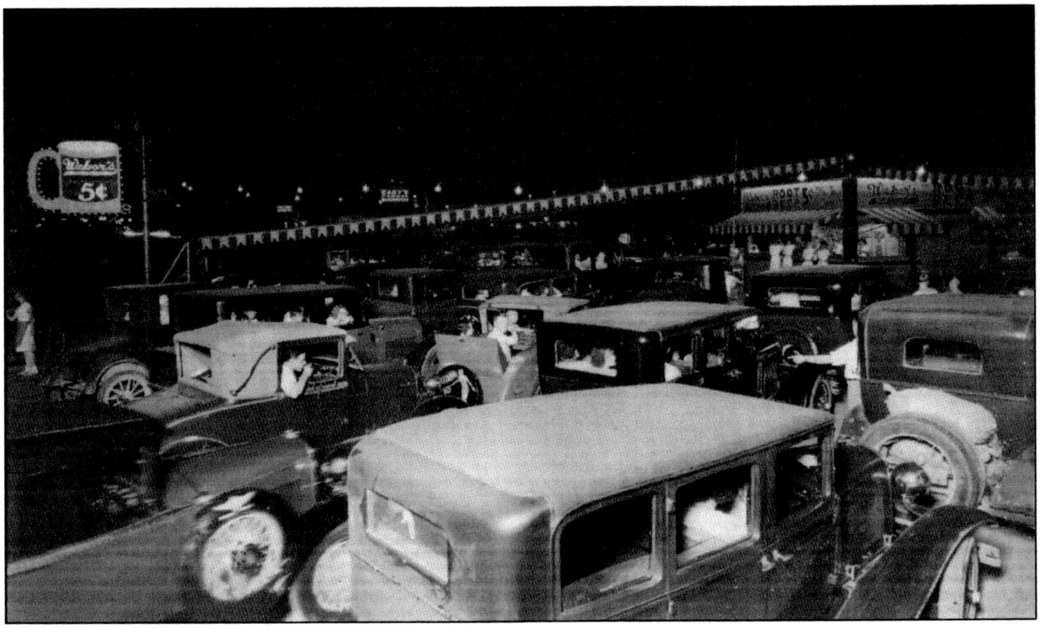

Automobiles began to proliferate in North Texas during the golden age. The increase in number and quality of paved roads made automobile ownership more practical and created a love affair between Texans and their automobiles. In the above 1920s photograph, rows of drivers in automobiles are enjoying service at Weber's Root Beer stand in Dallas. (Courtesy of the Dallas Historical Society.)

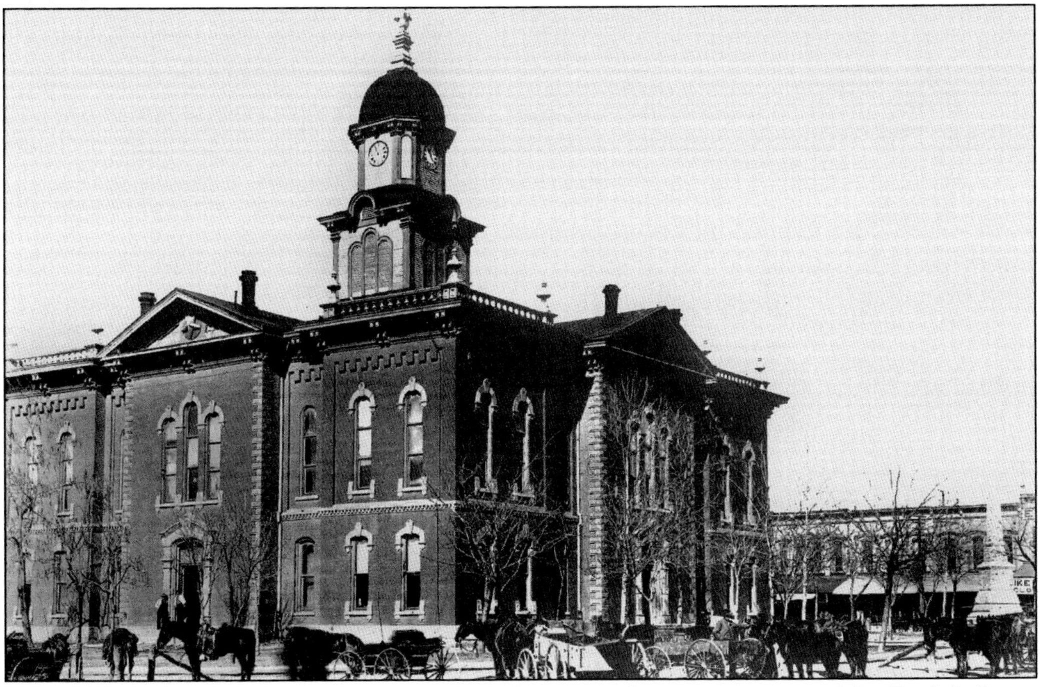

This photograph of the Grayson County Courthouse in Sherman was part of the Fred A. Jones 1905 Engineers Report and Survey commissioned to study the feasibility for construction of an interurban system to run from Sherman to Dallas. The courthouse building burned to the ground in 1930 during a mob riot.

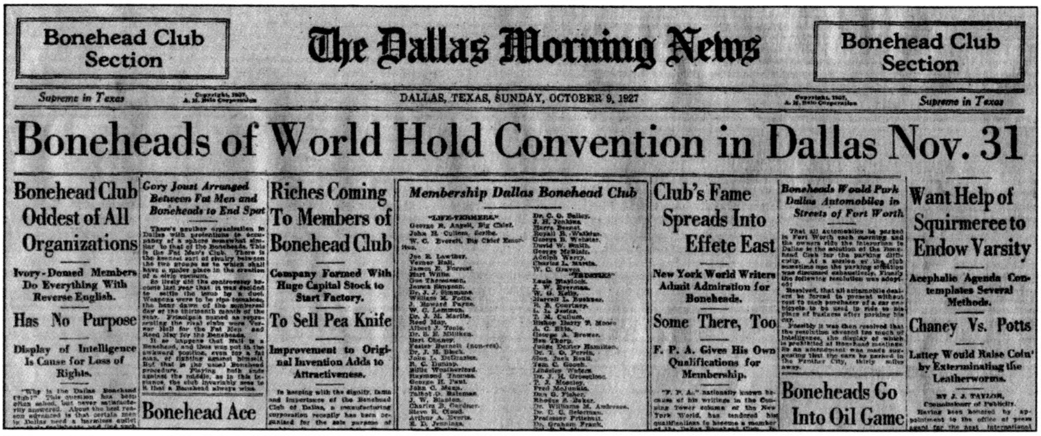

Bonehead Club Section

The Dallas Morning News

Bonehead Club Section

Supreme in Texas

DALLAS, TEXAS, SUNDAY, OCTOBER 9, 1927

Supreme in Texas

Boneheads of World Hold Convention in Dallas Nov. 31

Bonehead Club Oddest of All Organizations

Ivory-Domed Members Do Everything With Reverse English.

Has No Purpose

Display of Intelligence Is Cause for Loss of Rights.

Cory Joust Arranged Between Fat Men and Boneheads to End Spat

Bonehead Ace

Riches Coming To Members of Bonehead Club

Company Formed With Huge Capital Stock to Start Factory.

To Sell Pea Knife

Improvement to Original Invention Adds to Attractiveness.

Membership Dallas Bonehead Club

Club's Fame Spreads Into Effete East

New York World Writers Admit Admiration for Boneheads.

Some There, Too

F. P. A. Gives His Own Qualifications for Membership.

Boneheads Would Park Dallas Automobiles in Streets of Fort Worth

Boneheads Go Into Oil Game

Want Help of Squirmeree to Endow Varsity

Acephalic Agenda Contemplates Several Methods.

Chaney Vs. Potts

Latter Would Raise Coin' by Exterminating the Leatherworms.

Texas Electric Car No. 325 was burned in a fire accident in 1938. It was common for organizations to rent or charter one or a series of cars for a special event. While this car was on charter to the Dallas Bonehead Club, a coffeepot on board developed an electrical problem, caught fire, and set the entire car ablaze. All Bonehead members were able to escape the flames by hastily exiting at Elm Mott siding, north of Waco, but Car No. 325 was a total loss and had to be salvaged. Organized in 1919, the Dallas Bonehead Club "has no purpose or object and never hopes to accomplish anything." The group of local businessmen joined each other for the purpose of letting off steam by engaging in zany acts of hilarity and comic stunts. (Courtesy of the Dallas Public Library Archives.)

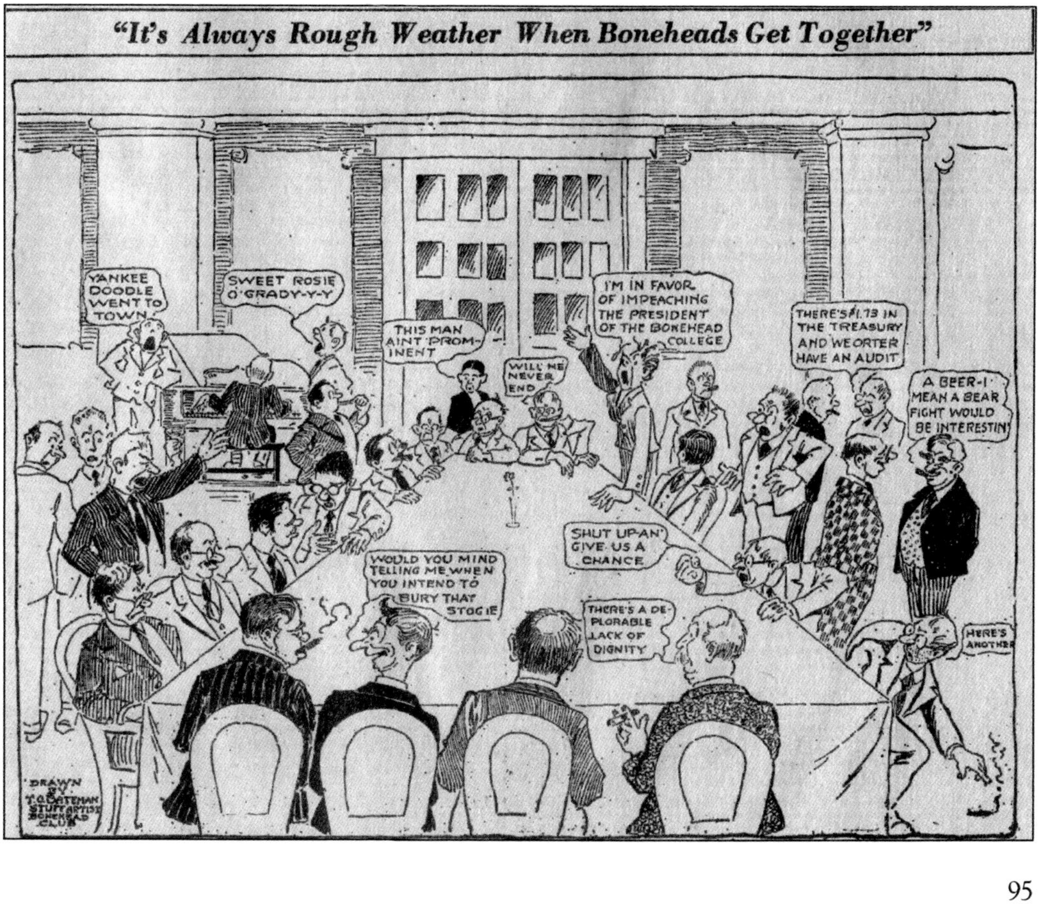

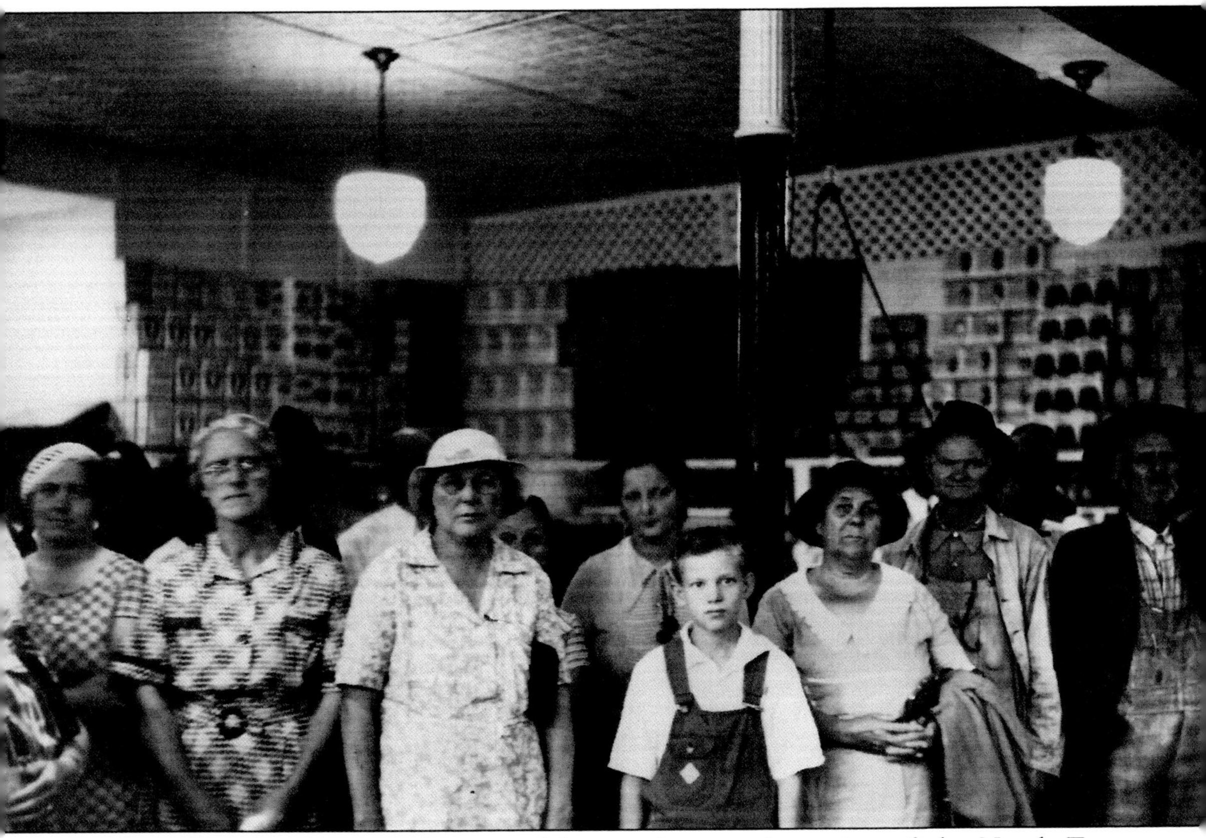

The golden age of interurban travel began the transformation of the North Texas rural population.

Four

Commerce Rides The Rails

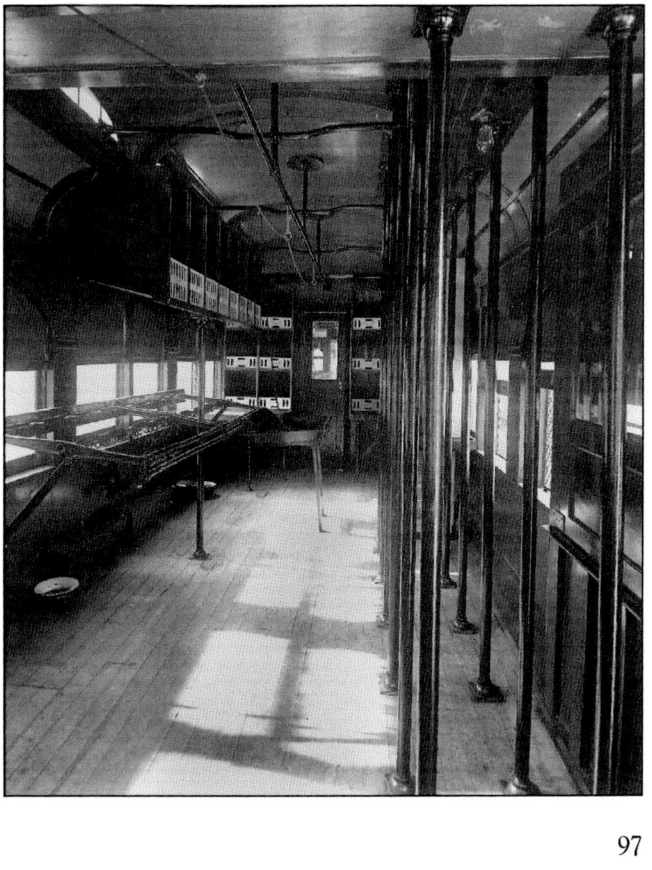

For rural areas such as early-20th-century North Texas, the RPO mail service delivered mail in a timely and efficient way. Drawing on the success of earlier railway postal efforts, the U.S. Post Office standardized the layout and floor plan of RPO cars. The typical car, such as the three used at Plano, looked like the photograph at right. The cars could handle most back-end post office processing functions. The postal officer in charge was required to carry a regulation handgun aboard the car to protect against theft and robbery. The overhead bins on the left side of car are for small packages and the metal rack underneath along the windows holds individual mail bags into which letters would be sorted en route to its destination. (Photograph by James R. McFarlane; courtesy of George Krambles.)

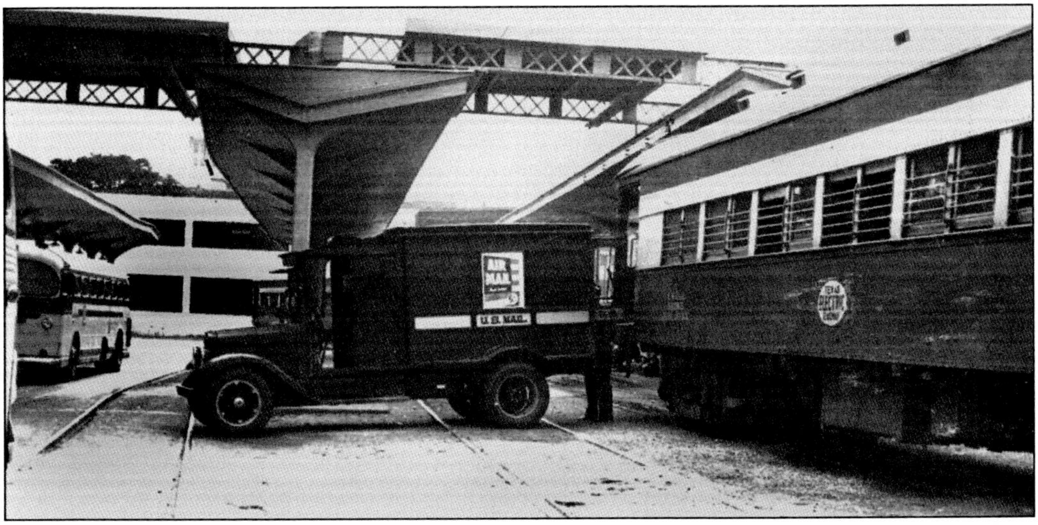

After a light Christmas Eve snow had fallen, a Texas motor coach bus ready for a run to Fort Worth shared the Texas Electric depot bays with electric railcars. A Short Route interstate bus stands waiting near a U.S. mail truck filled with mail and packages that will probably be delivered before Christmas morning.

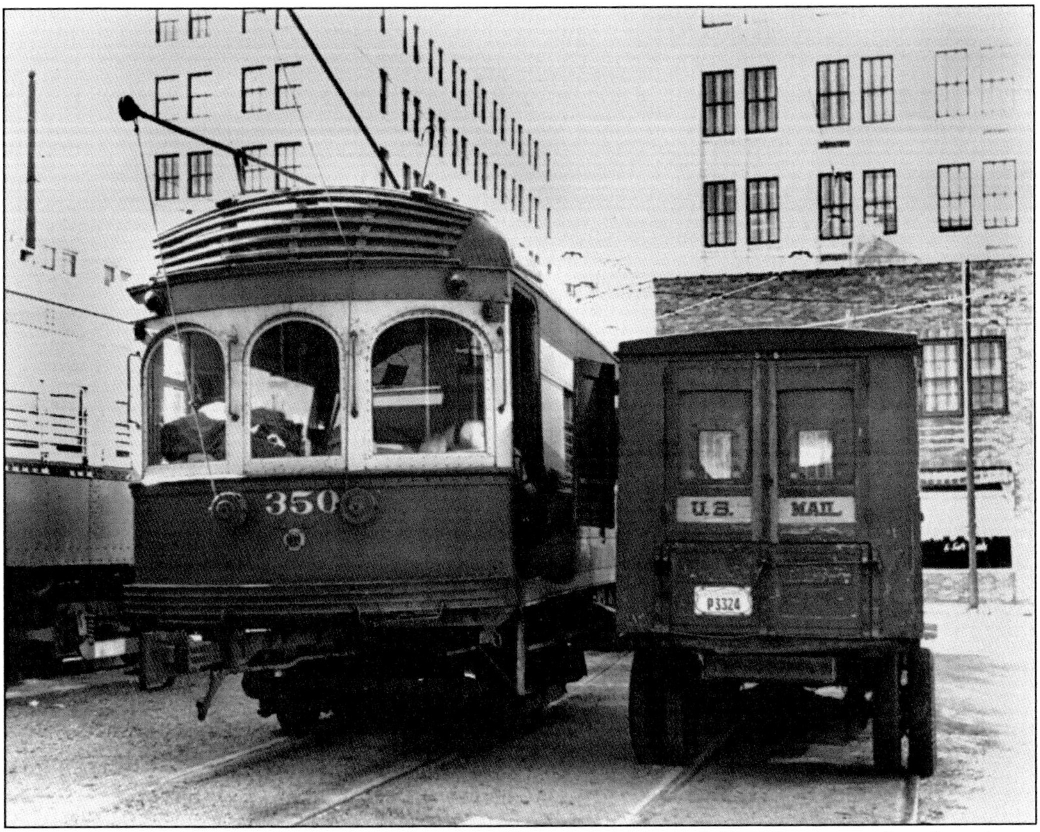

A U.S. mail truck stands parked beside Texas Electric Rail Post Office for a transfer of mail.

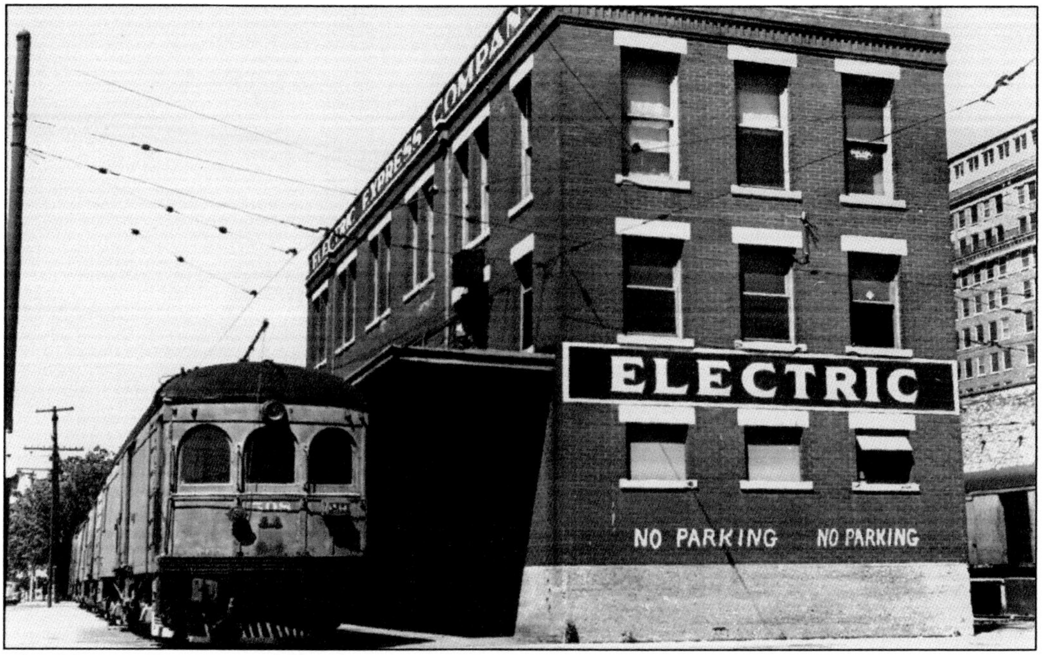

The Electric Express and Baggage Company, incorporated in 1913 by J. F. Strickland, became a subsidiary of Texas Electric Railway after it was created in 1917. A new terminal was built in Dallas, and the company enjoyed profitable freight runs throughout its existence. The principal routes were short hauls that were not profitable to the main railroads, such as shuttling a load from one railroad dock to another and carrying less than full freight carloads.

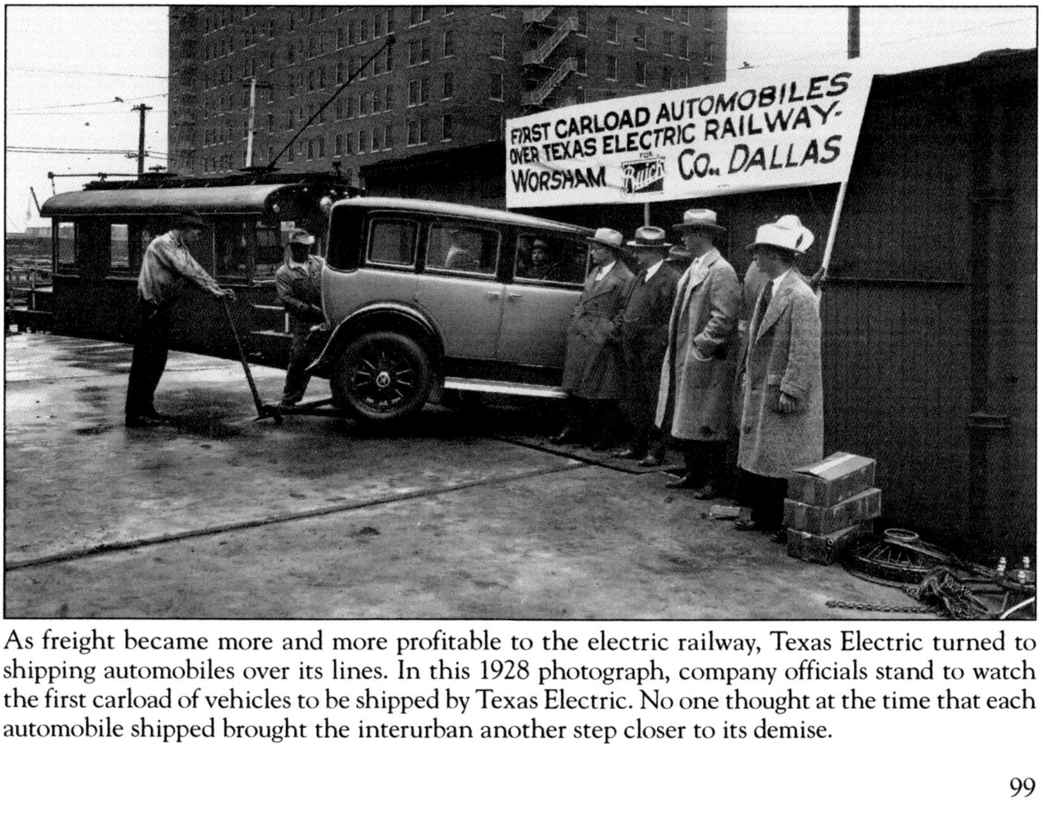

As freight became more and more profitable to the electric railway, Texas Electric turned to shipping automobiles over its lines. In this 1928 photograph, company officials stand to watch the first carload of vehicles to be shipped by Texas Electric. No one thought at the time that each automobile shipped brought the interurban another step closer to its demise.

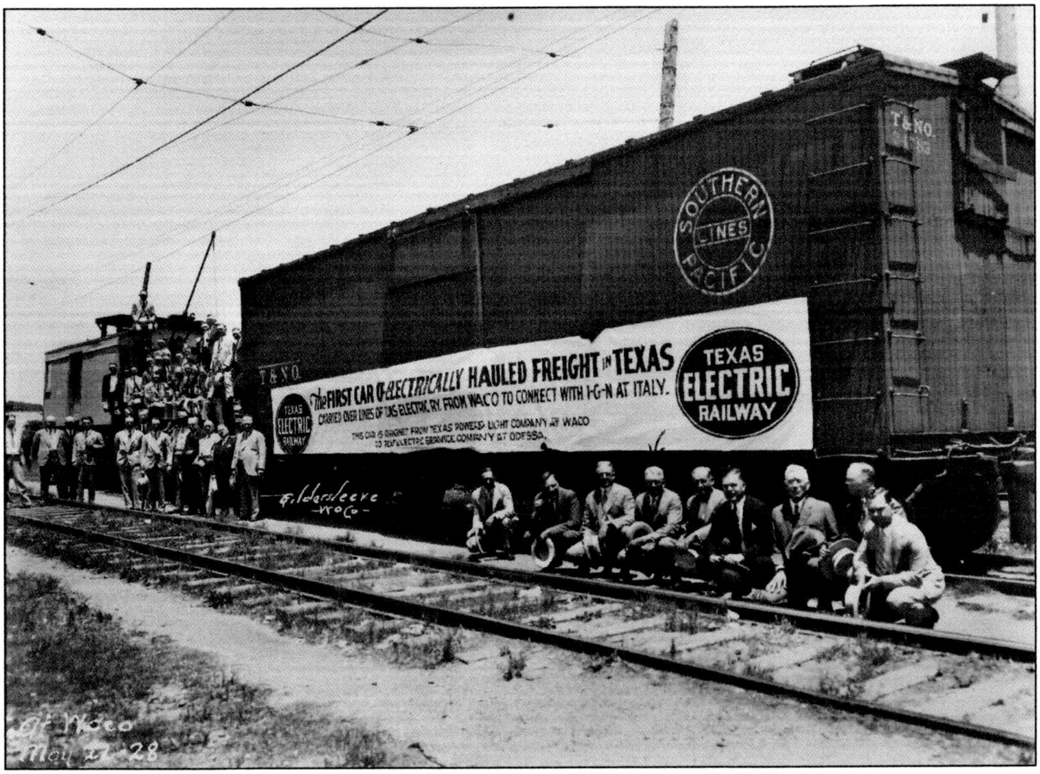

Frank Rogers, the official photographer for Texas Electric, was called to record the event of the first electrically hauled freight in Texas.

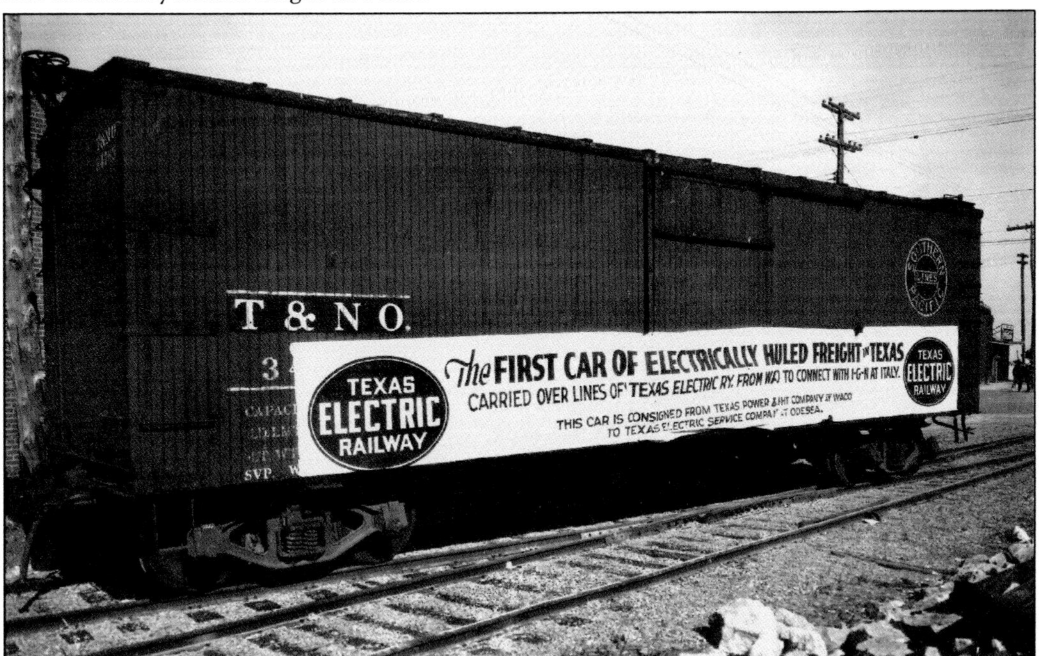

The decision to move freight would turn out to be a wise and profitable one for Texas Electric.

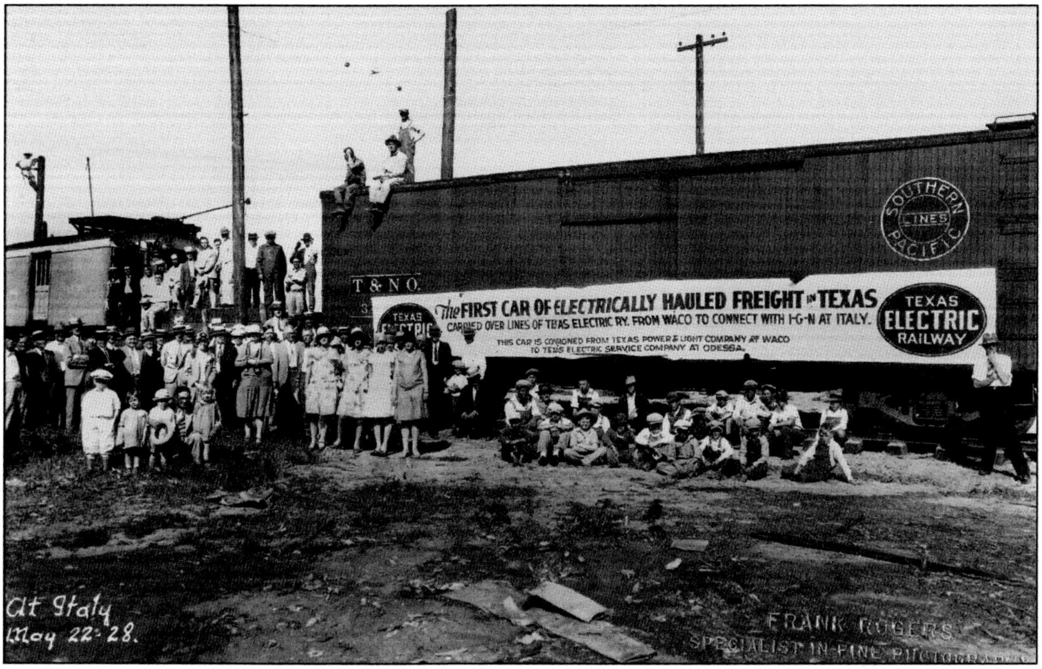

At Italy, Texas, most of the community turned out, including schoolchildren in their Sunday best, for a photograph of the occasion.

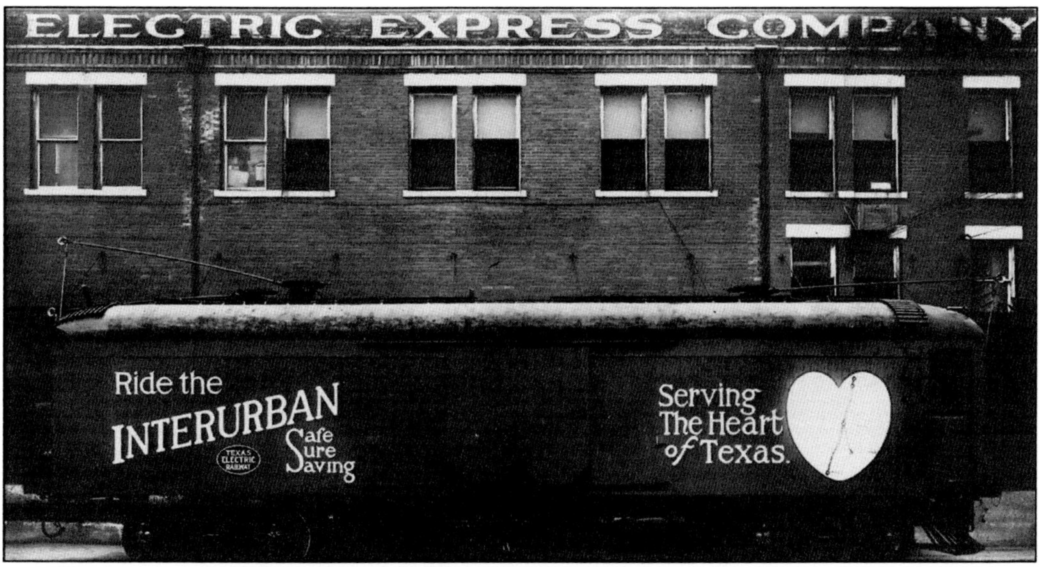

Texas Electric management found freight service very profitable; it could be made more so by adding advertising to the side of some freight cars.

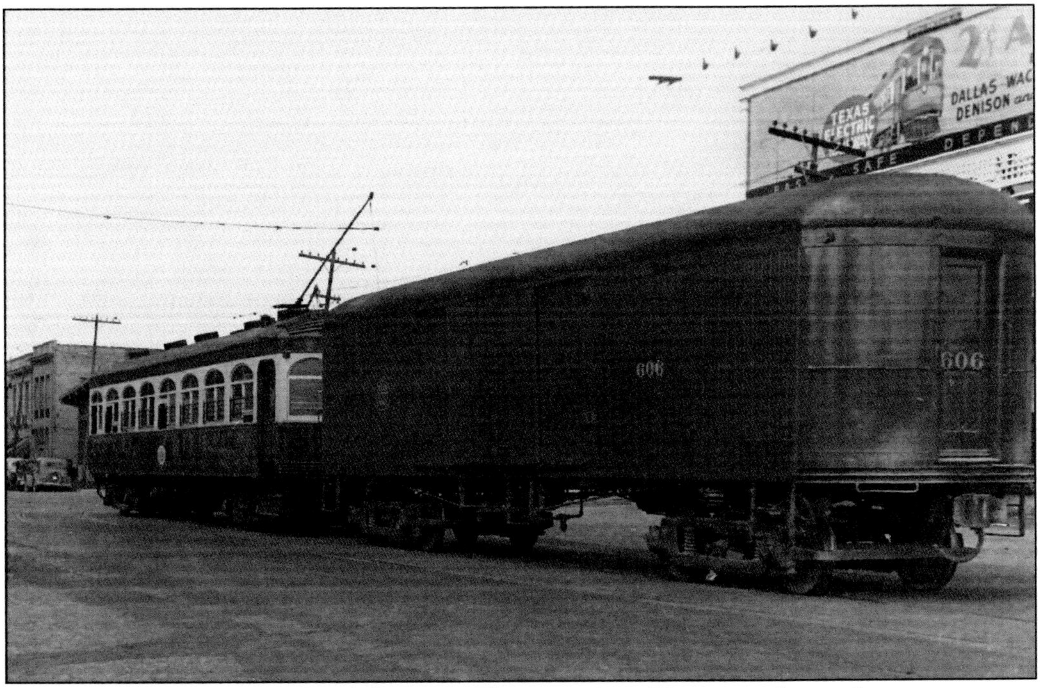

A freight trailer is pulled behind the Texas Electric railcar. Electric trailers without power were pulled through the center of cities until the sight of them coming down the center of town became unfashionable and unsightly.

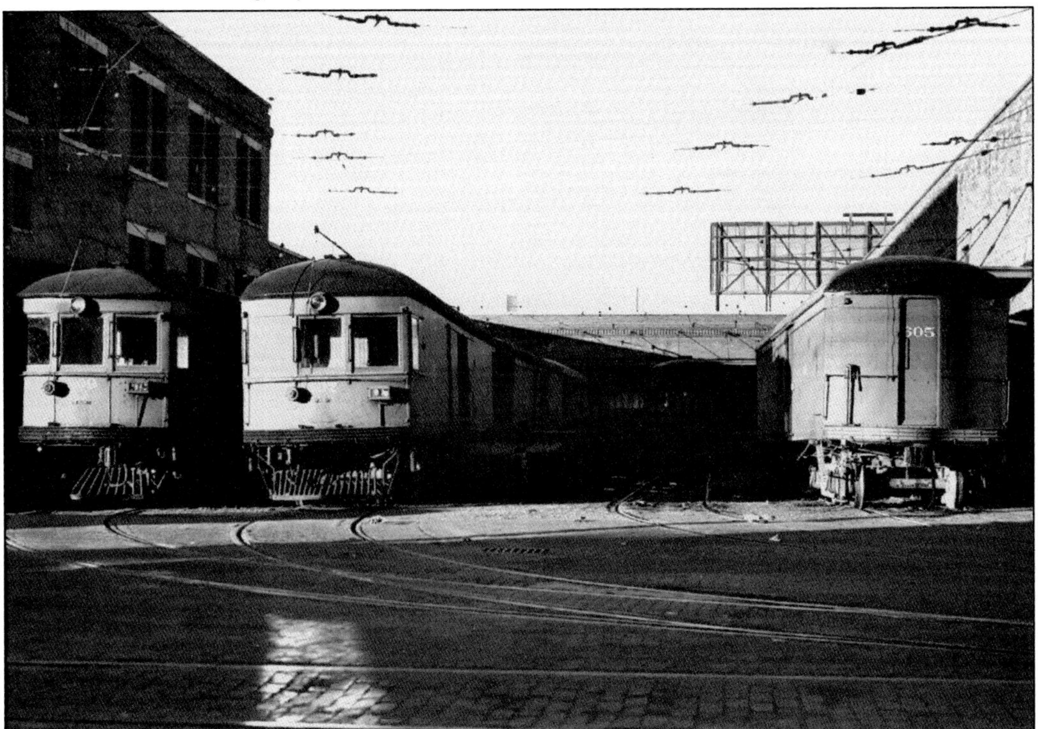

Texas Electric freight cars lined up at the freight depot in Dallas waiting for the next run.

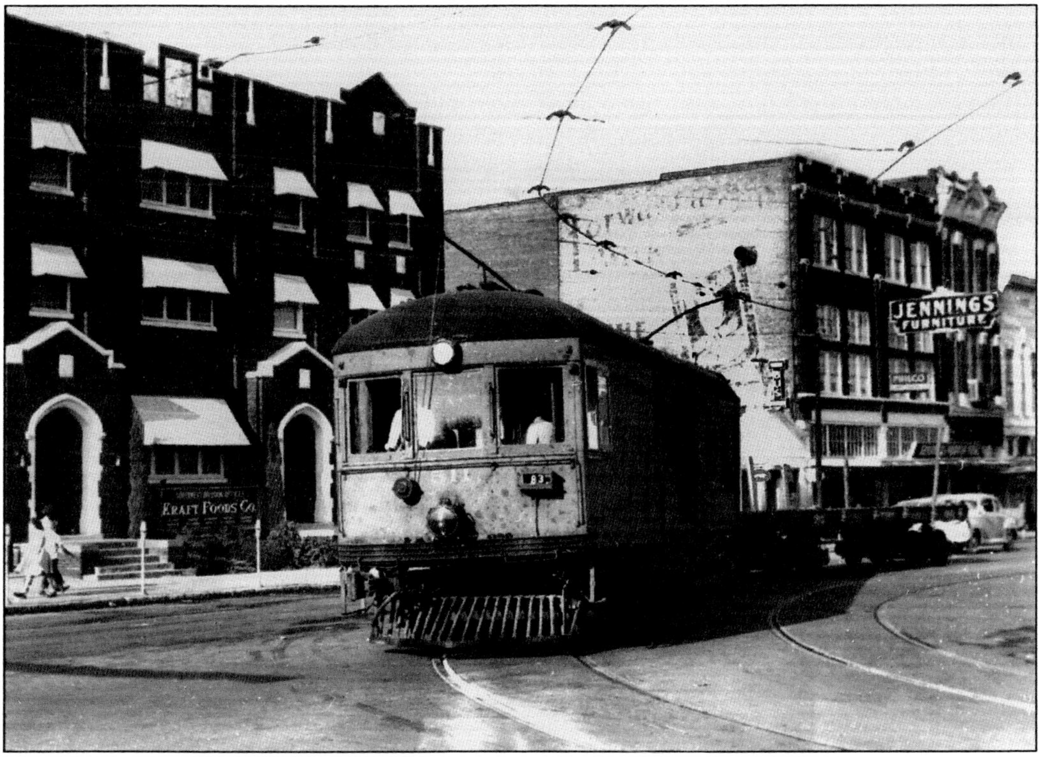

Texas Electric passes the Kraft Foods building in Denison. Although passenger service ended December 31, 1948, the very profitable freight service continued into 1949.

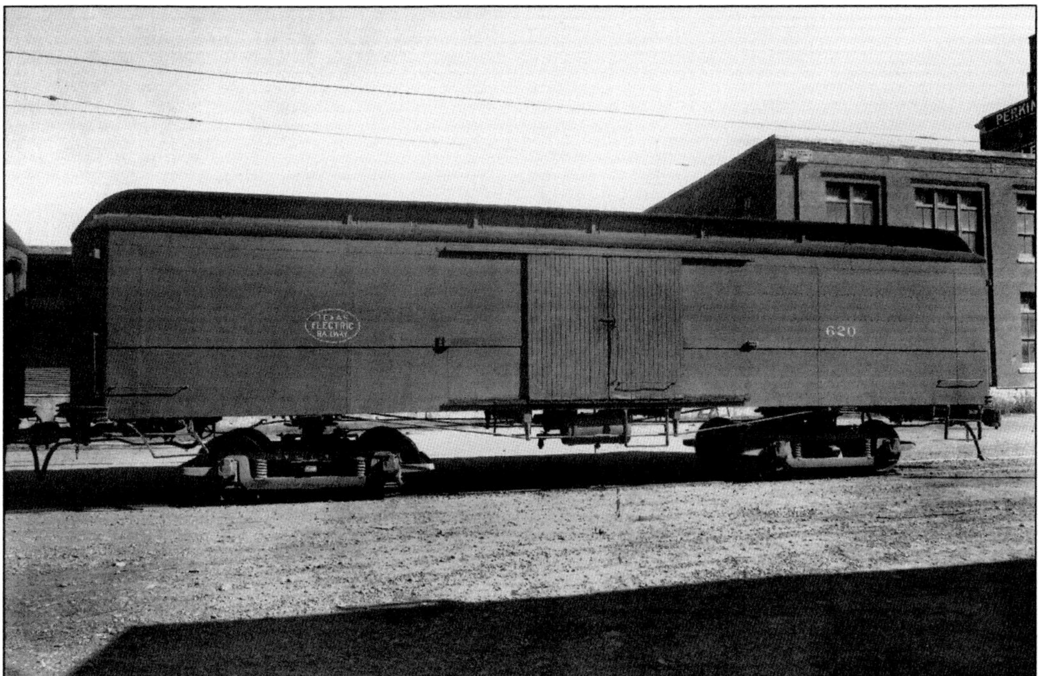

A number of freight cars had no motors and were used as trailers.

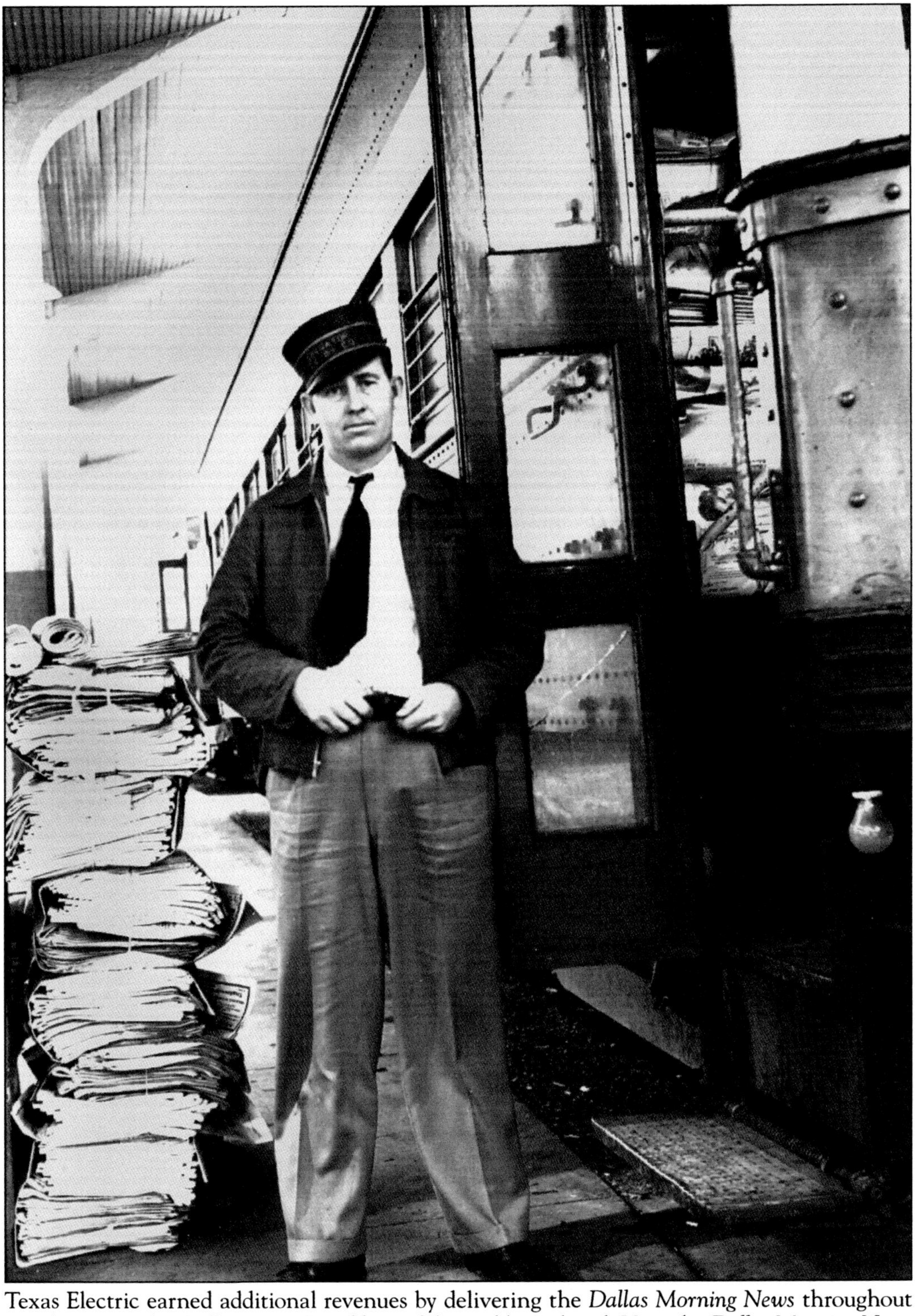

Texas Electric earned additional revenues by delivering the *Dallas Morning News* throughout North Texas. The *Dallas Times Herald* was delivered by railroad. Here the *Dallas Morning News* is stacked for delivery.

Five

Making It a Small World

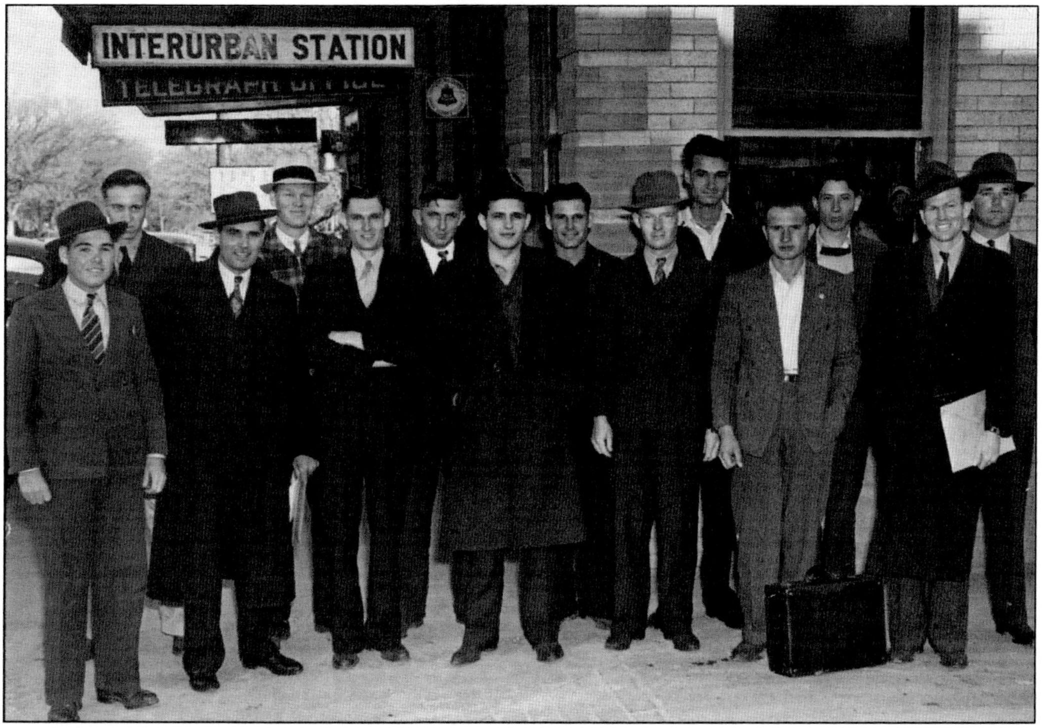

New draftees from Collin County meet for the first time at the McKinney Texas Electric Railway depot for a photograph just before boarding the train to head down the line to Dallas and transfer to troop trains going to basic training camps. Note the woman inside the station who appears to be looking out through the window. She may have accompanied one of the men to wish him farewell in spring of 1942. (Courtesy of Bryan Lean/North Texas History Center.)

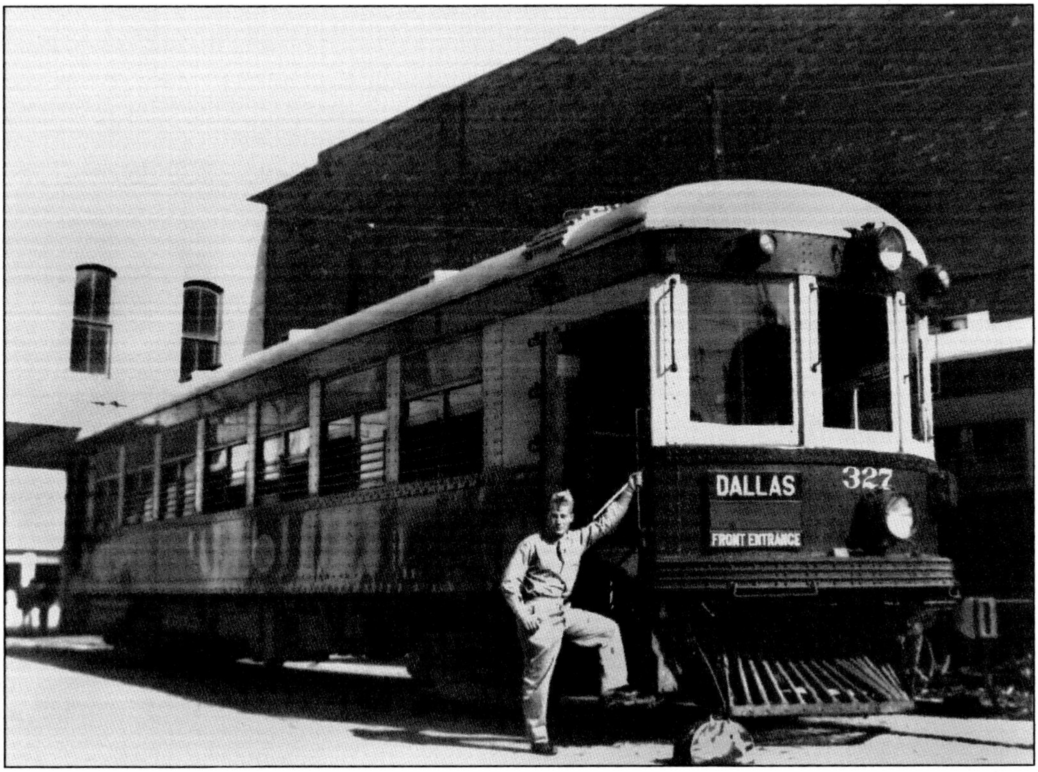

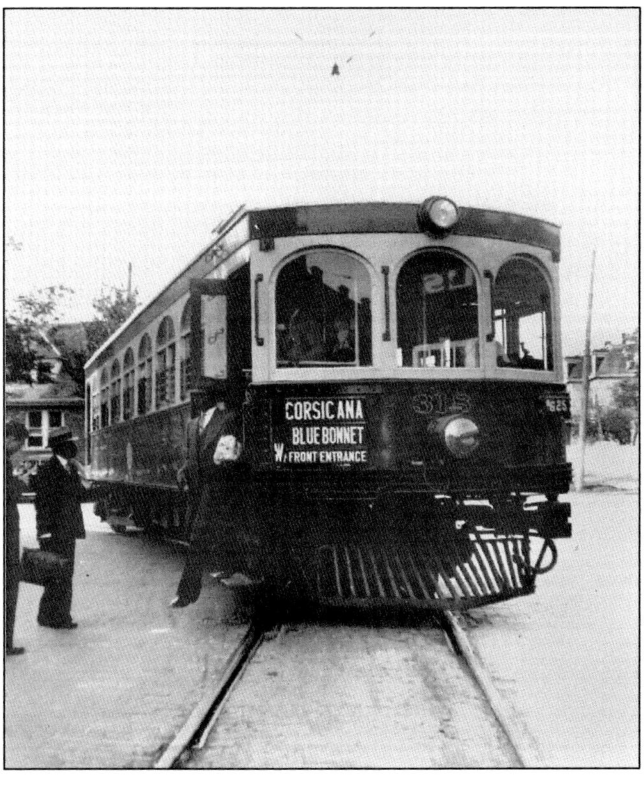

Wartime restrictions on travel and gasoline rationing increased the use of Texas Electric and other interurban systems.

The camera caught the stylishly dressed passengers in this 1941 photograph just as Texas Electric Railway *Bluebonnet* Car No. 318 had come to a stop. The discovery of oil in and around Corsicana created a healthy and strong economy in the Ennis/Corsicana region. Unfortunately, premature abandonment by Texas Electric of the Corsicana line just before the outbreak of World War II caused the company to lose wartime profits over the next four years as a result of gasoline rationing and other wartime restrictions. (Courtesy of John J. Myers.)

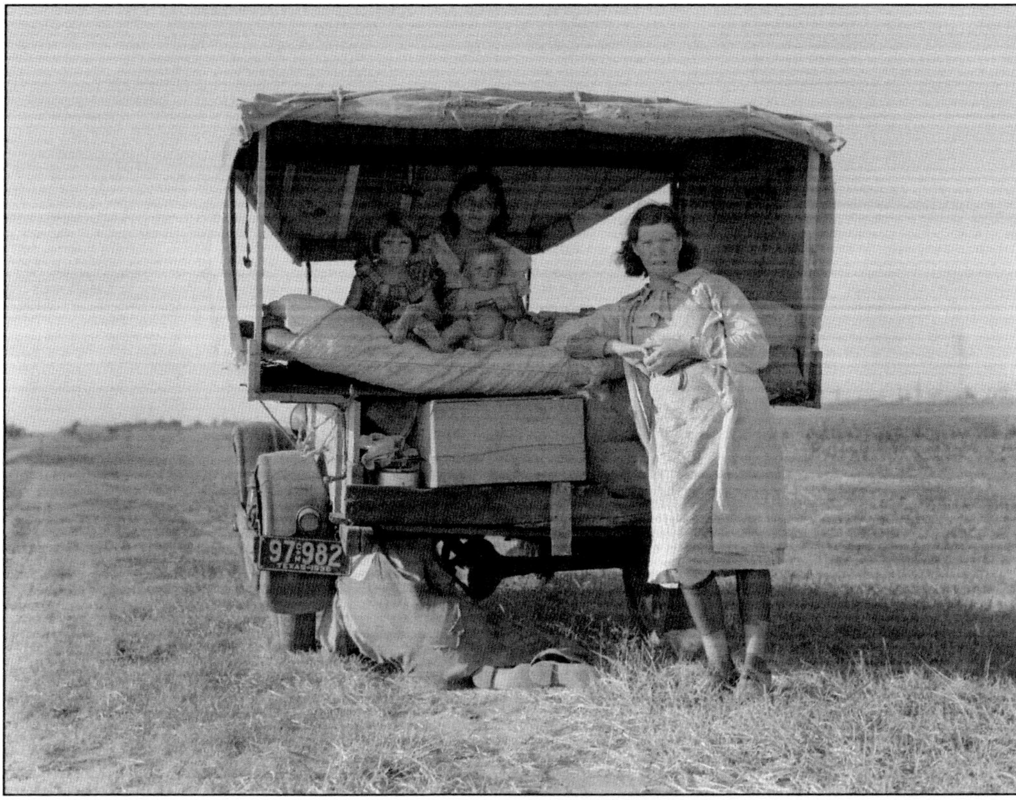

Interurban ridership declined during the 1930s when migrant agricultural workers also began to acquire automobiles to move from farm to farm. Whole families could move by car, and they found it was cheaper than using the interurban or railroad to get to their destination farms. (Courtesy of the Library of Congress.)

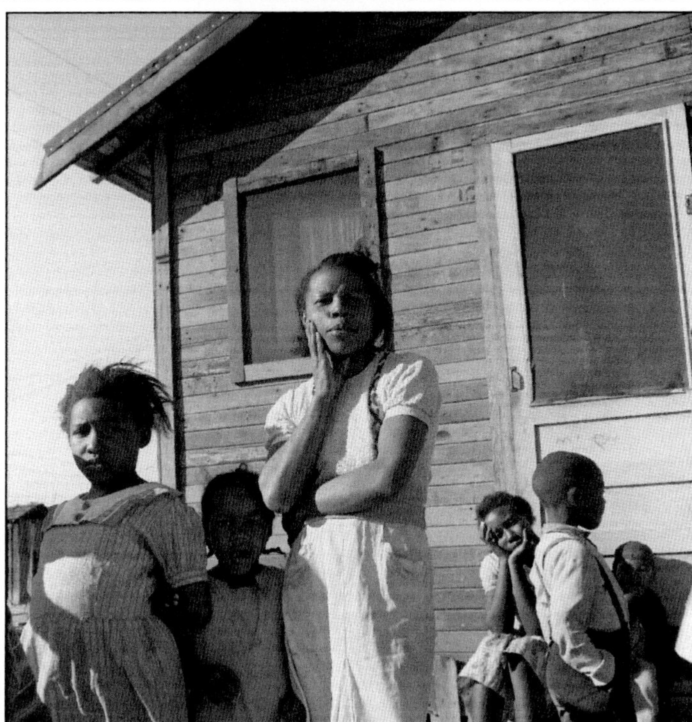

Dorothea Lang captured the faces of migrant workers who left Texas during the lean years of the Great Depression.

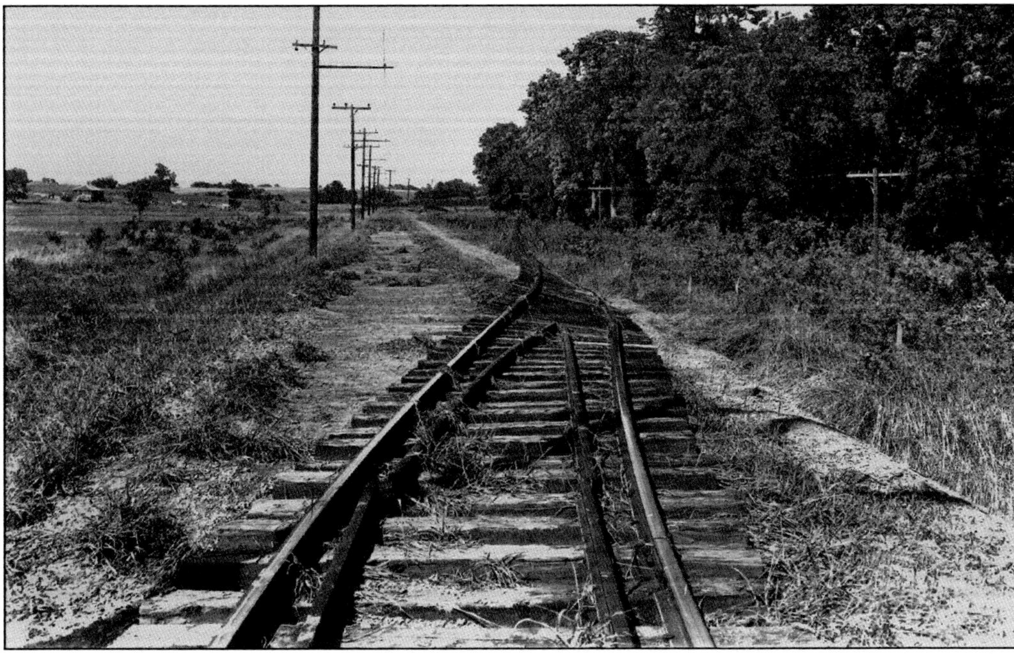

When rainstorms and floods happened on the prairie, Texas Electric Railway tracks could be washed out and had to be repaired before service could be resumed. Crews were always on duty to bring service back when needed. This track washout at Rowlett Creek north of the Kirkland siding happened during a heavy 1947 spring rainstorm.

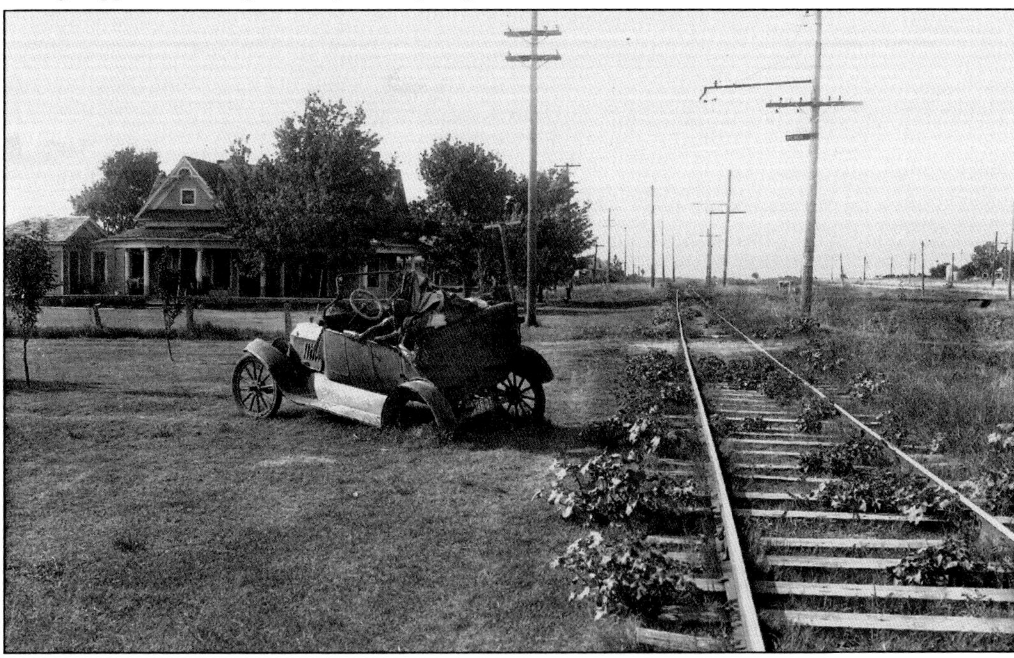

This early-1920s scene shows another automobile that lost a race with a Texas Electric Railway car. Frank Rogers was the photographer designated by Texas Electric Railway to document accidents. (Photograph by Frank Rogers; courtesy of the Interurban Railway Museum/Johnnie J. Myers Collection.)

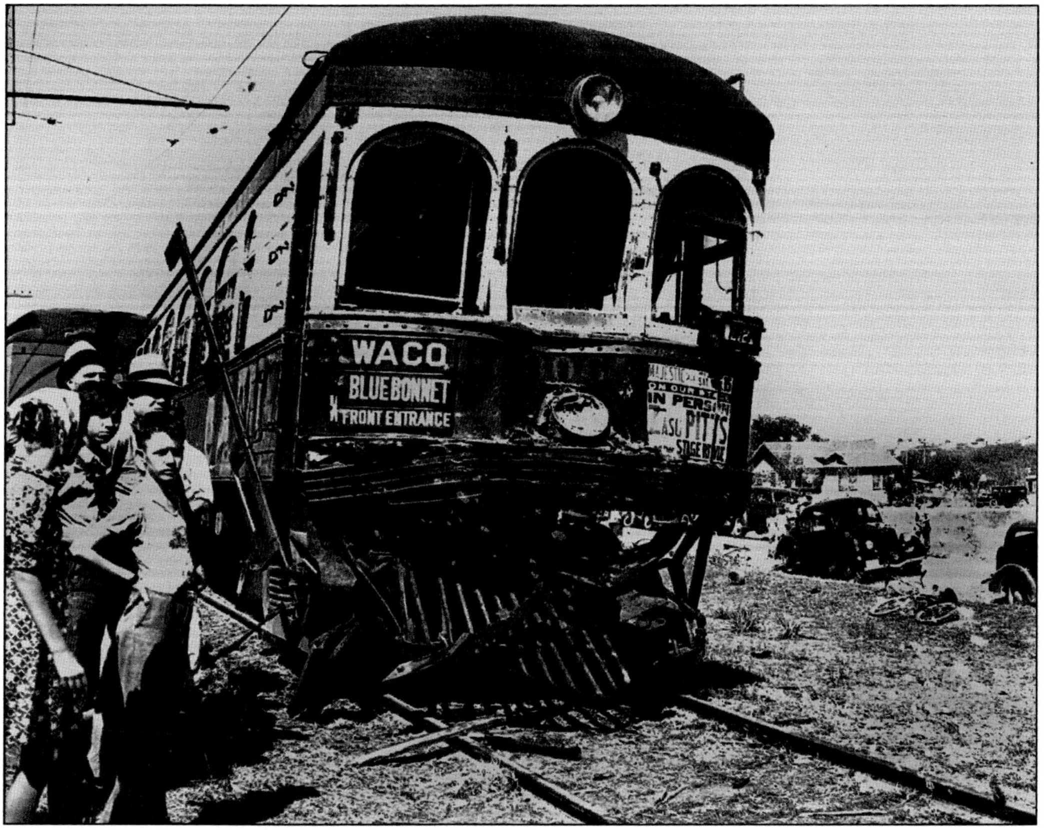

Accidents involving interurban railcars did occur infrequently in proportion to the number of miles traveled.

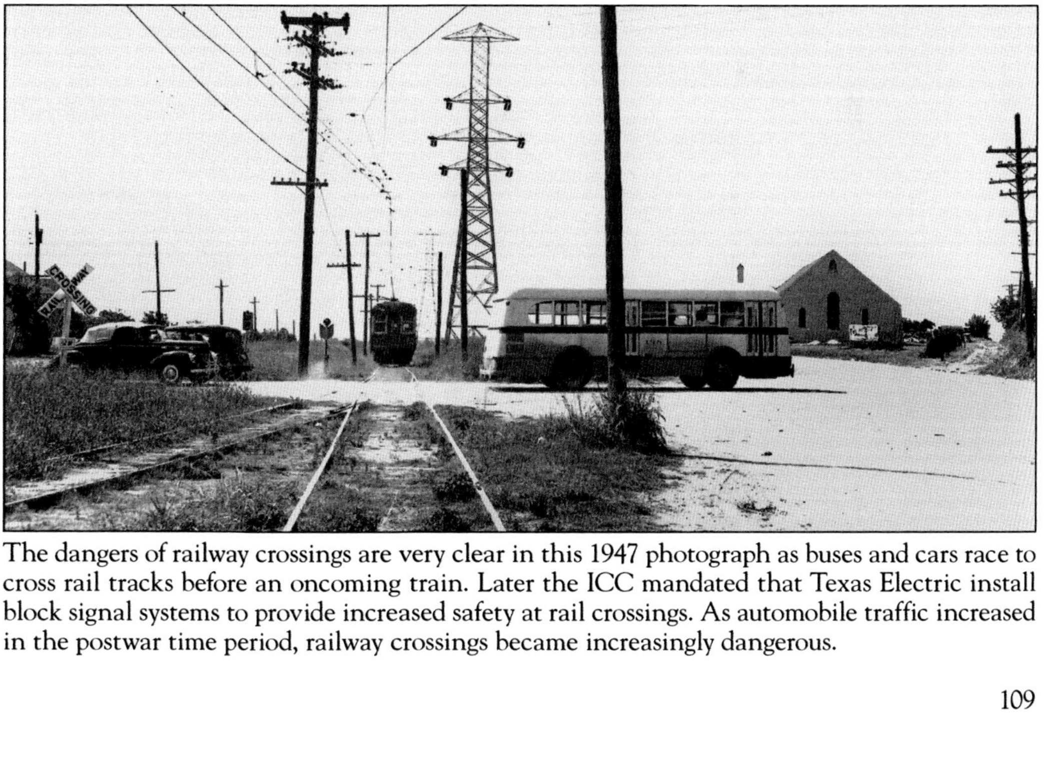

The dangers of railway crossings are very clear in this 1947 photograph as buses and cars race to cross rail tracks before an oncoming train. Later the ICC mandated that Texas Electric install block signal systems to provide increased safety at rail crossings. As automobile traffic increased in the postwar time period, railway crossings became increasingly dangerous.

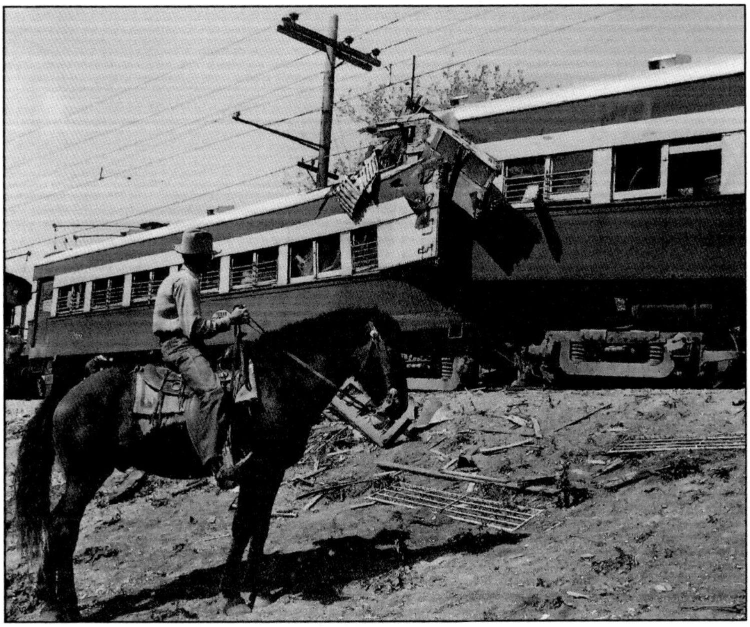

On Saturday morning, April 10, 1948, two Texas Electric interurban cars collided on a curve a mile and a half north of Vickery, about 100 yards south of White Rock Creek. Passengers were injured, but no one was killed. The force of the crash drove one car into the other, demolishing the front of both cars. Had one operator not locked his brakes in anticipation of impact and run to the rear of the car, he would have been crushed.

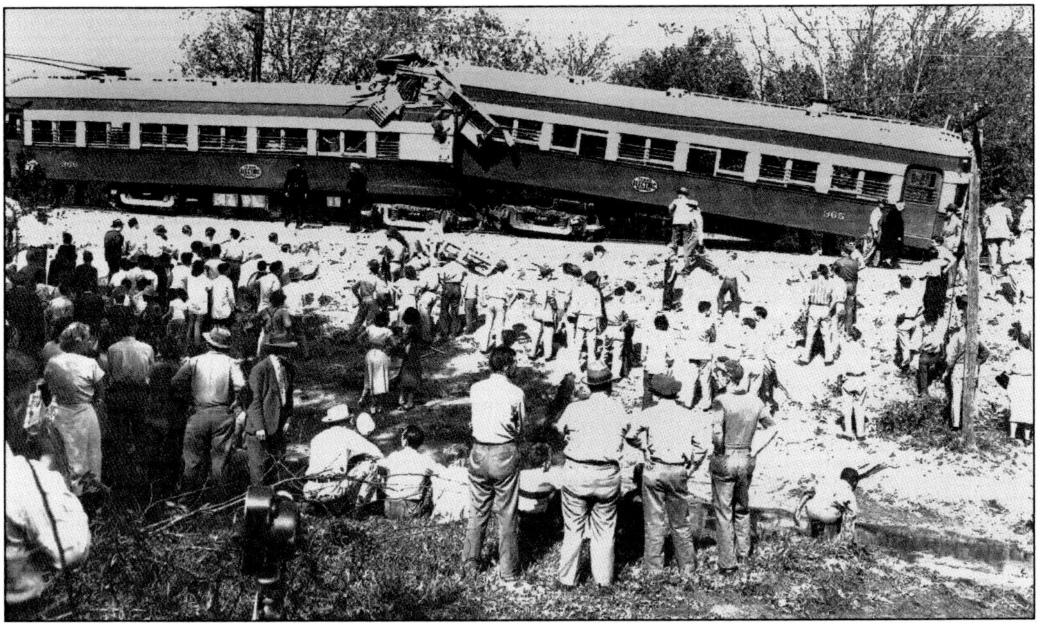

The April 10, 1948, accident was one of the most serious Texas Electric Railway accidents. The liability of claims and damage to equipment caused the company to seek abandonment of passenger service. The Interstate Commerce Commission's investigation of the accident and subsequent recommendations would have been extremely expensive for the company at a time when its revenues were already falling. Thus the company was unable to meet the requirement and decided to end passenger operations on December 31, 1948. The Vickery accident of April 10 was the final blow to a system struggling to survive in the post–World War II era as competition from automobiles grew rapidly along with expansion of tax-supported highways and turnpikes. Although there were no fatalities, the anticipated liabilities stemming from the accident dealt the death knell to the system.

Workmen begin the job of separating the two wrecked railcars.

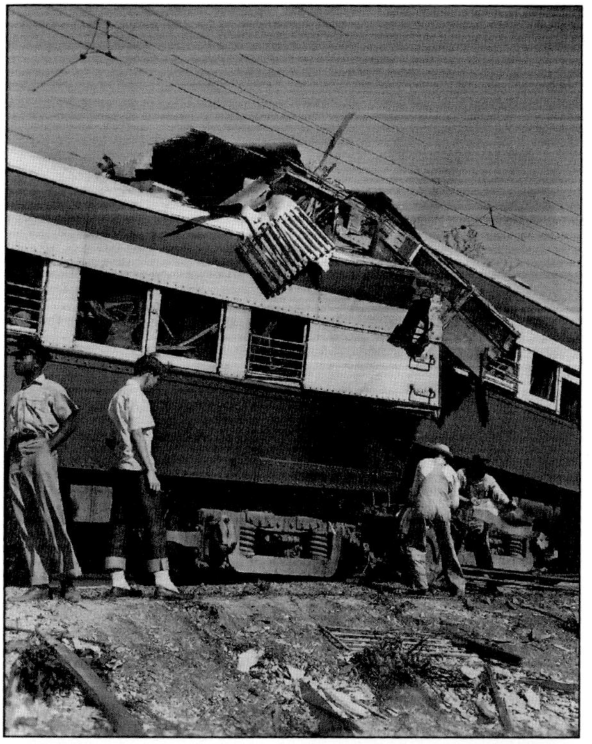

Pictured here is the ruined interior of one of the wrecked cars from the final disastrous accident of April 10, 1948.

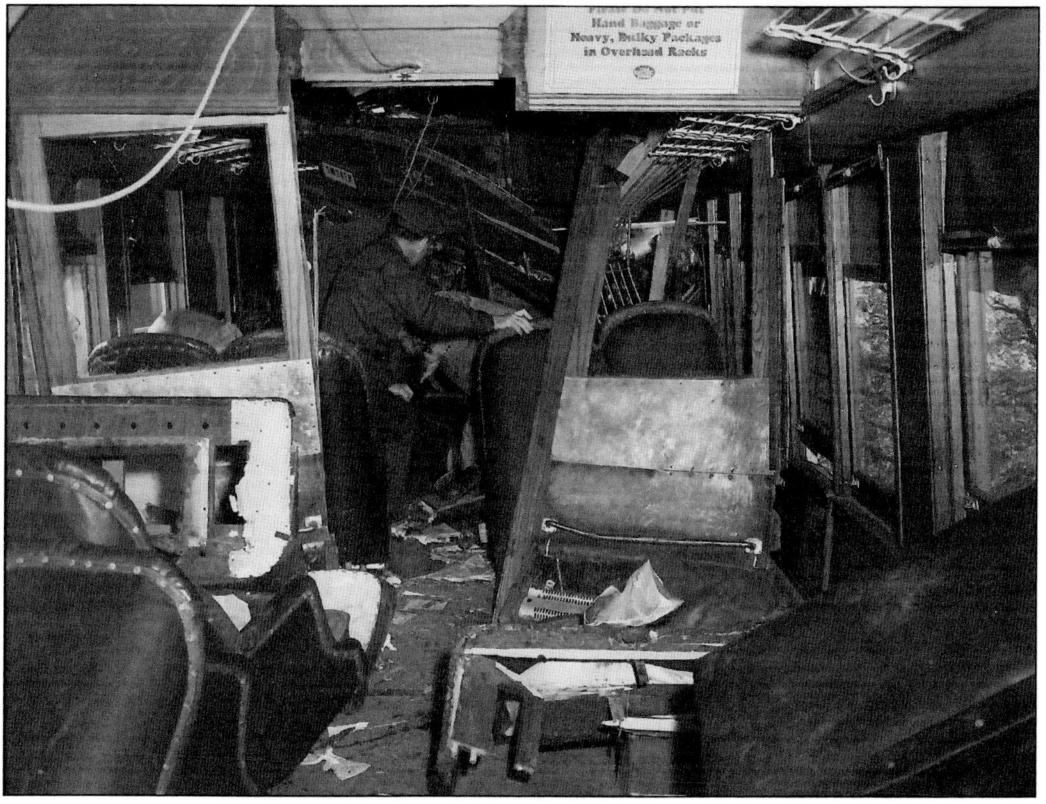

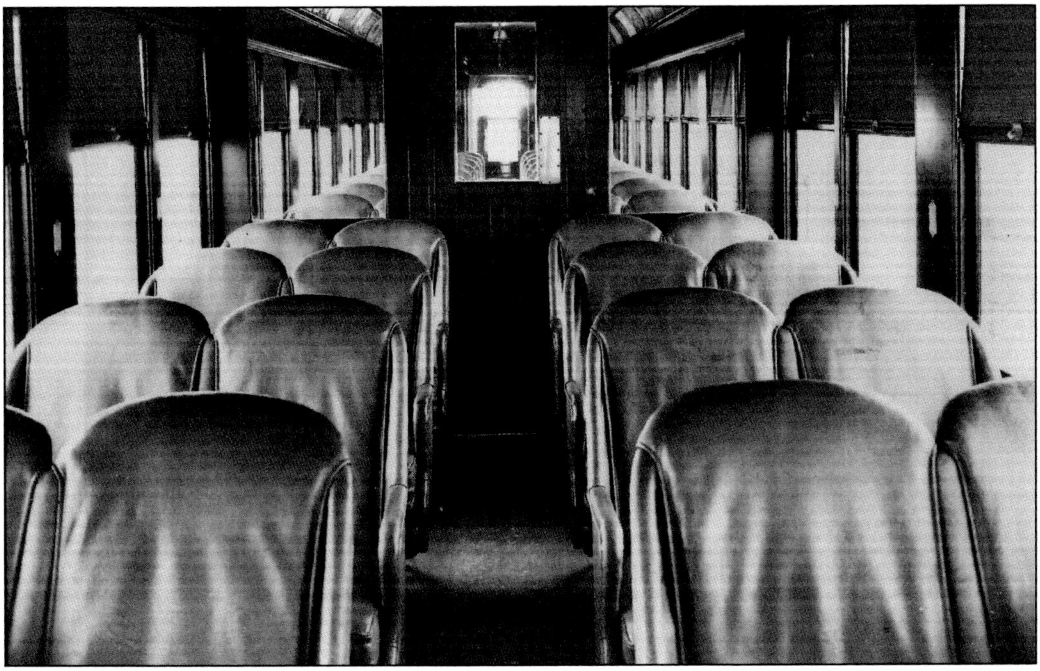

Although the company was in decline and the end was near, Texas Electric continued to maintain luxurious leather seats in the passenger cars and delivered service almost as effectively as during the golden era.

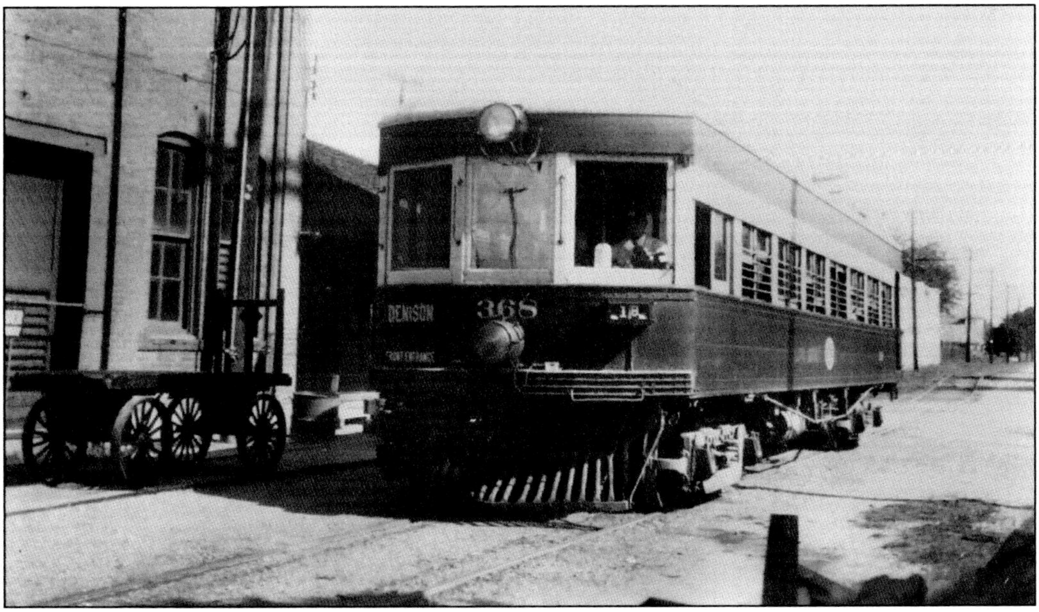

Car No. 368 pulls away from the Plano Depot on its way to Denison in July 1948. Note the tracks crossing Fifteenth Street just a few feet from where currently stands the restored Texas Electric Railway Car No. 360 in front of the Interurban Railway Museum. As the end drew near, the sight of Car No. 308 leaving the Plano station began to evoke nostalgia. Many in Plano did not wish to see the service end and hoped against hope that events would reverse and abandonment would not happen.

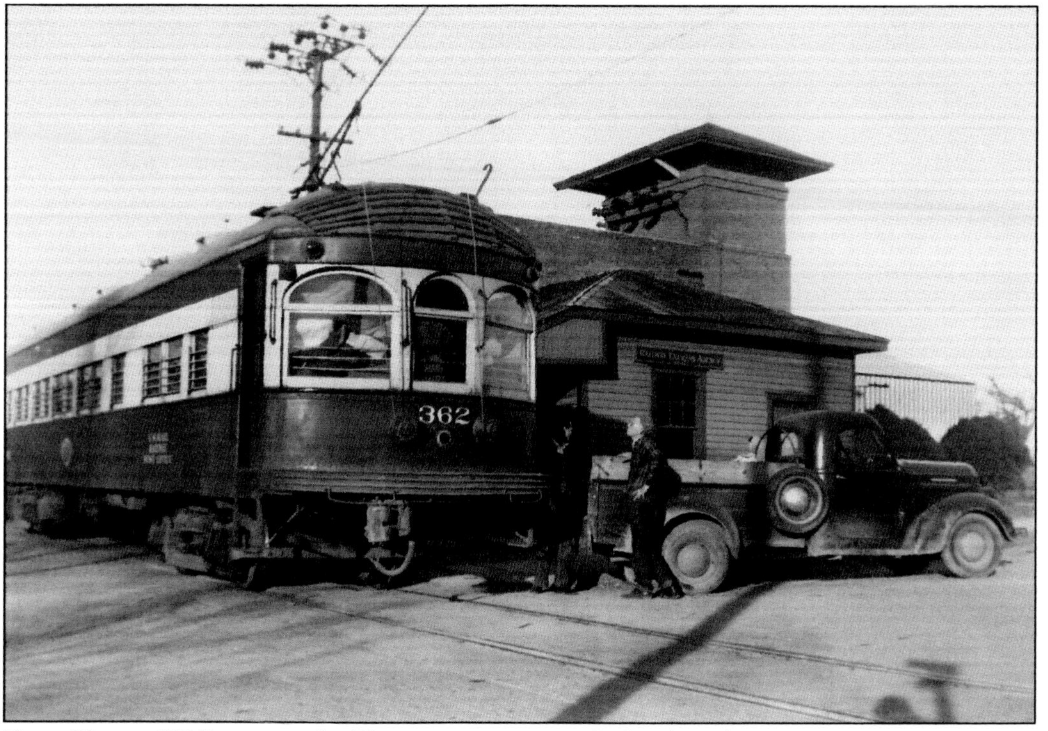

Texas Electric RPO stops at the Plano station to transfer local mail in 1948.

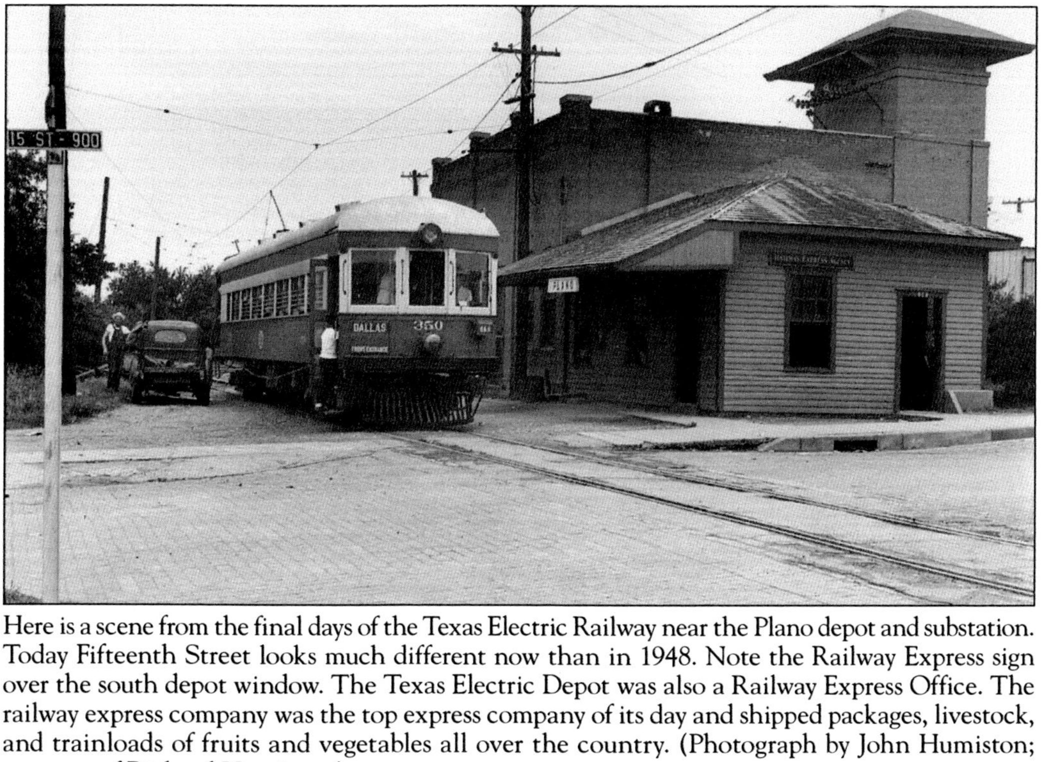

Here is a scene from the final days of the Texas Electric Railway near the Plano depot and substation. Today Fifteenth Street looks much different now than in 1948. Note the Railway Express sign over the south depot window. The Texas Electric Depot was also a Railway Express Office. The railway express company was the top express company of its day and shipped packages, livestock, and trainloads of fruits and vegetables all over the country. (Photograph by John Humiston; courtesy of Richard Humiston.)

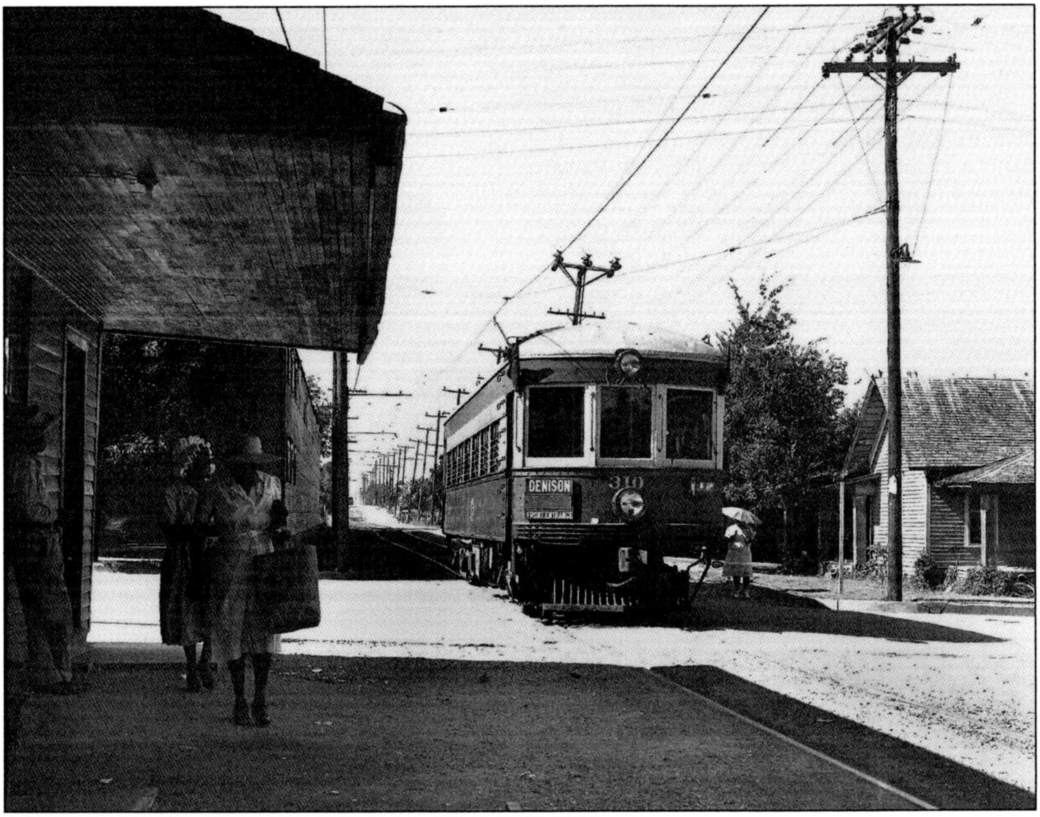

Crossing Fifteenth Street, Texas Electric Car No. 310 will pull into the boarding area in front of the station to pick up more freight and passengers on its way to its final stop at Denison. (Photograph by John Humiston; courtesy of Richard Humiston.)

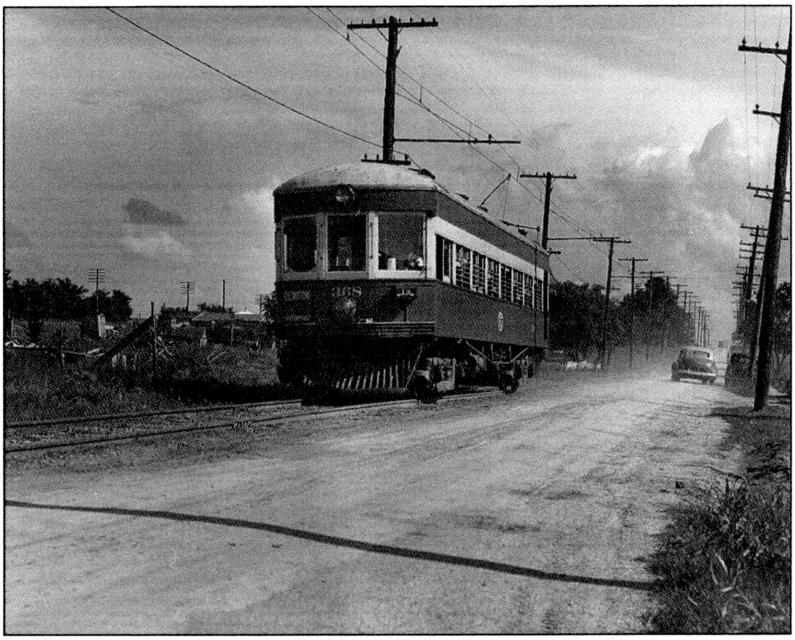

Approaching the Plano depot from a greater distance, Texas Electric Car No. 368 rolls through an area much less developed than it is today on Sunday, July 4, 1948. (Photograph by John Humiston; courtesy of Richard Humiston.)

Both patrons and employees posed for photographs on the last day.

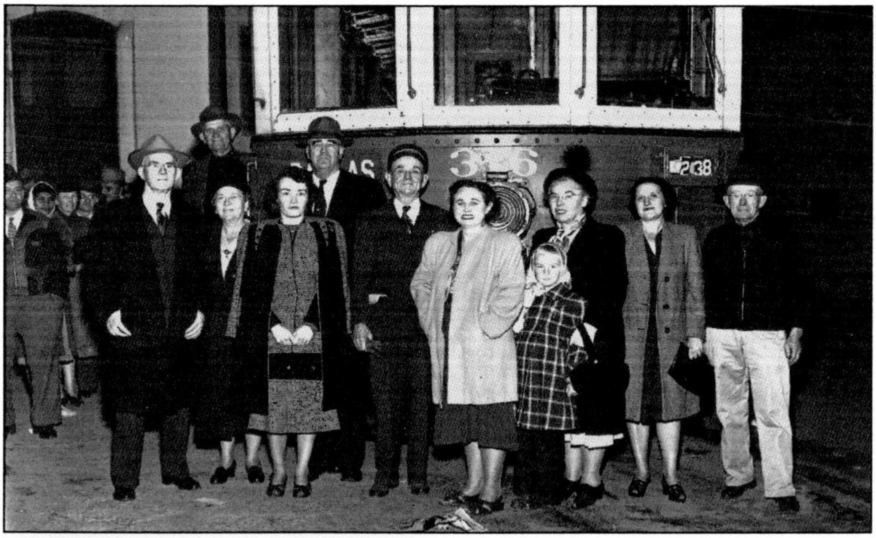

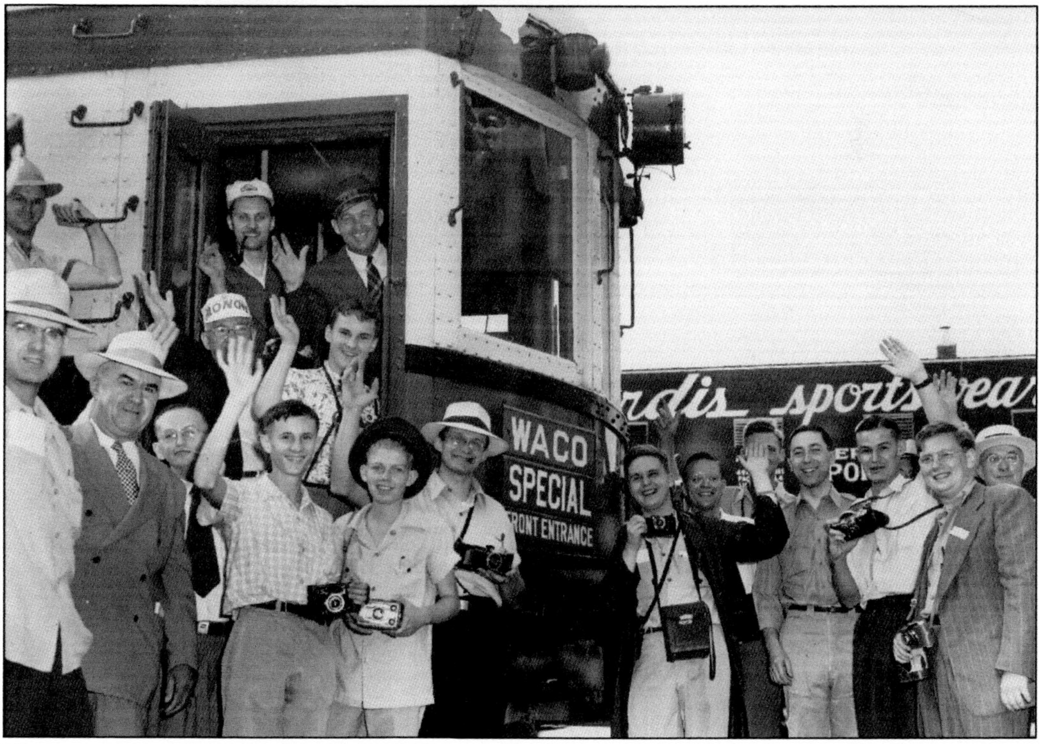

Twenty-six members of the Central Electric Rail Fans Association came to Dallas on July 3 and 4, 1948, to take a final ride on the Texas Electric Railway system after stockholders and management agreed to abandon the system. Some of the members came from as far away as Boston, Massachusetts; others came from Pennsylvania, Indiana, and Michigan. W. P. Donaldson Jr. and E. V. Nichols, both of Dallas, were joined by Texas Electric Railway general superintendent H. G. Floyd (first row, second from left); H. C. McIntosh, passenger traffic manager; and G. H. Peters, power superintendent. The car operator is J. A. Turrentine. They photographed and rode over the system in their special railcar, and when they arrived at Waco, Texas Electric treated the rail fans to a surprise chicken dinner. (Courtesy of the *Dallas Morning News.*)

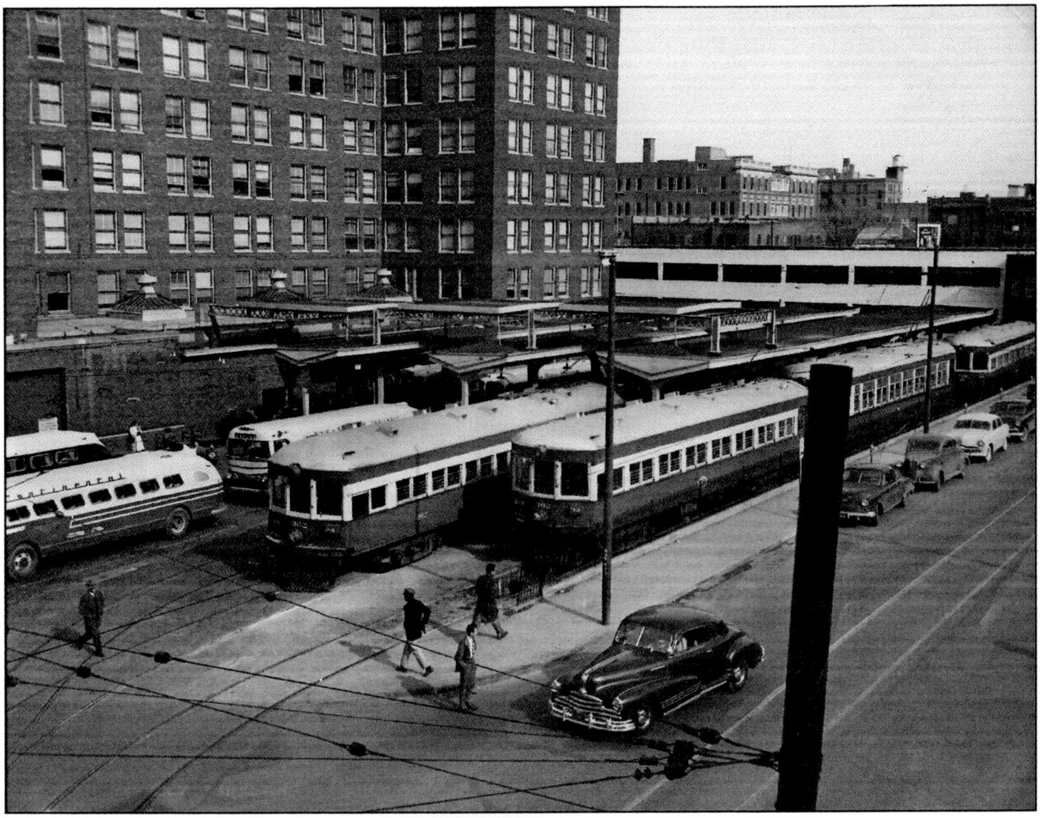

The last day at the Dallas Headquarters is pictured here.

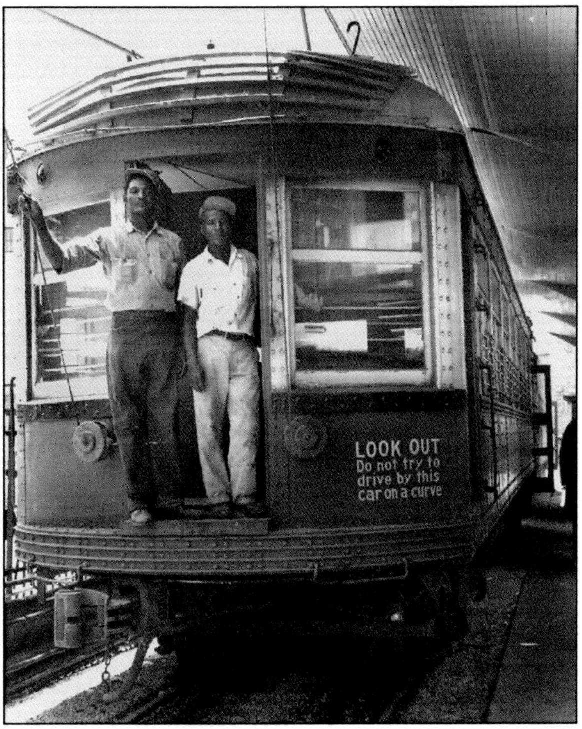

Employees of Texas Electric posed for final pictures as the system that had been one of the pillars of transportation in North Texas was prepared for shutdown and abandonment in December 1948. (Photograph by George Roush.)

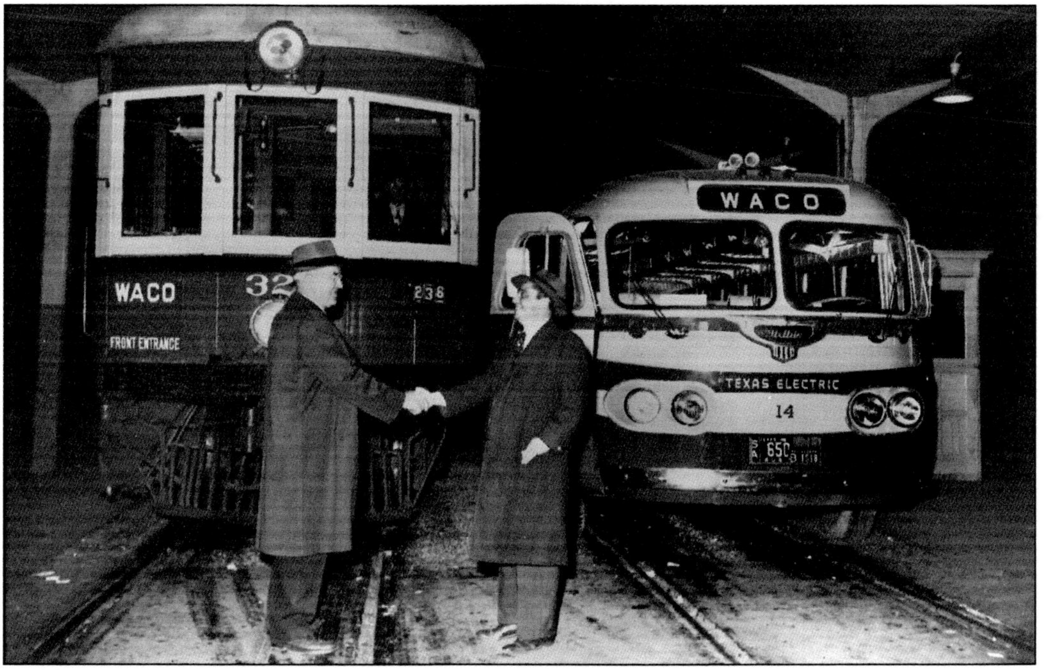

On the night of December 31, 1948, with a symbolic handshake between Supt. H. G. Floyd (left) and an unidentified man, the last aging Texas Electric Car No. 327 prepares to leave the Dallas terminal for the final run to Waco. The next morning would bring bus service on the interurban routes and a transportation era would pass into Texas history. (Photograph by Hank Tenny.)

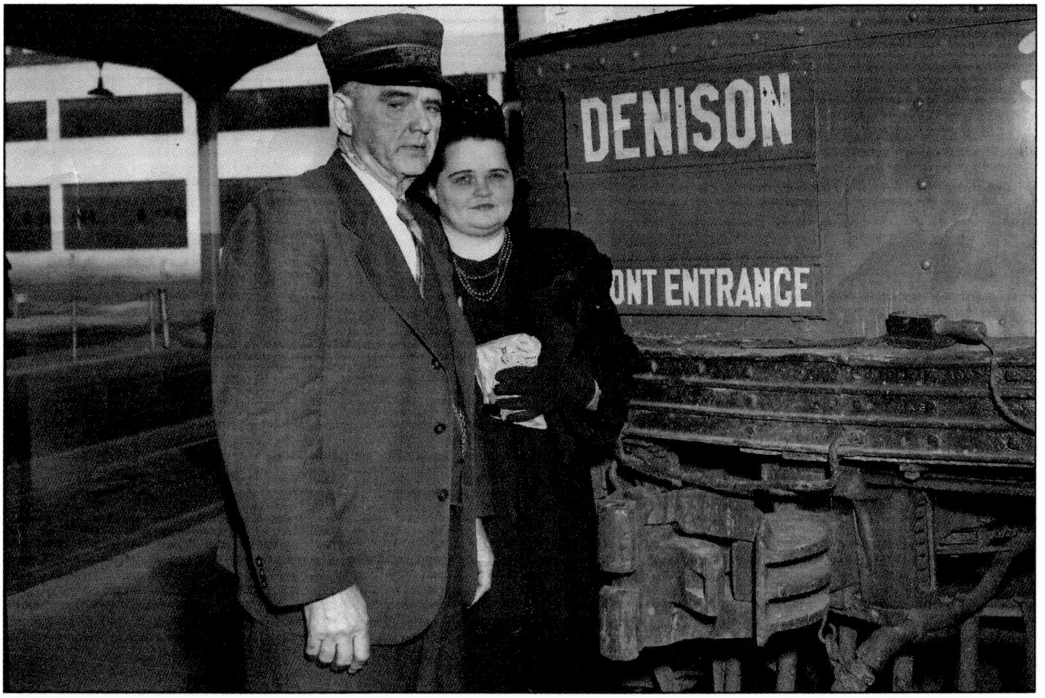

B. C. Cook and his daughter Helen C. Cook, stenographer at Texas Electric Railway, posed for the *Dallas Morning News* after abandonment on January 15, 1949.

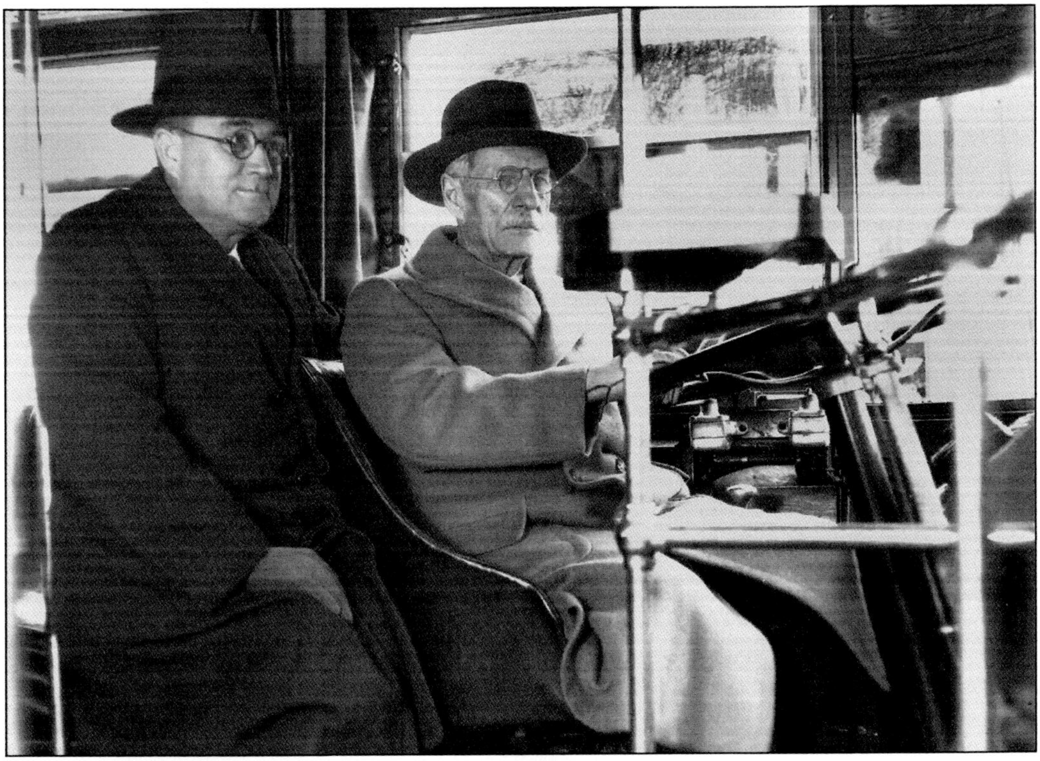

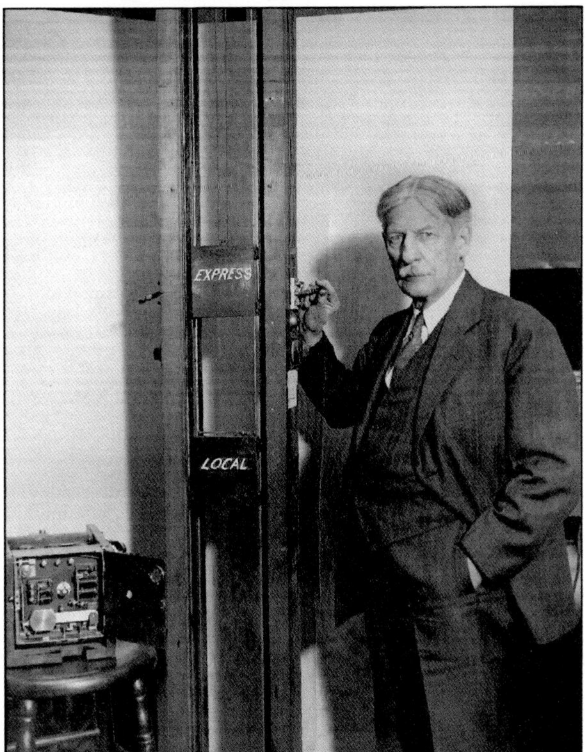

On November 13, 1931, as Texas Electric Railway was in receivership and most other interurban railway systems had disappeared or become victims of the automobile and bus transportation, F. H. Shephard of Westinghouse Corporation (left), the manufacturer of motors and other electric traction technology, is seated beside Frank J. Sprague (right), who is at the controls of an electric Chicago City Bus that runs on the technology Sprague invented. In his 70s, as the era of the electric streetcar and trolley car entered their twilight, Frank Sprague was celebrated many times for his contributions to the science of electric traction and many other areas of electrical engineering. (Courtesy of a private family collection.)

Frank Sprague stands beside a c. 1934 miniature working model of a new elevator system, one of his last projects, which ran two elevators at one time. (Courtesy of a private family collection.)

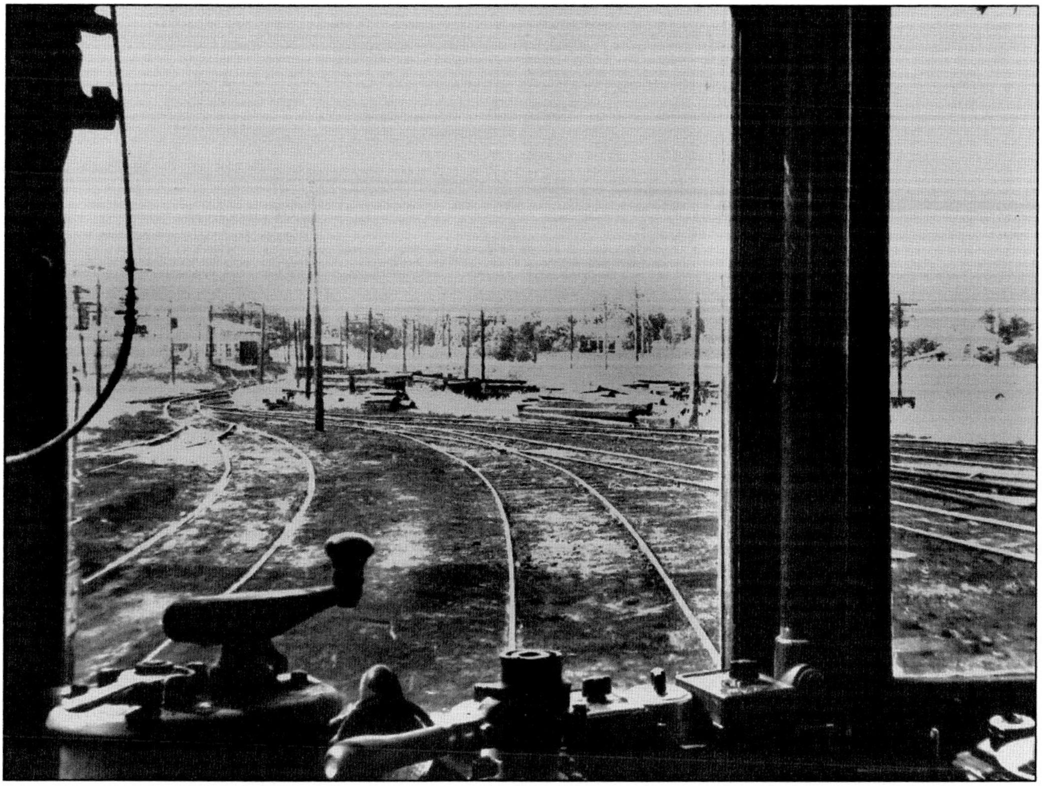

On January 1, 1949, the day after all Texas Electric Railway passenger service came to an end, the yard of the Monroe Shops appeared empty and abandoned. The photograph is taken from the interior of one of the railcars. Empty tracks and unused rail ties lie stacked to the right side of the yard. Part of the Texas Electric Railway fleet of cars is at the left and unseen. Most of the other cars were stored behind the car from which this photograph was taken.

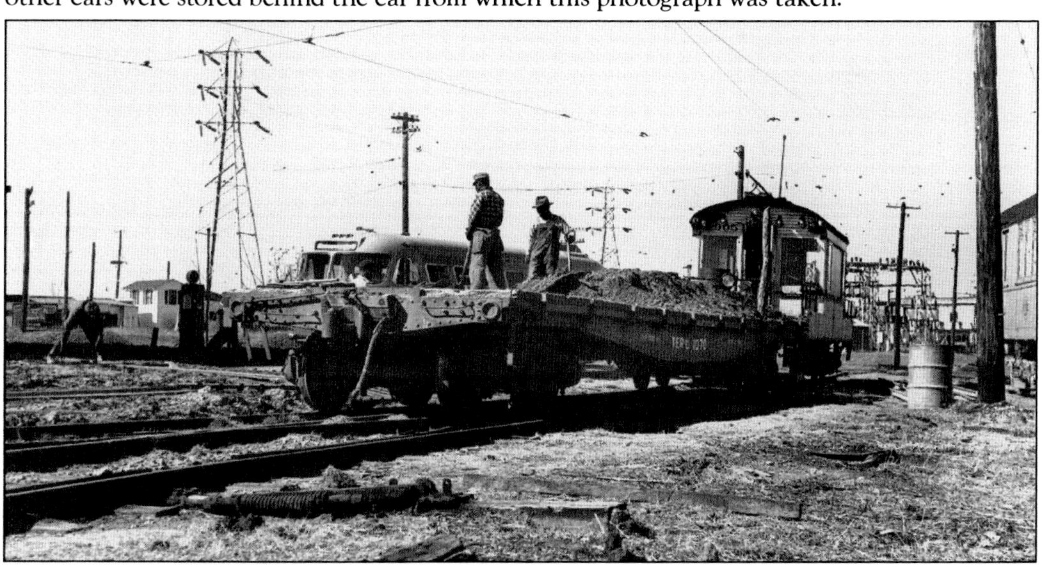

Soon after Texas Electric ended all passenger service, workers began the task of removing the web of tracks and ties that wove the system together.

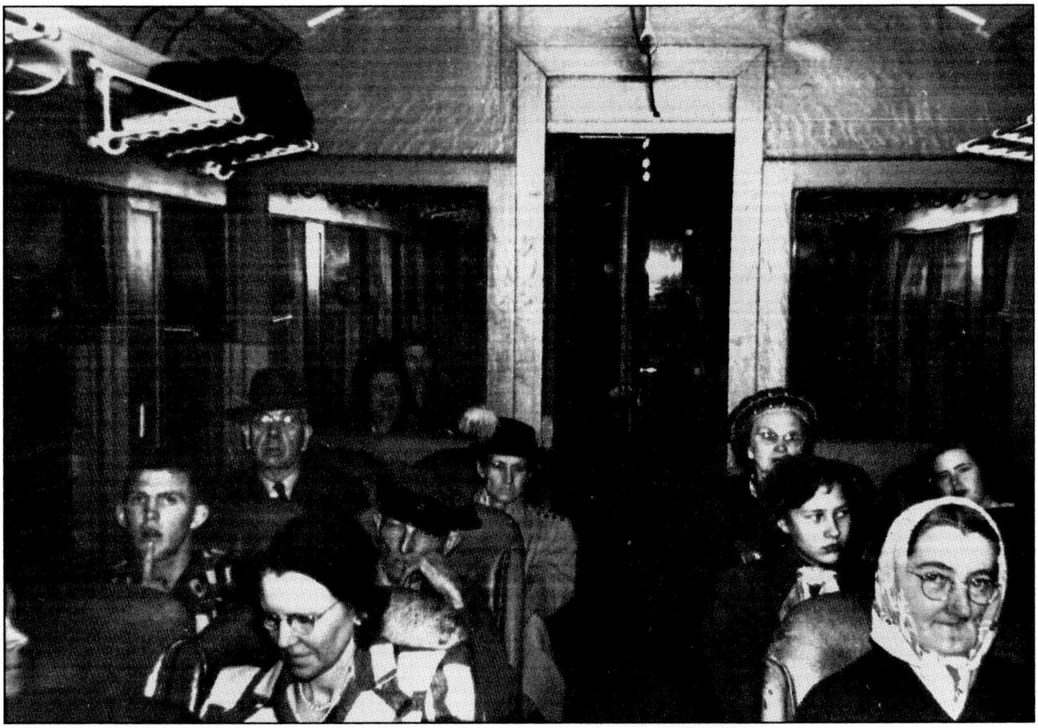

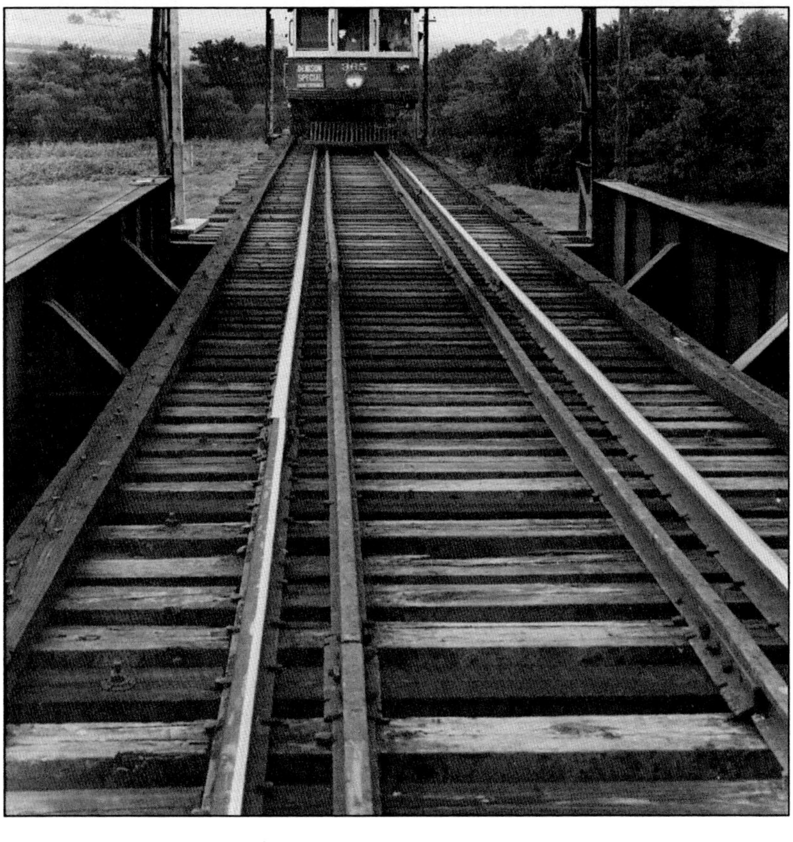

The lure of wartime work in the factories of North Texas brought large numbers of rural people from farms into the industrial cities of Dallas and Fort Worth, and most stayed, creating some sharp social differences in the populations of both cities.

There were many memories of the clickety-clack made by the wheels of the car running over joined sections of the track. Today's track is welded into a single rail.

Six

Their Future, Our Past

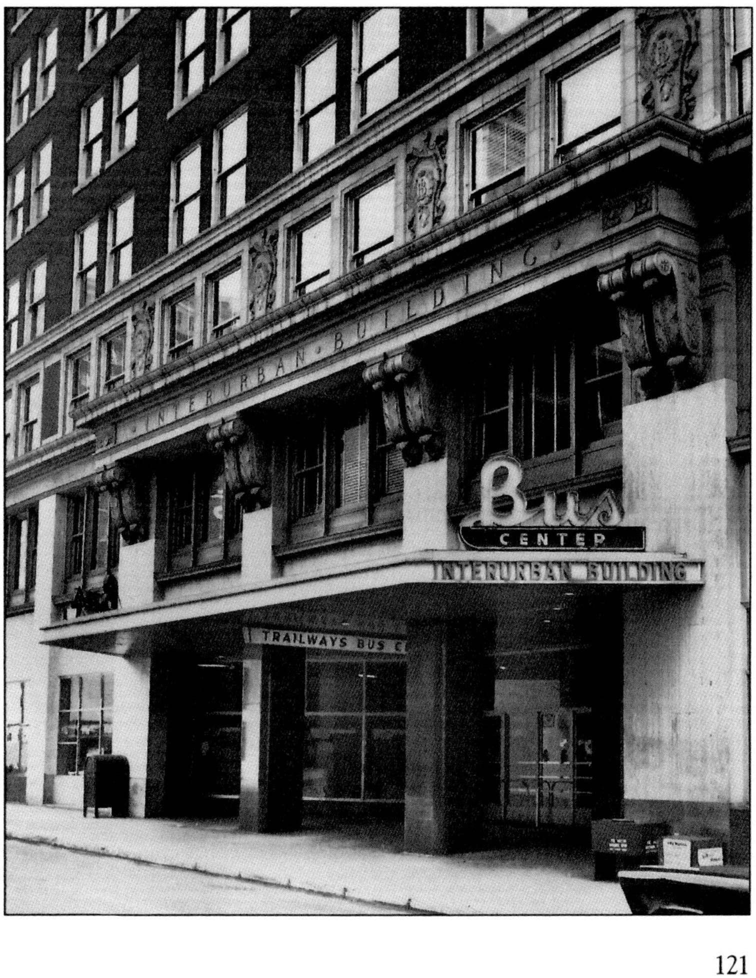

After abandonment, the interurban building became the depot for Trailways Bus Company. The building has now been converted to apartments.

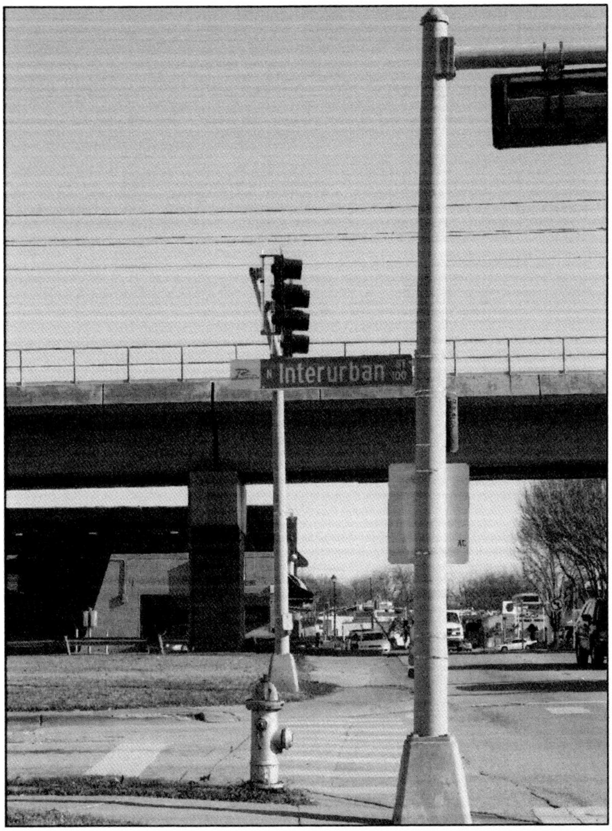

The route the interurban cars traveled when they departed the Plano station has been named Interurban Street. Note in the background that the Dallas Area Rapid Transit (DART) system nearly follows the original route to Dallas traveled by Southern Traction and Texas Electric Railway. (Photograph by Dave Lerry; courtesy of Plano Conservancy for Historic Preservation, Inc.)

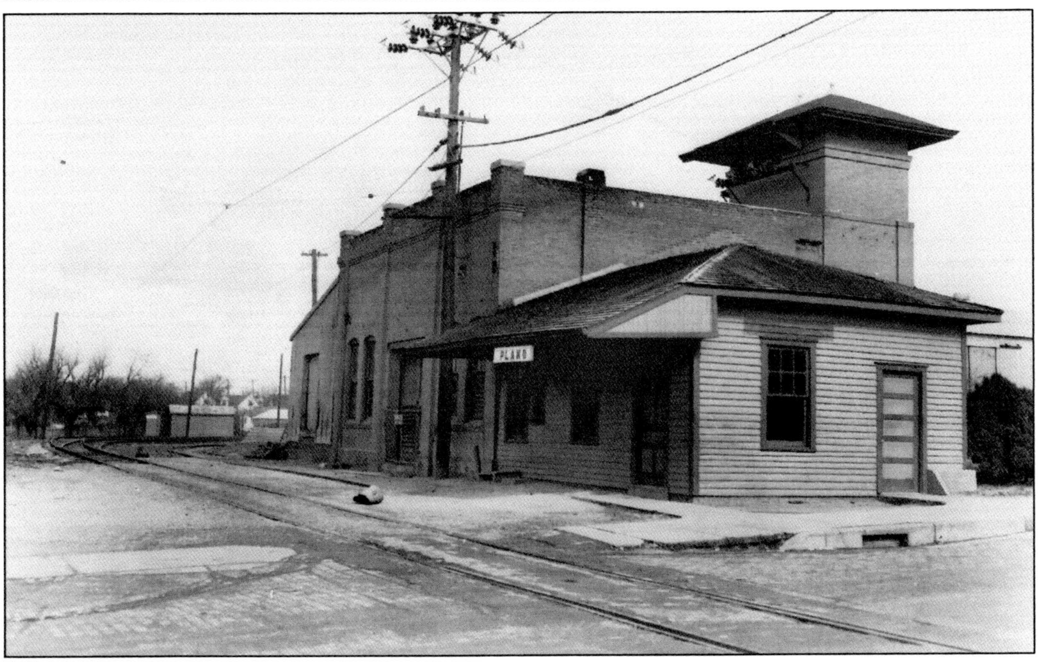

The Plano substation and depot are pictured in 1949 following abandonment by Texas Electric Railway.

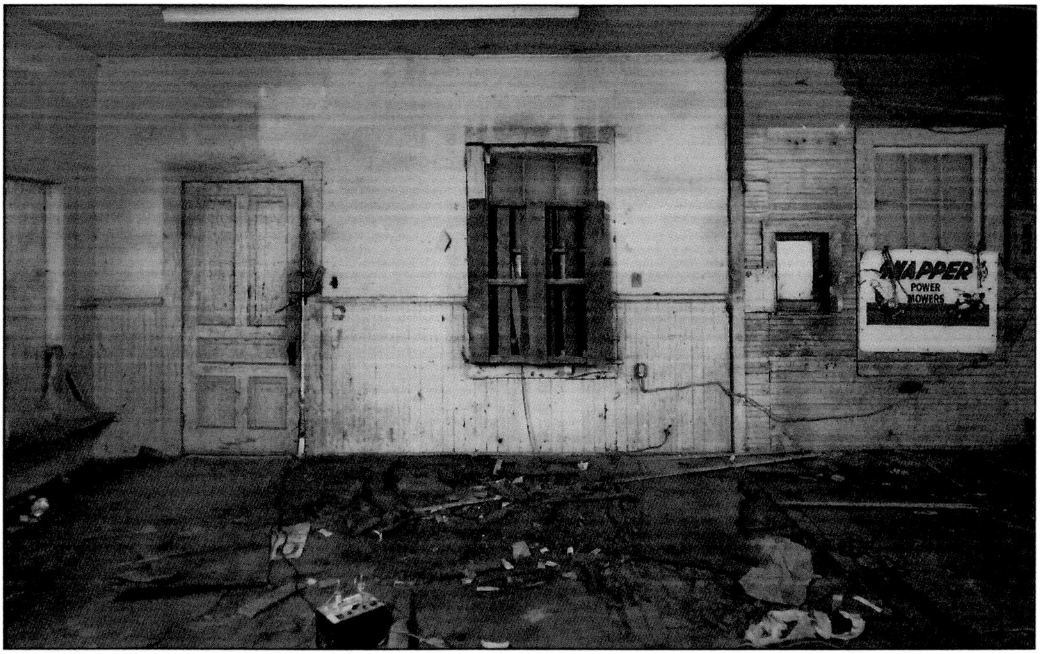

The deteriorated interior of the Plano depot and substation is shown here in 1980. The Plano depot building was rescued from demolition by the City of Plano, Department of Parks and Recreation. After serving as a lawn mower repair shop for many years, the station was restored in 1988 as the Plano Interurban Railway Museum.

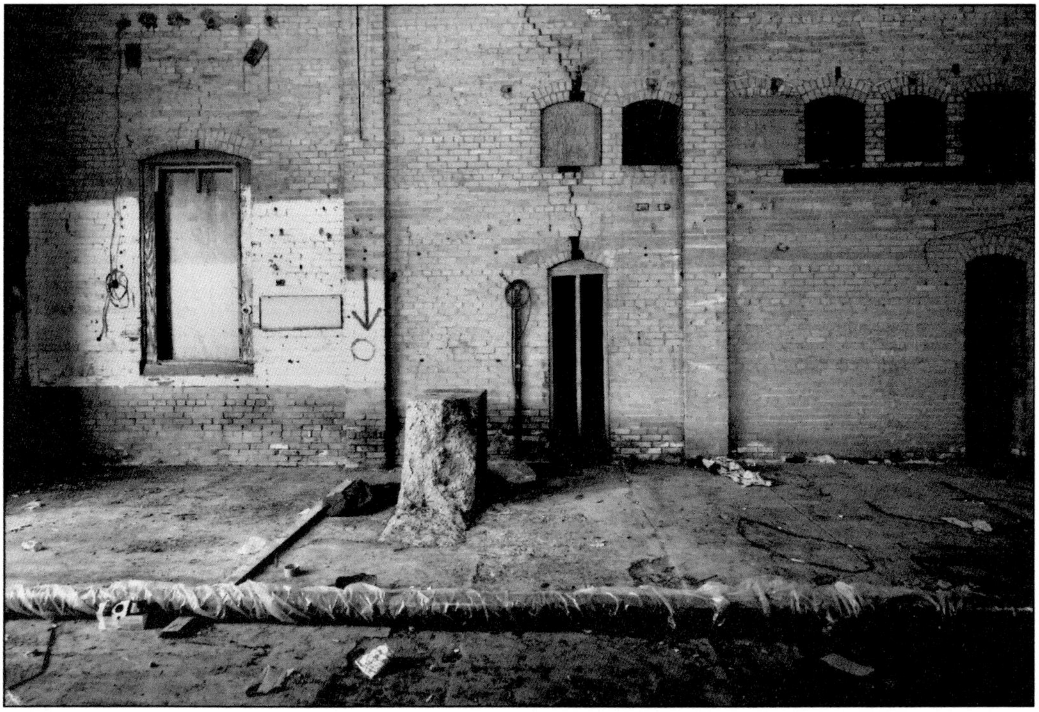

With the machinery long removed for salvage, the deteriorated interior of the Plano substation appears stark and bleak.

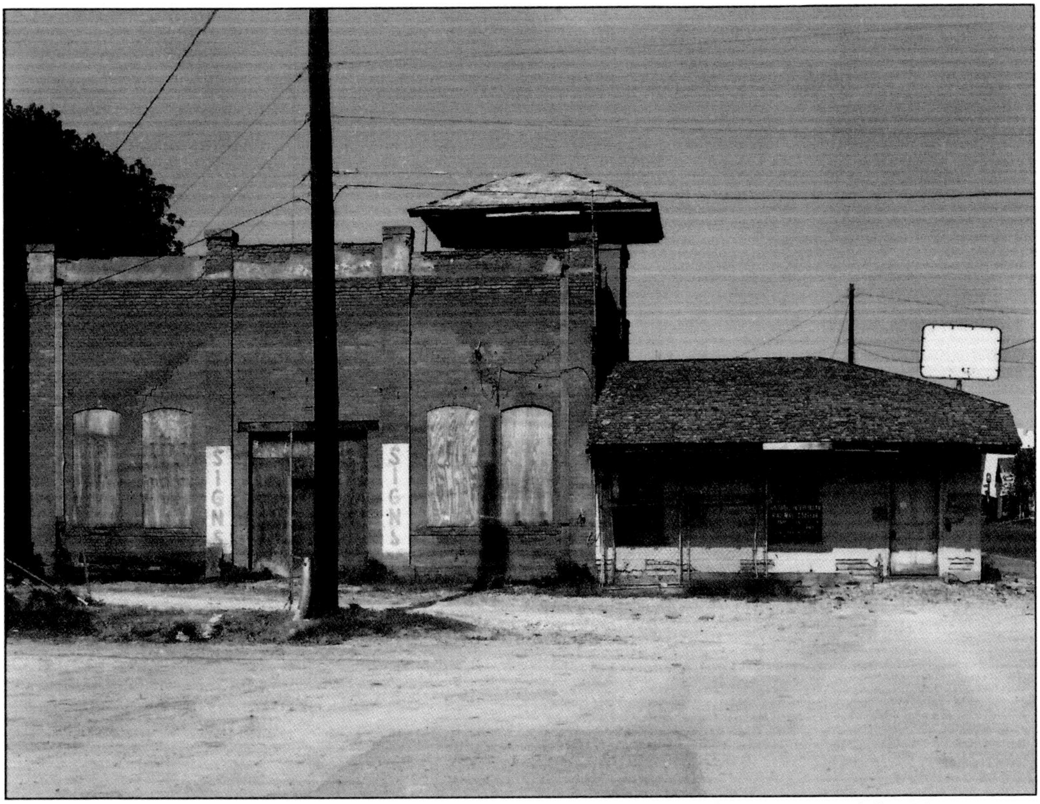

After 73 years, the exterior of the Plano station appeared ready for demolition.

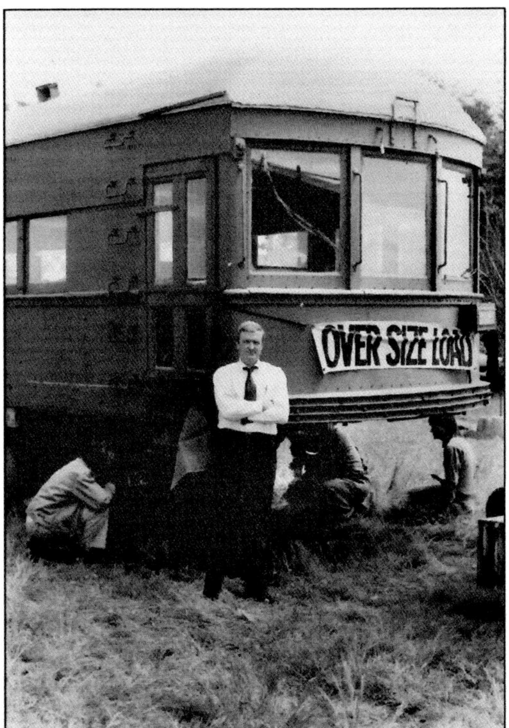

John J. Myers (left) and Jim Fox (not shown), of the City of Plano, Department of Parks and Recreation, were the principal proponents behind saving the interurban building and restoring railcar No. 360. A widely acknowledged expert on the era of electric rail transportation, John Myers directed relocation of the railcar from a farm to its present site and also personally worked to restore the car.

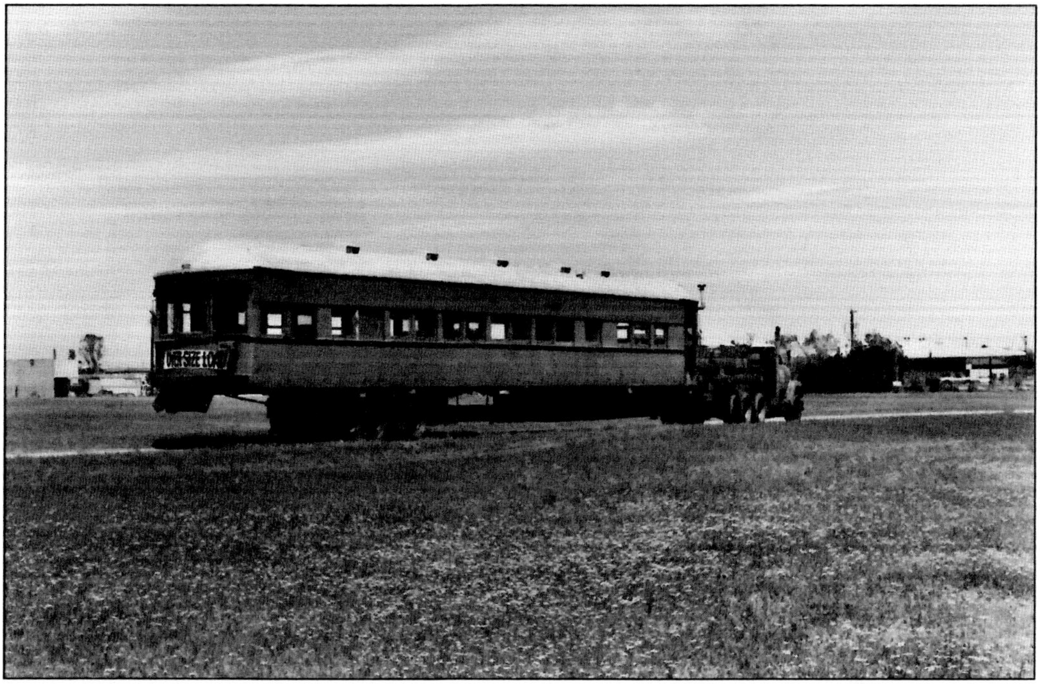

In 1988, the railcar was carefully trucked to Plano from a rural North Texas farm, where it had been used as a toolshed.

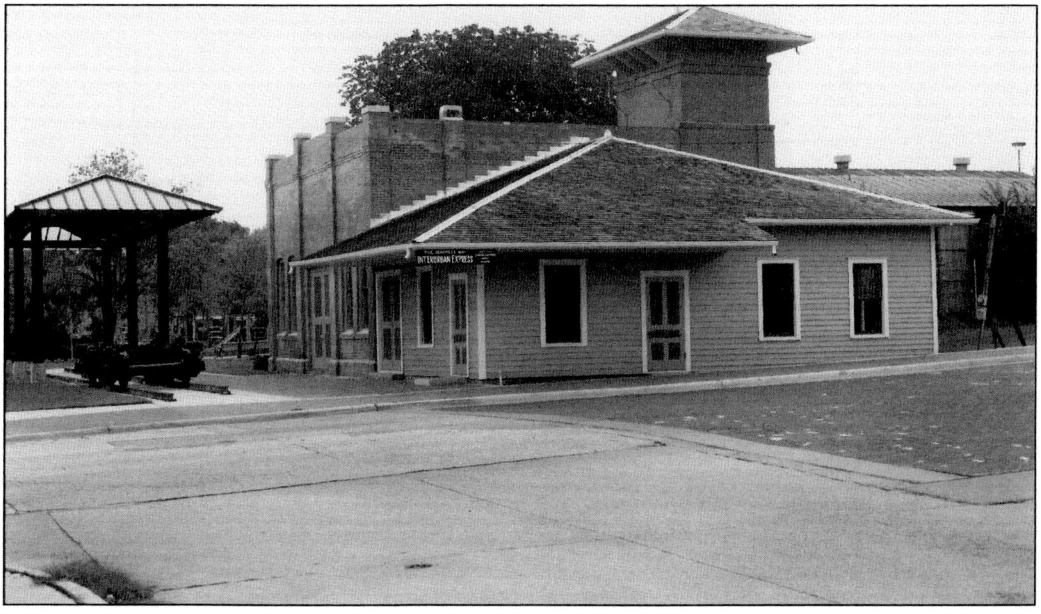

The restored Plano station awaits the arrival of Texas Electric railcar No. 360.

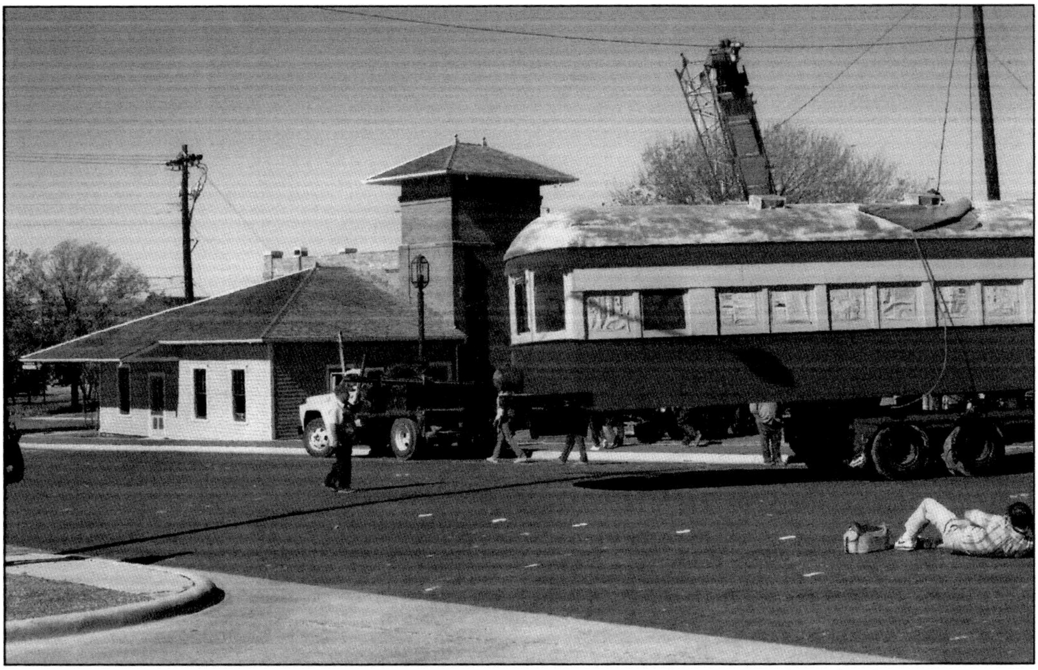

A heavy crane lifts the car from the truck bed to direct it to the canopy beside the museum.

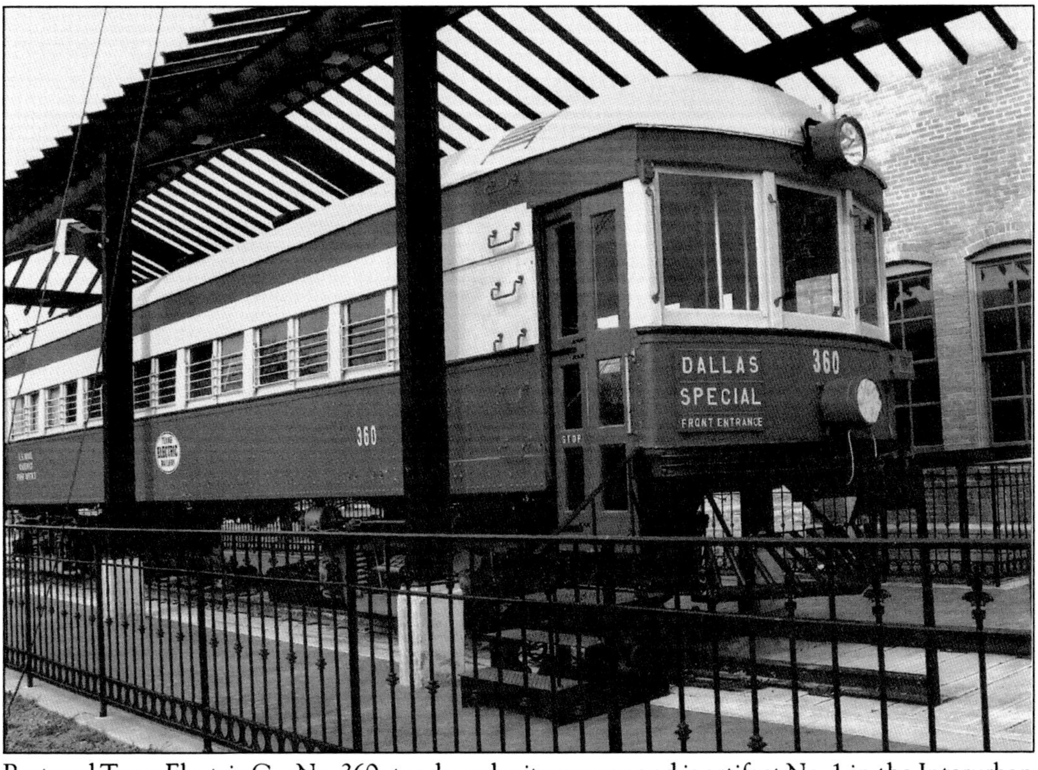

Restored Texas Electric Car No. 360 stands under its canopy and is artifact No. 1 in the Interurban Railway Museum collection. (Photograph by Dave Lerry; courtesy of the Plano Conservancy for Historic Preservation, Inc.)

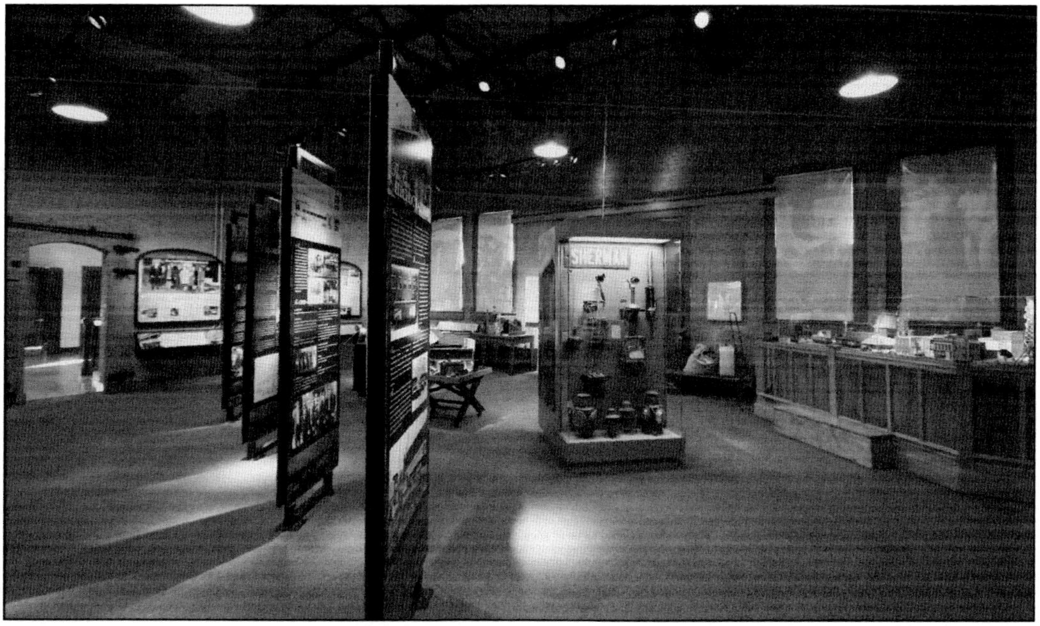

The interior of the former Texas Electric Railway station has been turned into a museum that tells the story of electric interurban travel in North Texas. Since 2001, the Plano Conservancy for Historic Preservation, Inc., has managed and directed the Interurban Railway Museum and provided educational outreach to the schools of the city of Plano and the North Texas cultural and academic community. Funding secured by this nonprofit organization has been used to develop new, exciting, and innovative exhibitions. (Courtesy of Museumscapes, Inc.)

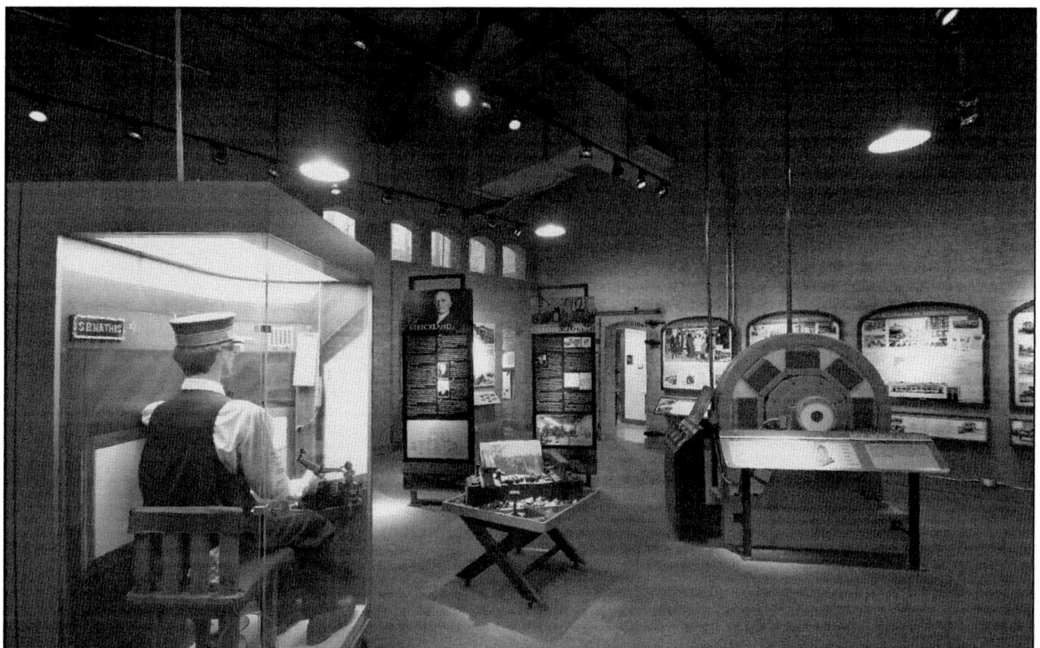

The interurban experience is recounted through artifacts, electronic media, and photographs. (Courtesy of Museumscapes, Inc.)

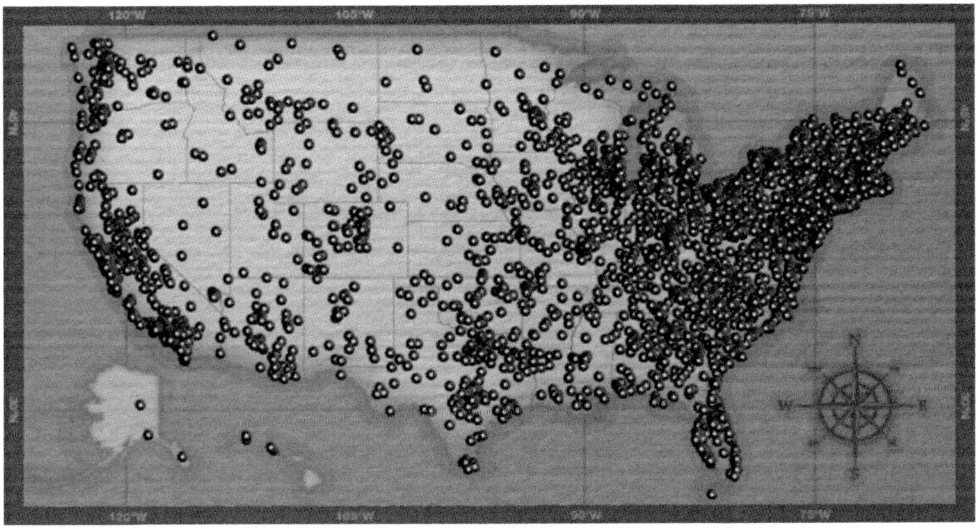